Intimate Friends, Dangerous Rivals

Also by the author:

Panic Behavior
Sensory Restriction: Effects on Behavior
A History of Modern Psychology
Psychology and Industry Today
Theories of Personality
Growth Psychology: Models of the Healthy Personality

Intimate Friends, Dangerous Rivals

The Turbulent Relationship
between Freud and Jung

DUANE SCHULTZ, Ph.D.

JEREMY P. TARCHER, INC.
Los Angeles

The author wishes to acknowledge the following:

Pantheon Books, for permission to reprint material from *Memories, Dream, Reflections* by Carl G. Jung; and from *A Secret Symmetry: Sabina Spielrein Between Jung and Freud* by Aldo Carotenuto.

Basic Books, for permission to reprint material from *The Life and Work of Sigmund Freud,* vol. 2, by Ernest Jones.

The Freud/Jung Letters: The Correspondence Between Sigmund Freud and C. G. Jung, ed. William McGuire, trans. Ralph Manheim and R. F. C. Hull, Bollingen Series XCIV. Copyright © 1974 by Sigmund Freud Copyrights Ltd. and Erbengemeinschaft Prof. Dr. C. G. Jung. Reprinted by permission of Princeton University Press.

Library of Congress Cataloging in Publication Data

Schultz, Duane P.
    Intimate friends, dangerous rivals : the turbulent relationship between Freud and Jung / Duane Schultz.
      p. cm.
    Includes bibliographical references.
    1. Freud, Sigmund, 1856–1939—Friends and associates. 2. Jung, C. G. (Carl Gustav), 1875–1961—Friends and associates. 3. Psychoanalysts—Austria—Biography. 4. Psychoanalysts—Switzerland—Biography. 5. Psychoanalysis—History. I. Title.
BF109.F74S378   1990
150.19 ' 52—dc20
[B]   89-38976
ISBN 0-87477-549-3   CIP
ISBN 0-87477-555-8 (pbk.)

Jeremy P. Tarcher, Inc.
5858 Wilshire Blvd., Ste. 200
Los Angeles, CA 90036

Distributed by St. Martin's Press, New York

Design by Gary Hespenheide

Manufactured in the United States of America
10 9 8 7 6 5 4 3 2 1

First Edition

To Sydney Ellen,
who makes everything better,
including this book

Contents

I could hope for no one better than yourself, as I have come to know you, to continue and complete my work.

Freud to Jung, April 7, 1907

Let me enjoy your friendship not as one between equals but as that of father and son.

Jung to Freud, February 20, 1908

❖

I propose that we abandon our personal relations entirely. . . . My only emotional tie with you has long been a thin thread—the lingering effect of past disappointments.

Freud to Jung, January 3, 1913

I accede to your wish. You yourself are the best judge of what this moment means to you. "The rest is silence."

Jung to Freud, January 6, 1913

Acknowledgments

It is a pleasure to record my gratitude to Jeremy Tarcher, a publisher who displays a genuine concern for the needs and fears—and the care and feeding—of authors. I am grateful to my editor, Connie Zweig, for her enthusiasm, her sound advice, and her frequent, cheerful, and encouraging telephone calls. My thanks also to production editor Dianne Woo, who maintained a masterful grip on the myriad details attendant to the publication of the book in a gracious and soothing manner. The professionalism and support of the entire Tarcher staff has made this the most agreeable publishing experience in a thirty-year writing career.

Preface

This book tells the story of a strange, doomed relationship. I wrote it to share with the reader my fascination with and curiosity about two highly creative, imaginative people who were also deeply troubled and perhaps more than a little weird.

We begin in the year 1906, when Sigmund Freud and Carl Jung made their first contact, and describe their personal and professional lives to that point. We review their early years—the influences that shaped their natures and the needs that would bind them to each other. If past is prologue, then the Freud/Jung relationship was immutably fashioned out of the torments and traumas of childhood, which drew an inevitable design for their future lives. The result of that preordained pattern—a friend and enemy in the same person—is discussed in the chapters covering the development of the relationship, which culminated in bitterness, disillusionment, and disaffection. Given their backgrounds and temperaments, the story could have no other ending.

This book is not an academic discourse. The reader does not need any background in psychology or psychiatry to be able to appreciate the closeness, the emotional nature, and the mutual dependence of the Freud/Jung relationship. Where Freudian and Jungian concepts and terms are used to elucidate personalities, motivations, and behaviors, they are explained within the text or in footnotes.

The book draws on primary sources—the numerous letters

exchanged among Freud, Jung, and their colleagues—as well as on the major biographies and histories in the field. I have told the story, however, from my own perspective as a psychologist, historian, and writer, and from my twenty years of experience in trying to make Freud and Jung come alive for my undergraduate and graduate students in the history of psychology.

An Uneasy Alliance

They were an odd pair, an alien mix, an uneasy alliance. Yet when Sigmund Freud and Carl Jung met for the first time it was truly a joyous event, the start of a six-year association that was at once the most rich, intimate, tortured, and bizarre relationship in the annals of psychoanalysis. Their eager expectations, which had developed through only ten letters written to each other in the closing months of the previous year, were amply and immediately confirmed.

Jung looked on Freud as the first person of real importance he had ever met. At last he had found what he had long been searching for—a father, a mentor, a spiritual guide on whom he could depend. Freud was equally impressed with Jung. He had not dared hope to find anyone so perfectly suited to becoming his spiritual heir, to assuming the leadership of the psychoanalytic movement upon his death. At last Freud had found what he had been looking for—a submissive son who would admire and affirm his greatness, a son on whom he could depend.

Both men had good reason to be delighted with their first meeting. Surely, they both thought, this new relationship will not end in disappointment and bitterness, as have so many others in the past. No, this one will last. But there was a clear signal, a sharp warning, a portent of the tragedy that lay ahead, and it appeared, appropriately, in a dream. Fewer than 24 hours after their first personal contact, the Oedipal theme of the son's wish to destroy the father asserted itself. It would haunt them for the next six years.

What is most surprising about the Freud/Jung relationship is not that it ended acrimoniously but that it occurred at all. The two men were poles apart in manner, background, and personal philosophy. Physically, the contrasts were striking. When they met, Jung was in his early thirties, a massive, rugged, broad-shouldered man, six feet two inches tall, of a decidedly Teutonic appearance. His hands were those of a workman—large, gnarled, and powerful—and they punctuated his speech with brisk, inelegant gestures. His dark brown eyes, described as crafty and cunning, peered at the world through gold-rimmed glasses. His cropped brown hair was thinning in front, above a high forehead.

Jung could be socially awkward. He was a bit of a country bumpkin, and his language was sometimes coarse, lacking the refinement expected of one in his professional position. He affected a pose of nonchalance to conceal his lack of sophistication, and a booming laugh became part of his act. He had the knack of feeling comfortable with persons of all social classes and could put them at ease. He also possessed a lively sense of humor and could be relied on to brighten any party by singing, yodeling, and dancing until the early morning hours. He was once described as a "breezy personality, domineering in temperament," and brimming with vitality.

Freud was in his early fifties when he met Jung. Several inches shorter, he had none of Jung's powerful, rough-hewn appearance. Freud's immaculately trimmed mustache and beard were by then gray, but his hair had remained dark brown, thick, and well groomed. His physique was slightly rotund, in the manner of one with a sedentary occupation. There was a soft, almost effeminate quality to his movements and gestures.

He was vivacious and quick, even restless, but also formal and ceremonious, and his eyes seemed constantly to be in motion, as though he did not want to miss anything. His gaze was described as piercing and unforgettable, looking at life "from the depths." He often showed the amiability and good humor typical of the sophisticated Viennese of the day. He was urbane and well versed in the art of conversation, being familiar with a variety of topics, and he possessed exquisite manners, a rich vocabulary, and a precise mode of speaking.

When the situation warranted it, though, Freud could be brusque and even rude. He was highly disciplined at his work and in his personal life, except for his passion for cigars. He seemed to be trying to keep himself under control, but he was not always successful.

The more significant differences between Freud and Jung went deeper—to their individual values, attitudes, and beliefs, all of which proved to be as resistant to change as their physical appearances. Freud was reared in a Jewish family in the cosmopolitan atmosphere of a major European city. Reason and intellect were his guides, hard-nosed science his faith. He rejected myths, superstitions, and the occult, and he believed mental and emotional life, like the external life of the city, should be controlled and ruled by the conscious forces of reason.

Jung was a product of a rural Protestant setting. He believed in myths, supernatural events, and the power of God. In the countryside, nature ruled: animals sensed storms and earthquakes, the dreams of old women foretold doom, and clocks stopped at the moment of death. All such events were real to Jung. His world was rich with secrets and symbolism.

Freud's adult preoccupation with unconscious forces—with the passions and the instincts—was based on a desire to subdue them. To Jung, unconscious forces were the sources of wisdom, not to be curbed but to be set free.

Ultimately, perhaps the only quality Freud and Jung shared was their mutual dependence. The relationship was much more emotional than intellectual, more directed by passion than by reason. The friendship was, for each man, a repetition of earlier attempts to satisfy needs that had goaded them since childhood.

Intimacy and interdependence characterized their six years together, but there were early hints that the relationship could not endure. Reliance turned to resentment, admiration to disgust;

imagined slights and fancied slurs became real. The loyal and devoted son began to disagree with the teachings of the father, and the father became angry at the growing independence of the son. Despite their genius for seeing into the souls of others, Freud and Jung, for a long time, did not see any of these signs in themselves.

CHAPTER ONE

———···✧···———

The Medallion: 1906

On Sunday evening, May 6, 1906, a strange and unsettling event occurred in the consultation room of Dr. Sigmund Freud of Vienna. A small band of loyal followers gathered to celebrate the momentous occasion of Freud's fiftieth birthday. Freud himself did not like ceremonies, but he indulged his adherents this once, letting them have their way.

Freud was dressed, as usual, in an unfashionable dark suit, dark tie, and stiff white collar. His beard and mustache were neatly trimmed, and his hair was combed back from his forehead.

The consultation room was not large. It connected the waiting room in the front of the house with Freud's office in the rear, which overlooked the garden in the courtyard of the apartment building. An Oriental rug covered most of the floor, and reproductions of Italian paintings and portraits of ancient pharaohs lined the walls. The guests were seated around an oval table. One of them made a short speech, offering congratulations and best wishes, and presented Freud with a gift from the group.

Freud was stunned. His face drained of color. He tried to speak but his voice choked.

The gift was a medallion. Freud picked it up and held it lightly in his fingers, turning it over and over. One side bore a profile of Freud, and the other showed a carving of Oedipus, King of Thebes, whose name had come to denote one of Freud's great discoveries. Around the face was an inscription from Sophocles' play *Oedipus Tyrannus:* "Who divined the famed riddle and was a man most mighty."

Freud glanced around the table and asked who had thought of the inscription. Paul Federn, who had joined Freud's circle three years before, said that it was his idea. Quietly, Freud explained why the words so unnerved him, why the choice of this quotation was so uncanny. Thirty years before, when Freud was a student at the University of Vienna, dreaming of recognition and fame, he liked to stroll around the university courtyard and contemplate the busts and statues erected to honor famous professors. He imagined that one day he would see his own likeness among them. It would bear a line from Sophocles, the same words Federn had inscribed on the birthday medallion.*

The quotation was highly appropriate for Freud by that time. Growing numbers of people in Vienna and beyond Austria's borders had come to believe that he had indeed divined the famed riddle, the riddle of the origin of neurosis and the nature of the human personality. Never had the future looked so promising for Freud as during the early years of the new century.

Ten years before, on Freud's fortieth birthday, there had been no gifts from admirers, no allusions to greatness, and little hope of professional recognition. His personal life was a shambles and his career a failure. His emotions were in turmoil, his mind beset by anxieties, and his body besieged by pain. The psychoanalyst who would achieve such acclaim for his work on mental illness was suffering his own neurotic episode. He described his mental agonies as "odd states of mind, cloudy thoughts and vague doubts, with barely here and there a ray of light." He worried about dying and feared for his heart. He became anxious about open spaces and fearful of travel. He complained of migraine headaches, urinary problems, and spastic colon. He later diagnosed his condition as an anxiety neurosis, which he believed was caused by an accumulation of sexual tension. But at the time, the genius who would reveal to the world the secrets of the unconscious could not yet see within himself those dark ruling forces.

---

*In 1955 a bust of Freud with the inscription from Sophocles was placed in the courtyard of the University of Vienna by Freud's first biographer, Ernest Jones.

Freud felt isolated and shunned. "No notice was taken of me," he claimed. His friend and mentor for more than ten years, the neurologist Josef Breuer, had broken with him, unable to accept Freud's emphasis on sexuality. Freud's father had died, and the death affected Freud profoundly, contributing to his inner torment. "I now feel quite uprooted," he said.

His work had reached an impasse. He had not achieved his great ambitions, his lofty dreams. There had been no formal academic position, no disciples, no success of any kind. With a large family to support, medical-school debts to pay, and a small private practice, Freud worried about financial matters. The situation fed his lifelong fear of poverty. His hopes were unfulfilled and his future uncertain.

But slowly his prospects improved. His neurotic symptoms finally drove him to undertake a program of self-exploration, an investigation of his own unconscious mind through the analysis of his dreams. He unraveled the threads of his past as revealed symbolically in his dreams, and his symptoms abated. He also noted an improvement in his sense of self-assurance.

His strong need for a father figure such as Breuer dissolved, to be replaced by a new kind of dependence, a need for followers who would admire him and pledge faithfully to carry on his work. In 1902, the first few of these surrogate children came to him. Responding to postcard invitations, four young men arrived to form the nucleus of the corps of psychoanalysts who would spread Freud's doctrine throughout the world.

The group met every Wednesday evening at 8:30 at Freud's home. This Wednesday Psychological Society included Wilhelm Stekel, Alfred Adler, Rudolf Reitler, and Max Kahane. Others joined the society—two more in 1902, another two in 1903—until by 1906 there were seventeen members. Like Freud, most of these early psychoanalysts were attracted to the field because of their own emotional problems. They sought as much to understand and heal themselves as to help others. Their discussions focused on personal conflicts, fantasies, and memories as well as on the problems of their patients.

Over black coffee and cigars, served by Freud's wife, Martha, the society members presented papers on various psychoanalytic concepts and discussed their case studies. Each new idea was hotly debated and criticized. Freud was highly pleased with the proceedings. Here was a stage for his ideas, a forum within which to elaborate on his work. Above all, here were loyal disciples who heeded the words of the master. Sigmund Freud had founded a movement.

With his heightened personal insight and emotional growth, the result of his continuing self-analysis, Freud's theories rapidly took on greater definition and shape. He spent a great deal of time writing, as much as his busy schedule of patients would allow, and produced several important books, beginning in 1900 with *The Interpretation of Dreams*, the result of his exploration of his own unconscious mind. Drawing on his childhood experiences, Freud outlined in this book the nature of the Oedipus complex, in which children become sexually attracted to the parent of the opposite sex and fearful of the parent of the same sex, whom they come to regard as a rival.

In Freud's view, the publication of *The Interpretation of Dreams* was almost totally ignored, and the few journals that deigned to review the book condemned it. In truth, although the book was not universally praised, it certainly attracted widespread attention. Professional journals in areas as diverse as philosophy, psychology, psychiatry, and medicine discussed the work, as did popular newspapers and magazines in Vienna, Berlin, and other major European cities. The book was said to contain "extraordinarily rich material of very accurately recorded dreams," and it was lauded as a work "thought through with genius." A German magazine judged it "interesting though strange," and in Zurich, Carl Jung read the book and mentioned it in his doctoral dissertation.

The following year Freud published *The Psychopathology of Everyday Life*. It became a popular success, drew some professional praise, and was translated into several languages. The theme of this book was how unconscious forces affect commonplace events, causing people to forget names, misspeak phrases, and utter embarrassing words.

Jokes and Their Relation to the Unconscious, his next major work, was published in 1905. In it, Freud discussed the similarity between jokes and dreams, arguing that both reveal unconscious thoughts and may serve as vicarious or symbolic means of fulfilling wishes. In *Three Essays on the Theory of Sexuality*, which appeared that same year, Freud emphasized the sexual themes that have become synonymous with his name and his system of psychoanalysis. He proposed the existence of sexual needs in infancy and discussed the changes in sexuality that occur with the onset of puberty. He also described and classified a variety of sexual deviations.

Freud was not too far ahead of his time in discussing sexual matters candidly. Free and frank discourse on sex was not unusual in Vienna at the turn of the century. Indeed, society was receptive to public debate of the topics Freud was raising in print. Not only was this open attitude toward sexuality evident in the culture at large, but for many years there had been a wealth of academic books about sexual pathology, many of them presaging Freud's ideas. His own works were received with considerable interest, which enhanced his professional stature.

The audience of those sympathetic to or curious about Freud's theories grew steadily. The daily mail brought inquiries from people who had read his books and wanted to know more about psychoanalysis. His correspondents wrote from Russia, Australia, India, the United States, South America, and Europe, and Freud considered each writer a potential acolyte. He answered each letter promptly, usually the day he received it.

His local following increased with his appointment in 1902 as Professor Extraordinarius at the University of Vienna, a position for which he had lobbied for five years. Although it was a part-time post and carried no regular salary, it enabled him to use the title of professor, which conferred immense prestige. The university affiliation also gave him the opportunity to seek converts for his movement.

Another sign of the continuing improvement in Freud's personal and professional situations was that he finally attained a small measure of financial security, brought about by a steady growth in the number of patients coming to consult him. He charged around eight dollars per hour, a sum considered expensive at the time, and soon he was able to indulge his passion for collecting such antiquities as Greek and Egyptian statues, vases, and busts.

The decade between Freud's fortieth and fiftieth birthdays thus saw significant changes in his personal life and the modest beginnings of an international reputation. Although he did not lack vocal detractors in Vienna and elsewhere, they were becoming outnumbered by his adherents. Through his writings and lectures Freud was determined to revolutionize the psychology of the human mind. He liked to suggest that opposition, rejection, and scorn were his constant companions, but this was not the case. By 1906 his ideas had influenced the younger generation of Viennese intellectuals, his private practice as a therapist was thriving, and he could even be called something of a celebrity.

With his movement well under way by 1906, Freud's daily routine assumed a comfortable rhythm organized around his work, and all of his activities were carefully structured. Martha Freud ensured that the large household—six children, her sister Minna Bernays, the housemaid, the governess, the charwoman, and visiting relatives—did not disturb her husband. The family occupied an apartment on the second floor of 19 Berggasse, in a respectable but unfashionable section of the city. They lived there for forty-six years, until 1938, when they fled from the Nazis.*

Freud's offices were originally on the first floor, but in 1908 he took over a sister's second-floor apartment so that his living

*In 1954 the World Federation for Mental Health placed a plaque on the building: "In this house lived and worked Professor Sigmund Freud." The apartment is now a museum, although Freud's books, mementos, and furnishings are in the London house in which he died in 1939. The London house was opened to the public in 1986.

and working quarters could be together. He rose at seven, usually unwillingly because of his habitual late-night hours, took a cold shower, and had his beard trimmed by a barber who came to the apartment. After a quick breakfast and a glance at the newspaper, he went to his office precisely at eight to see his first patient. He scheduled appointments throughout the morning hours, allotting 55 minutes to each. If anyone was late, Freud became quite perturbed.

At one o'clock he returned to the family quarters for the large main meal of the day—several courses, from soup to dessert. When he entered the dining room, he always indulged his youngest daughter, Anna, by "making a funny sound, something between a growl and a grunt." This was usually the only time the entire family was together. Freud took his evening meal too late for the younger children. At the table he devoted his attention wholly to the food, saying little to the others present. He was just as silent with visitors, forcing guests to make awkward conversation with family members instead of with the great man they had come to see.

Freud did listen to the conversation and always noted when anyone was missing. Gesturing toward the empty chair with a knife or fork, he would look expectantly at Martha. When she had satisfactorily explained the person's absence, Freud would nod and resume eating.

Whenever he acquired a new treasure—perhaps an antique coin or a small statue—he liked to place it on the table beside his plate and contemplate it along with his meal. He would do this once or twice until he found a permanent place for the object in his office or consultation room.

Freud waited impatiently for the daily mail delivery. During his five-minute respites between morning patients he frequently burst into the living quarters, demanding to know if the post had arrived. When a regular correspondent was tardy with a reply, Freud angrily counted the days since he had written to the thoughtless person. He kept meticulous records of the date on which he received each letter and the date he responded to it.

He reserved the afternoon hours between one and three o'clock for his first walk of the day. Freud descended the marble steps from the apartment, passed through the wide entryway leading from the courtyard to the street, and stepped out onto the cobblestones of Berggasse. Often he paused to look in the shop windows on the ground floor of the building—a butcher shop on one side and a food cooperative on the other. Much of Berggasse was steep; hence the name "Mountain Street." It stretched from the Tändelmarkt, the flea market, to the Votivkirche, a Gothic cathedral near the university. Occasionally one of the children accompanied Freud, as long as he or she could keep up the rapid pace. Friends liked to joke that Freud marched rather than walked.

Freud used these afternoon strolls not only for exercise but also for errands. He visited his publishers to deliver proofs of a book or article and stopped at the tobacconist to replenish his stock of cigars, of which he smoked twenty a day. By three o'clock he returned home, ready to receive patients for another six hours.

Following a light supper, at which he was usually more talkative than at lunch, Freud embarked on another brisk walk of two to three miles. Martha and Minna often joined him, and sometimes they stopped in at the Café Landtmann. The routes Freud chose were so predictable that students who wanted to speak with him knew exactly when and where to wait for his appearance.

Later in the evening Freud returned to his office to work on correspondence and manuscripts, often until well after midnight. When he finally went to bed he fell asleep immediately, waking precisely at seven the next morning.

Some evenings he deviated from this routine, but even these changes were predictable. On Wednesday nights, the Wednesday Psychological Society met at his home. On alternate Tuesdays he attended meetings of B'nai B'rith, a Jewish fraternal organization, at which he sometimes spoke about his theories. On Saturday evenings he presented a two-hour lecture at the university, and after class he indulged in a favorite pastime—a four-handed card game called tarock—at the home of his friend Leopold Königstein, an ophthalmologist.

And so it went from Monday through Saturday, a strict regimen centered on his work. But to Freud, the long and rigorous hours were not a burden he was forced to carry. His work was his life, his vocation and avocation, as necessary as the food he ate and the air he breathed. "I could not contemplate with any sort of comfort a life without work," he wrote to a friend. "I take no delight in anything else." And to another: "A man like me cannot live without a dominating passion. [Mine] is psychology."

On the seventh day Freud rested, but not completely. Despite certain social obligations, he contrived to do much of his writing on Sunday. The day began with a ritual call on his mother. Freud always complained of an upset stomach during these visits, so consistently that it became a family joke. He explained his indigestion as the result of the large dinner he had eaten at Königstein's the night before, but more than one Freudian analyst has suggested that Freud's visits to his mother triggered a regression to childhood, that Freud reverted to being a little boy in his mother's presence in an unconscious effort to win her sympathy and protection.

On Sunday afternoons Freud liked to take the children to museums and art galleries. The traditional evening meal was taken at his home, attended by his mother and five sisters, but the moment everyone had finished eating, Freud disappeared into his office.

The days passed with regularity from September through June, but in the hottest months of the summer the family left Vienna for a rented house in the mountains. There Freud walked for hours along the trails, often getting lost. (He had a poor sense of direction.) He enjoyed dressing in the Tyrolean costume of walking shorts, suspenders, and a green felt hat with a little brush at the brim.

His pastimes were identifying wildflowers and gathering strawberries, blueberries, and mushrooms. He was quite fond of mushrooms and took as much pleasure in discovering them as in eating them. He had an uncanny ability to ferret them out of the most hidden recesses of the forest, and when he uncovered an interesting specimen he would stalk it silently and pounce on it with his hat, as if he were capturing a butterfly.

After six weeks in this restful environment, Freud was ready to travel, either alone or with his sister-in-law Minna or a colleague. He liked the cities of Italy and was an energetic and enthusiastic tourist, although he suffered considerable anxiety just before setting out.

In the summer of 1906 the family spent a few weeks at Lavarone in the Dolomite Mountains of northern Italy before journeying to Riva on the northern tip of Lake Garda, a place Freud described as "paradise." Refreshed and restored, the family returned to Vienna in mid-September, and Freud immersed himself again in the development of psychoanalysis.

Although Freud continued to modify and elaborate on various aspects of his system throughout his life, by 1906 the foundation of his revolution of the mind was solid. Its structure had been built tall enough for onlookers to discern its shape and substance and to decide whether or not it was appealing. Despite Freud's repeated claims of being ignored and ostracized during his early years, his work had exerted a noticeable impact on the intellectual establishment. Justly he could say of himself, "I was one of those who have 'disturbed the sleep of the world.'"

The books published before 1906, especially *The Interpretation of Dreams,* outlined the fundamentals of psychoanalysis. Through the exhaustive examination of his own dreams, his patients' dreams, and his patients' revelations through the free-association technique,* Freud was convinced of the importance

---

*In free association (literally, to Freud, "free intrusion"), the patient responds to questions or to personal recollections and dreams with whatever comes to mind or intrudes into consciousness.

of unconscious forces in directing and controlling all human behavior, both normal and abnormal.

The power of the unconscious—its specific wishes and desires—is revealed not only in dreams but also in slips of the
tongue, memory lapses, and most human speech and action. We
repress unconscious desires that are personally abhorrent by hiding or barring them from conscious awareness. We do this for
our own protection, Freud said. If we were cognizant of these
thoughts, we might find them too distressing to live with. (A
trained analyst can probe the repressed material and interpret or
decode the symbolism of its manifestations in our dreams and
behaviors.)

Although the mechanism of repression keeps us unaware of
our powerful unconscious wishes, these wishes actively seek
some means of expression because merely submerging them does
not eliminate them. If they are not expressed in a healthy way
that permits us to accept them without shame or guilt, they will
show themselves in an unhealthy way through neurotic symptoms, such as the anxieties and physical discomforts Freud himself suffered. To Freud, life was a constant battle between the id
and the ego—between unconscious desires and wishes on the one
hand, and the more rational part of the personality, which attempts to control the id forces, on the other.

The unconscious id forces are predominantly sexual. Sexual
energy, which Freud called libido, is always pressing for expression and satisfaction. Suppressing sexual urges frustrates them,
transforming them into neuroses. Freud concluded that the cause
of every neurotic symptom he had seen among his patients could
be traced to conflicts relating to their sex life.

Although he recognized that adult sexual problems were
damaging, he believed that sexual conflicts dating from childhood were more destructive. His patients frequently told him
about sexual events in childhood, leading him to propose that
sexual awareness begins in infancy and not, as was then generally
held, at puberty. Many of Freud's colleagues, as well as the
general public, found this idea shocking.

Freud's patients recalled many childhood fantasies that focused on an unconscious sexual desire for the parent of the opposite sex, along with the wish to eliminate as a rival the parent of the same sex. And his own childhood fantasies as revealed in his dreams were persuasive—a longing for his mother and hostility toward his father. This was the idea Freud put forth in *The Interpretation of Dreams* as the Oedipus complex. He spoke from the depths of personal experience, an indication— one of many—of how much his psychoanalytic system was auto- biographical in nature.

Among Freud's supporters by 1906 was a small band of admirers in the somber Swiss city of Zurich. Freud was delighted. He saw the Zurich group as his most important conquest and held high hopes for the contingent of believers there. In the end, however, they caused him nothing but grief.

The city of Zurich surrounds the northern end of its lake with green parks, busy streets, and a disconcerting yet charming mix- ture of old and new buildings. The twin towers of the Roman- esque Grossmünster cathedral define the skyline of the old quarter, which rises steeply to the university and the mountains beyond. A mile and a half to the south, in the heights of the suburb of Reisbach, stands a severe block of stone buildings, the Burghölzli Psychiatric Hospital. In 1906 it was one of the best- known and most prestigious mental hospitals in all of Europe.

The Burghölzli was also the citadel of psychoanalysis, the only hospital in the world in which Freud's system of therapy was being practiced with patients. Psychoanalysis was also being taught at the medical school at the University of Zurich, for which the Burghölzli served as the psychiatric clinic.

It was Zurich rather than Freud's Vienna that supported the most active center of psychoanalysis in the early years of the twentieth century. The psychiatric clinic at the University of

Vienna was openly hostile to Freud's work. Although Freud lectured at the university there, his course was not a formal part of the primary curriculum for psychiatric training, and the awkward Saturday-evening schedule for his class was not designed to attract many students. Freud enjoyed the backing of a few intellectuals in Vienna but not the institutional sanction awarded his ideas in Zurich.

The support from the Burghölzli was enthusiastic and wholehearted. Its psychoanalytic circle held lively monthly discussions of Freud's views. Psychoanalytic terms were part of the everyday conversation of the staff, who were ever alert to their colleagues' slips of the tongue and other manifestations of Freudian mechanisms at work.

Psychoanalysis had been introduced to the Burghölzli by its director, Eugen Bleuler, who was one of Europe's foremost psychiatrists. Later known for his pioneering work with schizophrenia, Bleuler dedicated his life to the institution and was responsible for making psychoanalysis the Burghölzli's official doctrine. He lived on the hospital grounds and devoted his time to patient care and treatment. Fair and broad-minded, Bleuler allowed his staff doctors considerable freedom in their work, but in return he expected the same intense commitment he demanded of himself. A staff member likened the Burghölzli under Bleuler to a factory "where you worked very much and were poorly paid."

Bleuler was one of Freud's earliest adherents. He had read *The Interpretation of Dreams* shortly after its publication and had asked a junior resident, Carl Jung, to report on the book at a staff meeting. Bleuler wrote to Freud to say that he admired Freud's work and that he was applying Freudian principles to patient care at the Burghölzli. He described some of his dreams and asked for Freud's interpretation, and he expressed his agreement with Freud's ideas on the unconscious mind, infantile sexuality, and the sexual origin of neurosis.

Bleuler maintained a correspondence with Freud from 1904 until 1925. Freud admired—almost revered—Bleuler, although the relationship soured when Bleuler refused to join the official psychoanalytic organization.

Several ambitious and intelligent young psychiatrists were attracted to the Burghölzli, including some who became loyal, orthodox Freudians. Ernest Jones, Sandor Ferenczi, Karl Abraham, and A. A. Brill all took psychoanalytic training there.

Second to Bleuler, the major proponent of psychoanalysis by 1906 was his assistant, Carl Jung. He had been at the hospital only six years but had risen in the hierarchy and had earned considerable recognition in the psychiatric world.

Two weeks after graduation from medical school at the University of Basel, Jung appeared at the imposing stone entrance of the Burghölzli complex, baggage in hand, to begin his professional career. It was December 11, 1900. The doorman ushered him into a waiting room, where Bleuler welcomed him. Despite Jung's protestations, Bleuler hefted Jung's suitcases and led the younger man up three flights of stairs to his new home, a couple of small rooms directly above Bleuler's own.

Jung immersed himself in the rigorous work load expected at the hospital, describing his routine as "all intention, consciousness, duty, and responsibility." The day began with a round of the wards before the 8:30 staff meeting. Jung and three other psychiatric residents, who together were responsible for some four hundred patients, presented status reports on their cases. On many mornings a ten o'clock meeting followed to discuss new admissions. Bleuler believed in fostering a close emotional rapport between doctor and patient, although achieving this with psychotic patients who had little contact with reality required hour upon hour of intensive therapy.

Evening rounds took place between five and seven each day. Because the hospital employed no secretaries, not even for the director, Jung and the other physicians wrote their daily patient reports themselves, often working until eleven o'clock.

There was little time for a life beyond the hospital walls. The doors were locked at ten in the evening, and the junior residents were not permitted to have keys. Alcoholic beverages were prohibited because Bleuler was an ardent teetotaler. Jung quickly became an abstainer as well, referring to his time at the Burghölzli as a life "within monastic walls."

By his own account Jung was unhappy during his first months at the hospital and discontented with his choice of psychiatry as a specialty. He was horrified to discover that he "understood nothing at all." He felt incompetent at dealing with patients and guilty about being able to do so little to help them. His confusion increased when he discovered that his colleagues seemed to be satisfied with such work.

Jung soon learned that the other residents were having no more success with their psychiatric patients than he was, but they believed that they were doing everything possible. This realization did not alleviate Jung's doubts about his professional worth, so he cloistered himself more than the job required. He decided to read all fifty volumes of the German-language *Journal of General Psychiatry* in the hope of uncovering more effective treatments. The price he paid for his self-imposed isolation was alienation from his colleagues, who judged him to be distant and arrogant.

Despite this unpromising beginning of his career, Jung took consolation in Bleuler. Long seeking a spiritual hero and father, Jung found Bleuler an attractive candidate. For a time—a very short time—Jung felt a childlike mixture of adulation and respect for Bleuler, but within fewer than two years disappointment set in. The relationship provided a preview of the dynamics of Jung's involvement with Freud.

Jung later dismissed Bleuler as a "frosty old bachelor, a brilliantly successful pseudo-personality, festooned with complexes from top to bottom." So completely did Bleuler's influence fade from Jung's life that Jung made little mention of this onetime mentor when he wrote his autobiography.

In the winter of 1902 Jung took a brief leave of absence from the Burghölzli to go to Paris to attend the lectures of Pierre Janet. A pioneer in the study of hysteria and the use of hypnosis to treat emotional disorders, Janet had done extensive work on the unconscious mind, leading some to suggest that his conception of the unconscious predated Freud's. This was a point Jung would make years later.

Although Jung found many of Janet's ideas appealing, the man himself proved to be a disappointment, failing to live up to Jung's inflated expectations for a father figure. Perhaps Janet showed too little interest in the unsophisticated but sensitive young man from Zurich. Jung may have felt personally slighted. In any case, his bitterness toward Janet surfaced in his writings. He called the eminent Frenchman "a mere intellect devoid of personality" and "a typical mediocre bourgeois." Like Bleuler, Janet is mentioned only infrequently in Jung's autobiography.

In 1903, Jung married Emma Rauschenbach, whose wealth would alter his lifestyle considerably. It was also at this time that Freud became important to him. He began to apply Freudian ideas and methods to his own patients and devised a diagnostic tool with which to confirm some of Freud's conclusions. This technique—word association—brought Jung widespread recognition and acclaim, particularly among psychiatrists and psychologists in the United States.

The word-association technique had previously been used only with conscious ideas and thoughts. At Bleuler's suggestion, Jung attempted to use it to uncover unconscious material. He would read aloud a list of words to a patient and ask the patient to respond to each word with the first thing that came to mind. The procedure provided a way of organizing the nonsense typically uttered by psychotic patients. Jung developed a list of one hundred common words, such as *tree, blue,* and *lamp,* that he believed were capable of eliciting emotional responses. He recorded not only the response but also the time that elapsed until the patient replied.

After administering the test to a large number of patients, Jung concluded that the words to which they had difficulty responding—as evidenced by long delays or an inability to think of a response—revealed unconscious disturbances. Jung accepted the Freudian notion that unconscious and repressed material contributed directly to mental illness. Now he had a way of probing those repressed experiences and bringing them to the patient's attention. He could show experimentally that repressed material existed, and thus he could confirm the essence of Freud's theory.

Jung observed that the test words to which his patients showed abnormal reactions centered around common themes, which he called complexes. These complexes became clear to him when he interpreted his patients' word-association responses in psychoanalytic terms. Although this strengthened his belief in Freudian theory, he was puzzled to discover that the repressed wishes and desires of some patients did not involve sexual events. This planted the seeds of a crucial doubt in his mind about Freud's emphasis on sex.

By 1906 Jung's reports of his research had brought him considerable professional notice. When his relationship with Freud began, he was not an unknown student, as were most of Freud's Viennese followers. Jung's word-association studies had been published in prestigious English-language journals. His private practice was expanding and already included several wealthy American patients.

Two years earlier he had established a research laboratory for experimental pathology at the Burghölzli that attracted psychologists and psychiatrists from the United States. He was appointed as lecturer at the University of Zurich to teach clinical psychiatry, psychotherapy, and psychoanalysis. At the same time he was promoted to clinical director at the hospital, placing him second in authority to Bleuler, and he also became head of outpatient services. The career that had begun on such an inauspicious note a few years before was advancing brilliantly and rapidly.

In some quarters Jung's reputation was more respected than Freud's, partly because of his association with the Burghölzli and Bleuler. The major share of Jung's fame, however, stemmed from the ingenuity and innovativeness of his own work, and the inspiration for that work had come from the ideas of Sigmund Freud.

At first Jung was disturbed when the results of his word-association research so strongly corroborated Freud's position. Jung hoped for a university career, and he knew that Freudian theory was unacceptable to many in academic circles. He had been warned by two professors that his career would be in jeopardy if he publicly sided with Freud, but Jung said that he would not want any career based on hiding the truth. Thus Jung made his decision and became an open and vocal supporter of Freud and psychoanalysis.

In April 1906 Jung sent Freud a copy of his new book on the word-association research he was conducting with his patients. It contained several references to Freud's writings and showed how extensively Jung accepted psychoanalysis. Freud replied immediately, warmly thanking Jung for the book, although he had already purchased a copy in his eagerness to read it. He expressed his pleasure in seeing that Jung's work demonstrated everything Freud knew to be true about the unconscious. He said he was confident that Jung would continue to support him. That marked the beginning of a voluminous correspondence of more than 350 letters.

Six months later Freud sent Jung his latest work, *Collected Short Papers on the Theory of the Neuroses.* Jung's reply expressed the hope that Freud's followers would continue to grow in number. Jung mentioned that he had recently defended Freud's work in a confrontation with Gustav Aschaffenburg, a professor of psychiatry and neurology at the University of Heidelberg and a critic of psychoanalysis. Jung also championed Freud's ideas at a meeting in Tübingen, arguing against Alfred Hoche, a psychiatry professor from Freiburg. Jung told Freud that he agreed that the genesis of neurosis was predominantly sexual, but it was not, in Jung's opinion, exclusively so.

Freud answered at once. He recognized that Jung was not totally committed to the primacy of sexuality as the cause of neurosis, but he hoped that eventually Jung would accept his position. He charged that his detractors—Aschaffenburg and the others—were merely repressing their own sexuality! He closed the letter by saying that whenever he saw a new book or article by Jung or Bleuler, it gave him the great satisfaction of knowing that all "the hard work of a lifetime has not been entirely in vain."

Jung continued to state his doubts about Freud's emphasis on sexuality. Although he admitted that his reservations could be related to his inexperience in clinical practice, he nonetheless pressed the point. He asked Freud if neurotic behavior could be at least partially attributed to other factors such as basic physiological drives. As an example, he mentioned hunger, which is manifested in sucking and eating.

Freud professed to be pleased by Jung's question because it showed that Jung had, after all, grasped the underlying sexual nature of neurosis. The role of sexuality, he lectured, was obvious, so much so that virtually all other behaviors—such as sucking and eating—are expressions of its power.

Freud was gratified to have as a spokesman for his work someone of Jung's stature, a psychiatrist who was not part of the Vienna circle of psychoanalysts. None of Freud's Viennese followers was particularly distinguished in academic or psychiatric circles. Freud was intolerant of mediocrity, and he recognized that most of the loyalists in his immediate group were not exceptionally impressive or talented. Moreover, virtually all of them were Jewish, and Freud was concerned that his system would be labeled a Jewish science. He believed that the success of the movement depended on having a prominent non-Jew, such as Jung, identified with it.

Jung appeared to be the ideal promoter for psychoanalysis, the perfect candidate to assume leadership of the movement. Freud realized in 1906 that he had done little more than launch a system of thought and therapy, and he knew it would be many years before psychoanalysis would revolutionize the psychiatric world. He was already fifty years old and concerned about the impact of his death on the future of his ideas. Indeed, Freud feared that he would die within a year.

Wilhelm Fliess, the friend on whom Freud depended during the neurotic episode in his forties, had proposed a bizarre theory of periodicity and life cycles, which formed the basis of the popular notion of biorhythms. He predicted that age fifty-one would be critical for Freud and might even be his last year. Freud had doubts about Fliess's theory but was superstitious enough to become obsessed by the prediction. He dreamed about Fliess's calculations and about his own death. "I would so much like to hold out," he told Fliess, "until that famous age limit of approximately fifty-one."

The crucial time was just one year away, and there was still so much to be done for psychoanalysis. Freud's need for an intellectual heir was paramount, but the chosen one would have to be deserving, capable of brilliant research, and possessed of sufficient prestige to be accepted by the academic community. Freud believed he could make no better choice than Carl Jung.

In addition, Freud's emotional craving for admirers, for surrogate sons, was not being satisfied by his Viennese disciples, devoted though they were. Freud needed a son whose strength would match his own. Again, Jung was the obvious—and the only—choice.

To prepare Jung for his leadership role, Freud described the torments that he, as the innovator and founder, had been forced to suffer. Freud revealed to Jung

> [the] unavoidable necessity of passing, among my own support-
> ers, as the incorrigibly self-righteous crank or fanatic that in
> reality I am not. Left alone for so long with my ideas, I have
> come, understandably enough, to rely more and more on my
> own decisions. In the last fifteen years I have been increasingly
> immersed in preoccupations that have become monotonously
> exclusive. (At present I am devoting ten hours a day to psycho-
> therapy.) This has given me a kind of resistance to being urged
> to accept opinions that differ from my own.

Jung later referred to this attitude of Freud's as unyielding dogmatism, but early in the relationship Jung's reaction was to promise to trust Freud in all matters in which he had greater experience. Freud believed he deserved Jung's trust. He had asked for it from very few people.

For three years Jung had been collecting data from observations of his patients for a book to be entitled *The Psychology of Dementia Praecox.* In the preface he qualified his support for psychoanalytic theory. Noting his debt to Freud's "brilliant discoveries," Jung also warned of the danger of submitting uncritically to Freudian dogma. He reiterated that he did not place as much emphasis on sexuality as Freud did.

Jung's emotional need for Freud was equal to Freud's for Jung. The younger man was seeking a mentor, a spiritual and intellectual guide, a surrogate father, and he therefore adopted most of Freud's beliefs. His early research, his initial attempts to treat his patients, and his first writings all were sketched within the frame of the Freudian model. Freud and psychoanalysis loomed large in Jung's life, and yet he resisted, unable to accept all of Freud's ideas unreservedly. He felt trapped between dependence and independence, between the security offered by submission to an authority figure and the desire to find his own way.

Having just six years in the profession, Jung was unprepared to resolve the conflict. He chose to disagree timorously with Freud, tentatively substituting his own thoughts, but not too loudly or for too long.

Although he showed a small measure of independence to the public in the preface to *Dementia Praecox,* it was with trepidation that he sent the book to Freud on December 29, 1906. He apologized for not being a more dutiful son. "You cannot be anything but dissatisfied with my book," he wrote. He offered Freud an explanation, a rationalization for questioning his emphasis on sexuality. It was done for political reasons, out of consideration for the academic establishment. Psychoanalysis had to be presented tastefully.

Freud questioned the need for such diplomacy and for trying to make psychoanalysis more palatable to its critics. He admonished Jung for paying too much attention to their opponents. Surely they would not amount to anything.

The tension that would undermine their relationship was already evident by the end of 1906, when only ten letters had passed between them. Each man was hastily—and perhaps blindly—forging bonds of dependence. Jung decried the lack of personal contact with his mentor, and Freud urged Jung to trust him, support him, and follow him. Their needs were clear and visible, needs that had formed, grown, and festered in childhood.

CHAPTER TWO

The Dream of the Three Fates: Freud's Early Years

$\mathbf{A}$s his mother was carried into the room, seven-year-old Sigmund Freud watched in horror. He looked at her lovely young face and was puzzled by her peaceful expression of sleep. His gaze shifted to the people who were carrying her. They were unusually tall and draped in strange clothing, but it was the faces that frightened the young boy. They were not those of humans but of birds with long beaks. Sigmund awoke from his dream screaming and crying. He jumped out of bed and ran to his parents' room. When he realized his mother was still alive, he calmed down.

Even thirty years later the dream retained its emotional intensity for Freud. When he finally analyzed it, he understood the reason. The superficial meaning was obvious—a little boy's fear of losing his mother—but Freud found a more subtle and shocking interpretation.

He examined the visual content of the nightmare, concentrating on the images of the beaked figures, seeking the symbolic significance of the creatures. What could they reveal about the unconscious longings of a seven-year-old boy? He recalled a childhood friend, a boy more worldly than he, who had introduced him to the word *vögeln*, the German slang expression for sexual intercourse. The term is derived from *Vogel*, which translates in English as "bird." Instantly the meaning of the dream came clear. It represented for Freud at the age of seven a sexual longing for his mother; it was the familiar Oedipal theme.

As a boy Freud adored his mother, and Amalie Freud returned the love of her firstborn with equal intensity. She was only twenty-one when Sigmund was born (his father was forty-one) and was beautiful, vivacious, and intelligent. From the beginning she believed that Sigmund was destined for greatness and fame. Even in her later years she referred to him as *mein goldener Sigi*. In her eyes he could do no wrong.

She once met an old woman in a shop who offered a prediction. "You are a lucky mother," the woman said. "Someday the whole world will talk about this little fellow." The story was often repeated in the Freud household, and soon it was not only Amalie who believed in Sigmund's special destiny; he came to believe it as well. Dreams of glory, the ambition to succeed, and supreme self-confidence became part of his character, attributes he never lost. Reflecting on this as an adult, he wrote, "A man who has been the indisputable favorite of his mother keeps for life the feeling of a conqueror, that confidence of success that often induces real success."

Amalie Freud's hopes for her eldest son revealed much about her own desires, the yearnings she hoped to satisfy through Sigmund. She dreamed that she would live to attend his funeral, accompanied by the leaders of all the great nations of Europe; at Sigmund's seventieth-birthday celebration she wandered among the guests, announcing to anyone who would listen that she was "the mother."

If the child is father to the man, as Freud came to believe, then we can see the similarity between the seven-year-old boy who dreamed of losing his mother and the middle-aged man who unraveled the thread of that dream. We can understand how the favored son came to believe not only in his eventual greatness but in the correctness of his theories in the face of opposition.

Also apparent is the reflection of his childhood years in his theories, particularly in the suggestion of a boy's powerful sexual craving for his mother. His attachment to Amalie persisted until her death, but, curiously, he did not attend the funeral.

There was a price to pay for the unqualified adulation, love, and security Freud received from his mother. So powerfully seductive was this emotional support that he continued to need it as an adult. When it was withdrawn, his self-confidence was replaced by doubt, strength by weakness and vulnerability, and emotional security by anxiety and worry. The absence of mother love was crippling, and the craving for its reinstatement consumed him. Freud realized this when he examined the causes of his own neurosis by analyzing the symbolism of his dreams, the primary language of his system of psychoanalysis.

In one dream, which he called his dream of the three fates, Freud was searching for food. He wanted some pudding, went into the kitchen, and found three women there. One—the hostess of the inn—was making dumplings, working a doughy substance with her hands. Freud asked for something to eat but was told he would have to wait until she was ready. He became impatient, stalked away, and put on an overcoat, which, to his surprise, was trimmed with fur. That coat was too big, so he reached for one that had a long stripe and some sort of Turkish design. A bearded man prevented Freud from trying on the coat, claiming it was his. After discussing the Turkish designs, Freud and the bearded man became friends.

In Freud's interpretation of this dream, the three women in the kitchen represented the "three fates who spin the destiny of man." The hostess was his mother. He recalled many times as a child going into the kitchen and finding his mother standing by the fire.

According to Erich Fromm, a psychoanalyst who spent many years studying Freud's writings, the dream of the three fates shows the typical response of a boy who has been favored by his mother. He demands to be fed by her; the feeding symbolizes nurturing and protecting. Freud became angry when told he must wait because the esteemed son is used to being nourished by his mother immediately. He does not expect to wait, and he believes such attention is his right. In his impatience, he leaves his mother and tries to assume his father's role by attempting to don coats that are too large or belong to someone else.

Even after Freud resolved his neurotic problems through self-analysis, he continued to be dependent, seeking people who would in some sense care for him, love him, and admire him. This need was apparent in his relationships with his wife and with several mentors including Josef Breuer, two professors under whom he worked, and Carl Jung. Freud transferred to these people the craving for emotional sustenance that his mother had so amply satisfied.

This need, and the insecurity that accompanied it, were also evident in two fears that Freud believed stemmed from his childhood—a fear of poverty and starvation and a fear of traveling. In letters to friends Freud frequently referred to memories of not having enough to eat. "I came to know the helplessness of poverty," he told Wilhelm Fliess, "and continually fear it." In fact, Freud's childhood had not been marked by poverty. The family was reasonably comfortable financially when Sigmund was a child. The explanation for his fear of poverty cannot be traced to his early experiences but seems instead to be symbolic, indicating his apprehension about losing his mother's warmth, love, and protection.

This symbolism may also explain Freud's other manifestation of insecurity, the fear of travel. Freud traveled a great deal, so his anxiety did not hold him captive, but it did influence his behavior. Trains were the most common and convenient mode of transportation, and Freud always arrived at the railway station a full hour before departure so he would not risk missing the train. He preferred to travel with a companion on whom he could depend, usually his sister-in-law Minna or a colleague. If travel is symbolic of leaving the security of home and mother, of severing ties and becoming independent, then for people with a strong maternal attachment travel can appear dangerous.

Although Amalie Freud was a major shaper of her son's personality, she was not the sole influence. The childhood drama of the Oedipus complex involves three actors—mother, son, and father—the latter being the rival for the mother's affection. If the boy is to be the sole possessor of his mother's love, then he must displace the father and assume that role for himself.

Freud showed his feelings toward his father, Jakob, when he was about seven years old: one night he walked into his parents' bedroom and deliberately urinated in front of them. Jakob was irate. "The boy will come to nothing," he shouted. This scene frequently recurred in Freud's adult dreams, but it was always accompanied by a recitation of his accomplishments, as though Freud was saying to his father, "You see, I *have* come to something."

In formulating his theory of psychoanalysis, Freud believed that the father has a great impact on the son's development, and one trait that evolves from this relationship is ambition. Freud saw this in himself. "I have come to something," he kept reminding himself. To conquer and displace his father meant that Freud would have to excel continually, moving on to ever greater success.

It also meant feeling superior to his father, an attitude that Freud recognized he had shown by the age of two. He recalled wetting his bed and being admonished by his father, but the boy's reaction was not remorse or guilt but smugness and self-confidence. "Don't worry, Papa," he said. "I will buy you a beautiful new bed." Sigmund had not been impressed by the scolding but instead imagined himself to be the adult, the one who could present the father with a new bed. These were words of superiority, of aspiration and ambition.

In the Oedipus complex the son not only hates the father but fears him as well; after all, the father is bigger and stronger. But a son also needs a father's protection and desires to respect the father as a person of strength. Freud's father, to him, was a weakling. As a child, Freud identified with such historic giants as Napoleon and Hannibal. His father could not measure up to these heroes. As an adult, Freud wrote that he would have become successful sooner if only his father had been a professor or someone of similar stature instead of a mere merchant.

Freud never forgot a story that he had heard at the age of twelve from his father. When Jakob was a young man he had been walking along a street when a passerby knocked his cap off and shouted, "Jew, get off the pavement!" What did his father do? "I went into the roadway," Jakob said, "and picked up my cap." Freud recalled that "this struck me as unheroic conduct on the part of the big strong man who was holding the little boy by the hand."

By identifying himself with heroes, Freud had to rebel against a father who might have been good enough for an ordinary son but not for one who bore the supreme self-confidence derived from his mother's love.

Other members of the Freud household helped to shape his personality. Freud's early years were enmeshed in a web of relationships that were a source of confusion and disillusionment, providing rich soil for the roots of his neuroses. His nanny, an old, ugly, and clever woman who looked after the child until he was nearly three, was a practicing Catholic who regularly took him to church and taught him about heaven and hell. After church services, the boy liked to preach to the rest of the family about God. The nanny praised him, reinforcing his growing sense of self-importance.

Freud assigned sexual overtones to this relationship. He wrote of being seduced by the nanny and being washed in reddish water in which she had bathed. In his memory she had instructed him in sexual matters. She was stealing from the family, however, and had on occasion induced young Sigmund to steal. His brother reported her to the police, and she was arrested and jailed. Her sudden disappearance from Sigmund's life was a shock. He had grown fond of her.

Throughout his life Freud repeatedly was disappointed by other people, believing that many who once were close had deserted or failed him. The experience with his nanny was the prototype for the wrecked relationships of the future.

An array of three generations of family members within the Freud home led to assorted sibling rivalries and hostilities. Amalie was Jakob Freud's third wife. His two sons by an earlier marriage, Emanuel and Philipp, were approximately Amalie's age. Emanuel's son, John, was a year older than Sigmund, and his daughter, Pauline, was two years older, yet Sigmund was their uncle. John and Pauline addressed Sigmund's father as grandfather. Which of these people belonged together? It would not have been unnatural for the boy to pair off the older people, the ones in authority—his father and his nanny. Emanuel belonged with his wife, but that left the young adults, Philipp and Amalie. This couple might have seemed reasonable to young Sigmund were it not for the fact that his father, not Philipp, slept with Amalie.

Sigmund's nephew, John, being about the same age, exerted a great influence on his early years. Freud came to believe that this association was the source of the neurotic component of all future relationships and of his combative temperament. Sigmund and John were companions as well as adversaries. Although Freud later complained that John had treated him badly, he also noted that he had opposed the tyrant with considerable courage.

In his thirties Freud described John's impact on his adult friendships. "All my friends have in a certain sense been reincarnations of this first figure. My emotional life has always insisted that I should have an intimate friend and a hated enemy. I have always been able to provide myself afresh with both, and it has not infrequently happened that the ideal situation of childhood has been so completely reproduced that friend and enemy have come together in a single individual." Carl Jung would be another of these reincarnations.

Together, Sigmund and John behaved cruelly toward John's sister, Pauline, and the relationship had a sexual side, revealed in Freud's fantasy that he and John raped her. One of Freud's biographers, a psychoanalyst, interpreted this fantasy as follows: "Freud's sexual constitution was not exclusively masculine. To hunt in couples means sharing one's gratification with someone of one's own sex."

When Freud was not quite a year old he faced a rival for his mother's love. Amalie gave birth to a boy, Julius, and she could no longer respond on demand to Sigmund's wishes and whims. He grew intensely jealous of Julius and wished him dead. Eight months later that desire was fulfilled. Freud's remorse, guilt, and self-reproach never left him.

When Freud was two, his mother had another child, a girl named Anna. Again Sigmund showed his jealousy of the usurper and his anger at having to share his mother's love. But he was old enough then to consider the mystery, the unanswered question: he wanted to know where this infant had come from.

His emotional turmoil increased when, during Amalie's confinement, his beloved nanny disappeared. Freud suspected that his older half brother Philipp was involved in the disappearance, so he asked him what had happened to the old woman. Philipp, making a joke, said she had been "boxed up," meaning imprisoned, but Sigmund took the remark literally.

Some time later, when Amalie was out, Sigmund became frantic, believing that she had left him. Recalling Philipp's explanation, Sigmund dragged him to a large cupboard and cried for him to open it. When Sigmund looked inside, he was crestfallen. His mother was not in the box.

In an attempt to interpret the incident three decades later, Freud wrote:

> The child of not yet three had understood that the little sister who had recently arrived had grown inside his mother. He was very far from approving of this addition to the family, and was full of mistrust and anxiety that his mother's inside might conceal still more children. The wardrobe or cupboard was a symbol for him of his mother's inside. So he insisted on looking into this cupboard and turned to his big brother, who had taken his father's place as the child's rival. Besides the well-founded suspicion that this brother had had the lost nurse "boxed up," there was a further suspicion against him—namely that he had in some way introduced the recently born baby into his mother's inside.

His mother's "inside" did conceal more children. Five girls and a boy were born over the next nine years, but their arrival did not instigate the jealousy occasioned by the births of Julius and Anna.

❖

Another aspect of Freud's childhood that helped to mold his character was his sense of Jewish identity. This underlies his personality and his relationship with Carl Jung; part of Jung's importance to Freud lay in the fact that Jung was not Jewish. Freud's educational and intellectual progress were influenced by the Jewish tradition of learning and the supremacy of logic and reason. The Jewish heritage also affected his emotional development. "I have often felt," he wrote, "as though I had inherited all the defiance and all the passions with which our ancestors defended their Temple."

The word *defiance* applies to much of Freud's attitude toward the world, particularly the organized medical and psychiatric establishment that opposed him and the colleagues who tried to modify the orthodox religion he called psychoanalysis. He worked steadfastly to protect his temple of faith. Born and nurtured as an outsider, a member of a traditionally oppressed minority group, he became a professional outsider in proposing and promoting psychoanalysis. Freud actively courted that role, sometimes playing it to excess.

He took pleasure in depicting himself as resolute in the face of opposition, persecution, and vilification, although the opposition was not as fierce as he pretended. He fostered the legend of the psychoanalyst, the Jew, encircled by the enemy, brilliantly and courageously repelling attack after attack.

In that sense, then, Freud wrapped himself in the cloak of his Jewishness and wore it as a challenge. If there was criticism of his theoretical system, it was because he was a Jew. He believed that if his name did not sound Jewish, his ideas would meet with less resistance.

During the years he was growing to maturity, anti-Semitism

in Vienna was largely dormant, and all professions were open to Jews. "This was a time when Jewish schoolboys, Freud and others, caressed in their fantasies a general's uniform, a professor's lectern, a minister's portfolio, or a surgeon's scalpel." Jews had been granted formal political equality in 1867 but had unofficially enjoyed full political rights at least ten years before.

No ethnic quota had been imposed on admission to the universities. The faculty of the University of Vienna and its medical school included many Jewish professors. In 1869, 30 percent of the medical-school faculty was Jewish, and twenty years later the figure was nearly 50 percent. On the surface, then, an individual's religion was not an issue in career decisions.

Anti-Semitism increased during the 1870s and 1880s, although not on the scale it would assume following World War I. Nevertheless, Freud developed an early sensitivity to manifestations of anti-Semitism, which probably derived less from personal experience than from his father's stories about the old days in Moravia and the enforced restrictions against Jews.

Years later, at the age of forty-five, while Freud was on a fishing expedition in Bavaria with his sons, they were jeered by a group of men yelling anti-Jewish slogans. The Freuds later encountered the same men, armed with sticks, blocking their path. According to Freud's son Martin, Freud "charged the hostile crowd, which gave way before him and promptly dispersed."

This defiance and anger, this defensiveness and hostility, were part of Freud's personality, along with ambition and self-confidence. These traits gave him "the strength to defy public opinion and to accept, like his ancestors, a sort of intellectual exile." Allied with these characteristics were a suspicion and distrust of people who were not Jewish. He spoke more than once of the "suppressed anti-Semitism of the Swiss" and, by extension, of Carl Jung.

Freud had not been taught to practice Judaism as a religion. His father did not adhere to the Orthodox customs and rituals, and the family never observed the Sabbath or the holidays. As an old man Freud considered himself to be "completely estranged from the religion of his ancestors." If he were asked what about him was Jewish, he said he would answer, "Not very much, but probably the main thing"—the main thing being the defiant, defensive, suspicious part of his nature. To Freud, his Jewish identity was not a set of practices but an attitude that permeated his adult thoughts and behavior.

In his psychoanalytic theory, Freud proposed that personality is formed by the age of five or six and that the character shaped in those early years is the basis for the character of the adult. Thus, childhood experiences assume a lifelong importance. In the crucible of Freud's childhood were forged the traits that made him a scientific innovator and discoverer, a fighter for his cause, a neurotic, an authoritarian leader, and a friend and rival to those with whom he worked. Ambition, self-confidence, insecurity, dependence, defiance, and hostility became the qualities with which he—and Jung—had to contend.

Freud's first three years of life, from 1856 to 1859, were spent in Freiberg, a small town in Moravia about 150 miles from Vienna. He later remembered the town and its rural surroundings with pleasure. He also recalled that he felt financially secure during those years because his father's textile business was prospering. In 1859, however, Jakob Freud's financial affairs suffered severe reversals as part of a general decline in the textile trade. His sons Emanuel and Philipp lost a considerable amount of the family money investing in ostrich-feather farms in South Africa. Adding to Jakob's anxiety was the rise of anti-Jewish sentiment in Moravia, so the Freuds moved, first to Leipzig, where they stayed for a year, and then to Vienna. Later, Emanuel took his family (including Freud's friend and enemy, young John) and Philipp to England.

Sigmund was not happy to leave his home in the country for a small apartment in the crowded city. His usually phenomenal memory for childhood events failed him during these unpleasant years, and he reported few recollections between the ages of three and seven. "They were hard times and not worth remembering."

The Freud family lived in a succession of buildings in the mostly Jewish Leopoldstadt district of Vienna and finally settled in a roomy, three-bedroom apartment on Kaiser Josefstrasse. It was here that Sigmund lived until his graduation from medical school.

The source and extent of Jakob Freud's income during the early years in Vienna continue to puzzle biographers. He is not listed in the city's tax records or register of tradesmen, so it is possible that he was not formally employed. Amalie's family provided some financial assistance, and Emanuel may have sent funds from England, but wherever the money came from, Sigmund's childhood was not spent in the poverty he often described. The family could afford summer vacations in the country, oil portraits of the children, books, theater tickets, and a piano. Theirs was one of the first dining rooms in the neighborhood to boast a new petroleum lamp, a luxury at the time.

Sigmund, the favorite child, was given the best of whatever was available, including the only private room. Although small, it was his alone, crammed with a desk, chairs, bookcases, and a bed. The other children did their schoolwork by candlelight; he had an oil lamp.

He spent a great deal of time in that room, disappearing as soon as he came home from school. As he grew older, he took his evening meal in his room so he could devote more time to his studies. The household routine revolved around the budding scholar, and every sacrifice was made to enable him to concentrate on his books, which soon overflowed his cubicle.

When his sister Anna began piano lessons at the age of eight, she practiced in a room quite distant from Sigmund's. Still, he found it too noisy and told his mother that he would move out if she did not get rid of the piano. The instrument was removed, and the other children were not given the opportunity to play.

This incident may mark the onset of Freud's aversion to

music. None of his own children received music lessons, and despite his residence in Vienna, the international city of music, he rarely attended concerts. A disciple recalled the "pained expression on [Freud's] face on entering a restaurant or beer garden where there was a band and how quickly his hands would go over his ears to drown the sound."

Freud's parents allowed little to interfere with his studies, and their efforts were soon rewarded. Freud consistently performed at the head of his class and received many academic prizes. His determination to succeed was so great that he devoted the bulk of his boyhood and youth to his schoolwork. These years set a pattern; for the rest of his life, little mattered to him except work.

He read everything his teachers prescribed as well as books to satisfy his own wide-ranging interests. He could read and converse in German, Hebrew, Latin, Greek, French, and English, and he later became fluent in Spanish and Italian. He was fond of English-language books and at the age of eight discovered Shakespeare. American culture intrigued him, and he read each new book by Mark Twain as soon as it appeared. The American form of government also interested him, and he memorized Lincoln's Gettysburg Address. Anna recalled Sigmund reciting Lincoln's famous speech to the assembled siblings and explaining its meaning.

His youth and adolescence brought an enthusiasm for military history. He received a set of toy soldiers and named each of them for an officer in Napoleon's army. He also collected war books. During the Austro-Prussian war in the summer of 1866, Jakob took the ten-year-old Sigmund to the railway station to see the troop trains bearing wounded men returning from the battlefield. The boy watched spellbound as blood-spattered figures were loaded into carts for transport to the hospitals. So affected was he by this experience that he asked his mother for used linen to make dressings for the wounded. Women and schoolgirls were preparing thousands of bandages, and Sigmund persuaded his teachers to let the boys make them as well.

Four years later, France declared war on Prussia, and Sigmund followed the battles with meticulous attention. He kept a map of the war zones in his room and plotted the movements of the armies with tiny flags. In somber tones he lectured his sisters Anna and Rose about the progress of the fighting and the strategies represented by the flags.

The boy dreamed of military glory, which was not uncommon in children at his age, but he also made it a serious and thorough study. His plans for a military career faded with time, but the effects lingered. In his writings on psychoanalysis, he often employed military terms such as *defense* mechanisms; other military references have been lost in translation from German to English.

Nothing in Freud's writings or in those of his colleagues indicates that he believed his dedication and commitment to scholarship in his youth was unusual or that he felt he was sacrificing social or recreational pursuits to his desire to learn. He was intensely ambitious and eager to fulfill his aspirations and those of his parents. In accordance with Jewish culture, the path to success and self-fulfillment lay in education. An intellectually gifted Jewish boy should work to maximize his talents.

Social life and play were peripheral. Young Freud's friends often visited him, but he would draw them into his room for serious discussions about their lessons. Anna called them his study mates, not playmates. Although he had no time for sports or games, he became an avid walker, hiking energetically along the trails in the Vienna woods. But even this activity was partially to foster his studies, and he invariably returned with specimens of plants and flowers to examine and classify.

Social dating was an uncommon practice in the time of Freud's youth, and he reported only one romantic experience. At the age of sixteen he visited his hometown of Freiberg and became enchanted by its charming country setting. There he became reacquainted with Gisela Fluss, a childhood playmate, and was captivated by her black hair and dark eyes. Freud imagined himself to be in love. Although he was a guest in the Fluss home and saw Gisela often, he was too shy to speak to her.

Frustrated and distraught, Freud spent his days wandering through the forest indulging in erotic fantasies, angry with his father for having taken him away from such a pretty place and such a remarkable girl. How pleasant it would be to stay in Freiberg and marry Gisela! Years later Freud admitted that he had probably been more in love with an idealized image of his infancy in Freiberg than with the girl herself.

The following year, 1873, when Freud graduated from the *Gymnasium*,* Vienna was in chaos. A cholera epidemic caused thousands of residents to flee. The stock market collapsed, precipitating bankruptcies and an economic recession. These financial conditions apparently had little effect on the Freud family, however, because Sigmund was able to enroll in medical school. At first his father objected, claiming that the boy was softhearted and horrified by the sight of blood, but Sigmund overrode his father's objections. Jakob agreed to support him during the prolonged years of medical study.

In the meantime Jakob harbored other plans for his son. In consultation with his son Emanuel he hatched the idea that Sigmund should move to England, join Emanuel's business, and marry Pauline (the niece about whom Sigmund had rape fantasies as a child). To foster this scheme, Jakob sent him to Manchester for a vacation after he completed two years of medical training. He enjoyed the trip but found he was not attracted to Pauline. Later, when he was having difficulty launching his medical career, Freud considered this "lost opportunity of an easier life" and decided that his father's plan had merit.

Freud returned to Vienna and resumed his medical studies but had no intention of becoming a practicing physician. He considered himself a scientist, not a doctor, and wanted a career in the research laboratory. "I lack that passion for helping," he wrote. "I have no knowledge of having had in my early years any craving to help suffering humanity. In my youth I felt an overpowering need to understand something of the riddles of the

*A high school/junior college preparatory for the university.

world in which we live and perhaps even to contribute something to their solution."

He felt the same way even after he became the founder of psychoanalysis. He was much more interested in uncovering the secrets of the human mind than in curing his patients. His psychotherapy was a tool for discovery more than for healing.

Freud's motivation stemmed from two sources—an intense curiosity about how things worked and a desire for fame. He could not hope to attain the greatness promised by his mother's faith in him if he were an ordinary physician treating runny noses and backaches. His future lay in making important scientific discoveries.

To prepare himself for this career, Freud spent more years in medical school than were necessary for graduation. He took extra courses in zoology, chemistry, and physiology, a field that held the promise of scientific acclaim. He also found a professor of heroic stature to serve as a symbolic father and mentor.

Freud discovered in the study of physiology "rest and satisfaction," and in Professor Ernst Brücke, director of the physiological institute of Vienna's medical school, a figure of authority. Brücke was one of Europe's leading physiologists, a highly respected Prussian whom the easygoing Viennese considered too stern, an alien in their midst. Most of Brücke's students feared him, but Freud regarded him with awe and reverence. Brücke was forty years Freud's senior, about the same age as Freud's own father.

Freud spent six years working in Brücke's laboratory, bent over a microscope to investigate the anatomy of the brain and nervous system. He wrote the requisite technical papers that were the first step along the path to a university career. His research was thorough and showed sufficient imagination and diligence to impress his exacting taskmaster.

Already as a student Freud struggled for recognition, hoping to make the scientific breakthrough that would advance his name and his prospects. He came close to finding the neuron—the basic unit of the nervous system—but *almost* in science means nothing at all.

In March 1881 Freud was awarded his medical degree at a ceremony attended by his proud family. Although Freud's parents regarded the event as significant, it was relatively unimportant to him. After graduation he continued his lonely work in Brücke's laboratory as a poorly paid research assistant doing some teaching on the side. He earned so little money that his father continued to support him.

These years of borderline penury, feverish work, and professional frustration were, to Freud, the "happiest years of [his] youth." He was successful in pursuing the only vocation he envisioned for himself. A steady if slow sequence of steps lay before him, culminating, in many years' time, in the position of professor of physiology. All that he lacked was a major discovery.

On a pleasant June day Freud's life changed. His careful plans for the future shattered. Sigmund Freud fell in love, not with some idealized vision from his youth but with an attractive and highly cultured woman of twenty, Martha Bernays.

Sigmund and his beloved Marty became engaged on June 17, 1882. Realizing the necessity for making more rapid progress in his career, he went the next morning to discuss his situation with Professor Brücke.

Brücke heartily congratulated the young man on his engagement, but when Freud inquired about his prospects at the physiological institute, the professor's expression became glum. There was no better job for him, Brücke said, and no way to continue his research and support a wife and family at the same time. Nor would there be any hope of such a position for many years.

The problem was not Freud's talent or ability, Brücke assured him, but a lack of money. Few academic positions paid a satisfactory salary, and anyone who aspired to such an appointment needed an independent income to sustain him until such time as a senior professor retired, died, or made a rare move to another university, freeing a coveted slot. Brücke had two other assistants, each with ten years' seniority over Freud, and thus it was conceivable that Freud would have to wait several decades before earning a university salary sufficient to maintain a family. (Freud would be sixty-nine years old before a position at the institute became available.)

Brücke was telling Freud that if he expected to marry, he would never achieve success in scientific research. He advised Freud to undertake a hospital residency instead, so that he would be qualified to open a private practice as a physician and thus make enough money to marry. This was a devastating blow to Freud. Although he was aware of the situation long before Brücke spelled it out, it was not until his engagement to Martha that he was forced to think realistically about the future. He did not mention in his writings that he had been forced to abandon his cherished plans because he was now engaged. "No doubt [Freud] found it painful to admit that in his youth the passion of love had once, at least, triumphed over intellectual passion."

Freud had received a few small research grants, but these were trifling sums, and he had borrowed money from friends. The only solution he saw to the economic impasse was to jettison his dreams and pursue a field in which he had no interest—the practice of medicine. But even that, as repugnant as it was, would not offer a quick remedy. Three years of hospital residency would have to be financed by more loans from his father and his friends.

A month after his disheartening talk with Brücke, Freud began a hospital residency in surgery, soon rotating to other departments to gain experience in different specialties. His months of work with surgical and medical patients only reinforced his conviction that he did not want to be a physician.

He spent a term in the psychiatry department, his first encounter with that field, and adopted a new mentor and father figure to replace Brücke. The head of psychiatry was Professor Theodor Meynert, whom Freud described as the "most brilliant genius" he had ever met. He remained with Meynert for five months before moving to dermatology, neurology, and ophthalmology.

Freud continued with his research, still hoping to make some marvelous discovery that would bring him international recognition. In a letter to Martha he described himself as "chasing after money, position, and reputation." Once again, he almost succeeded. In 1884, he began to experiment with the drug cocaine, which was then considered harmless. He took it himself and gave it to Martha, to his sisters, and to friends. More than anyone else, Sigmund Freud became responsible for introducing cocaine into medical practice. Wildly enthusiastic about this "magical" drug, he found that it turned his depression into cheerfulness and even improved his digestion. He told Martha it would make her strong and "give her cheeks red color." And he came to believe that in cocaine he had discovered the cure for everything from seasickness to sciatica. His place in medical history would be assured.

Freud used cocaine to cure a friend's addiction to morphine. But the friend, Ernst von Fleischl, one of Brücke's assistants, soon became addicted to cocaine, which was worse than his morphine dependence. Freud later confessed that he was troubled by the thought that Fleischl's death might advance his own career, and he experienced profound guilt about his role in Fleischl's illness.

In casual conversation with two of his colleagues, the ophthalmologists Leopold Königstein and Carl Koller, Freud mentioned his observation that cocaine produced numbness in the tongue. Someone searching for a topical anesthetic might instantly have seen the possibilities in that reaction, but Freud had no interest in anesthesia. Koller did, and he followed up on Freud's comment, conducting his own experiments with cocaine. He found that it could be used to anesthetize the human eye, thus making eye surgery possible.

Freud, at that time eager to join Martha for a vacation, or so he said later, hurriedly wrote an article for a scientific journal about cocaine, referring briefly at the end to its potential as a local anesthetic. He later admitted that he had not been sufficiently thorough in pursuing the matter. Koller's research, based on Freud's idea, won him international acclaim.

Freud's haste to meet his fiancée may have served as his

excuse for failing to see the implications of his work on cocaine. He did not actually join Martha until three months later. But the bitterness and frustration at having come so close to the fame he craved remained with him. Nearly thirty years later he wrote: "It was the fault of my fiancée that I was not already famous at that youthful age, but I bore my fiancée no grudge."

Life was not working out as Freud had hoped. Perhaps he had been wrong to believe in his own greatness. There would be no university career as a scientist, no laboratory in which to make great discoveries. He was condemned to spend years as an unknown physician treating patients with commonplace ailments. He spent many hours wandering the grounds of the medical school, contemplating the busts of the famous professors, the men whose accomplishments had won them honors. He had little hope of joining them then.

CHAPTER THREE

He Died in Time for You: Jung's Early Years

There was a rattling in his throat, and I could see that he was in the death agony." Carl Jung was fascinated. He had never seen anyone die. "Suddenly he stopped breathing. I waited and waited for the next breath. It did not come."

The twenty-one-year-old Jung turned away from his father's bed and went into the next room where his mother, Emilie, was waiting, her hands busy with her knitting. Carl told her that his father was sinking, and together they returned to the bedroom. "How quickly it has all passed," his mother said.

The man whom Carl loved and resented, who proved to be such a terrible disappointment, died in 1896 as Carl was on the threshold of his career in his first year at the University of Basel, Switzerland. It is easy to discern in the timing of this death the shadow of Freud's Oedipal theme, the sacrifice of one generation for the next, the father making way for the son.

Jung's mother sensed it, too, with the fey, otherworldly wisdom she possessed. Jung heard her say, whether to him or to herself he did not know, "He died in time for you." The words were shattering, perhaps because Jung recognized their truth. He knew that his father might have become a hindrance, but now he was free of the elder man's dogmatism and was no longer con-

43

strained by his father's refusal to recognize Jung's need to rely on his own experience instead of on his father's beliefs.

So strong had been this basic disagreement between father and son that one Jungian follower suggested that Jung needed his father's death "to be free to develop his own ideas." Some years later, the same could be said about Jung's relationship with his symbolic father, Sigmund Freud.

Along with sadness at his father's death, Jung experienced a sense of liberation, of release. He felt manly, he said, and demonstrated this in a direct and practical way by moving into his father's room and assuming the role of head of the family, replacing his father physically as well as symbolically.

Such behavior was not undertaken without guilt. Six weeks later, Jung's father returned to him in a dream, explaining that he had only been on holiday and would soon come home. Jung grew concerned that his father would be angry that he had moved into the master bedroom, but his father was not. Then Jung felt ashamed in his dream for unconsciously wishing for his father's death.

Two nights later the elder Jung reappeared. The dream's theme was the same—he had recovered from his illness and would return home. In his dream Jung reproached himself for believing that his father was dead. But soon the dreams ceased and Jung was free.

It is consistent with Jung's recollections about his father to suggest that death may not have been unwelcome to the fifty-three-year-old Paul Achilles Jung. It would have brought relief from the emotional difficulties that plagued him for much of his life. His adult years were marked by overwhelming frustration, by a pervasive sense of futility and failure. In his last months his body had wasted away, reflecting the deterioration of his spirit, his loss of the will to live.

A photograph taken of him ten years before showed a broken man. "He looked drained, as though his energies were hemorrhaging through a gaping psychic wound." As a clergyman torn by religious doubts, trapped in a bitter and loveless marriage to a neurotic woman who was stronger than him, and at odds with his brilliant son, Paul Jung was also worried about financial matters. In addition, he was a hypochondriac. He had felt unfulfilled since leaving the university with a doctoral degree in Oriental languages. Hoping for a career as a professor of philology and linguistics, he settled, for reasons unknown, for the life of a small-town parson, never to recapture the excitement and optimism of his university years.

The dramatic nature of this contradiction in his father's situation had been made clear to Carl a few months before his father died. Carl had joined the same student fraternity at the University of Basel to which his father had belonged. He invited his father to a fraternity party and was surprised by the man's exuberance: "The gay spirit of his own student days came back again." Jung instantly realized that his father's life had come to a halt at graduation. "Once upon a time he too had been an enthusiastic student in his first year, as I was now; the world had opened out for him, as it was doing for me. How can it have happened that everything was blighted for him, had turned to sourness and bitterness?"

Jung had long been aware of his conflicting feelings of love and resentment for his father. From an early age he viewed his father as weak and powerless, moody and irritable. He sensed that his mother was the stronger of the two; yet in his memory it was the father who attempted to provide emotional stability for the boy. In a reversal of roles, Paul Jung may have behaved in a more traditionally maternal fashion than did Emilie.

One of Jung's early memories was of a time in infancy when he was so restless and feverish that he could not sleep. His father comforted him, cradling him in his arms and walking with him, softly singing songs from his student days. "To this day," Jung wrote, when he was in his eighties, "I can remember my father's voice, singing over me in the stillness of the night."

The emotional ambivalence of Jung's relationship with his father began early, but the intellectual ambivalence came later, during Jung's school years. It centered around the young boy's growing religious doubts and culminated in a crisis of confidence that never passed.

At about the age of twelve, Jung reported an extraordinary event. He said that he personally experienced the will of God and reached a state of grace. This led him to question everything his father preached. The words sounded to him "stale and hollow, like a tale told by someone who knows it only by hearsay and cannot quite believe it himself." Convinced that his encounter with God was genuine, Jung wanted to share it with his father, to help his father resolve his own religious confusion. But for years Jung remained silent, too shy to mention the incident. When he finally spoke up, at the age of eighteen, his father said he was talking nonsense. "You always want to think," Paul Jung said. "One ought not to think, but believe."

Repeatedly he admonished the young man that understanding would come only with belief and trust and not with thought and experience. Jung pleaded with his father to recognize the validity of his revelation, but his father ended every discussion abruptly by shrugging his shoulders and walking away.

As the adolescent Jung viewed the situation, his father would not—or could not—help him in his quest for truth. The man had failed to be the strong authority figure the son needed. This failure set in motion a twenty-year search for a surrogate father.

Jung realized that his father's abilities were limited and that he would have to rely on himself for guidance on his journey to adulthood. "I must take the responsibility; it is up to me how my fate turns out." Jung believed that he was more creative than his father and destined to achieve greatness.

These themes were captured in an event that occurred when Jung was fourteen. He and his father were traveling to Lucerne and had stopped at the village of Vitznau, at the base of towering Mount Rigi. At the depot, the departure point for the cog railway to the mountain's peak, Paul Jung gave Carl a ticket; he could afford only one fare. "You can ride up to the peak alone," the father said. "I'll stay here." Jung analyzed this as clearly symbolic of his destiny. He would become more successful than his father, and his father knew it.

The influence of Jung's mother on his development was different from that of his father, and, befitting her personality, her impact was stronger. Emilie Jung was quite strange, as was her father, a clergyman who believed in ghosts and who, to frighten the ghosts away, forced his daughter to stand behind his chair while he composed his sermons. Jung remembered that his mother could change instantly from a cheerful homemaker to a witch, mumbling incoherently and gazing unseeing into the distance. She sometimes seemed like a prophetess and spoke to herself aloud, although Jung knew that "what she said was aimed at me and usually struck to the core of my being, so that I was stunned into silence."

As a child Jung came to regard his mother as two people inhabiting the same body, a realization that disturbed him. It triggered nightmares, which were reinforced by terrifying sounds emanating from her bedroom. "One night I saw coming from her door a faintly luminous, indefinite figure whose head detached itself from the neck and floated along in front of it, in the air, like a little moon. Immediately another head was produced and again detached itself. This process was repeated six or seven times."

Emilie Jung's ghostly appearances were not always a product of a child's imagination. When Jung was in his forties she appeared to him in his study, whispered a few eerily appropriate words, and vanished. Jung, unnerved, "shook like an aspen leaf for hours afterward."

Jung recalled being wary and distrustful of his mother from the time he was three. She was hospitalized in Basel for treatment of some unnamed illness, which may have been emotional, and during her absence a spinster aunt came to care for the boy. She was not a satisfactory substitute. Jung believed his mother had deliberately abandoned him. He prayed nightly for her return, but she did not come back for several months. Fearful and anxious, he would toss in bed, unable to sleep, and when he finally did doze off, he was tormented by dreams. This experience, he decided later, made him suspicious of the word *love*. And for much of his life he associated women with the notion of unreliability.

His apprehension about his mother intensified when he was nine. As an only child, he demanded her constant, if erratic and unpredictable, attention. The birth of a sister was unwelcome and distasteful. "It took him completely by surprise and led him to banish his sister forever after to the most remote corner of his universe."

The boy had not noticed the changes in his mother's body, nor had he thought it strange that she spent so much time in bed, something he considered an "inexcusable weakness" anyway. When he was shown the baby, he confessed to being disappointed. But he was more disturbed by the explanation provided for the infant's arrival. Having witnessed the births of farm animals, he could not be fooled by the old tale about the stork. "This story was obviously another of those humbugs which were always being imposed on me. I felt sure that my mother had once again done something I was supposed not to know about." He suspected that something "regrettable" was associated with his sister's birth.

Thus Jung had long felt that he could not rely on his mother or share with her his troubling thoughts and questions. He built a protective emotional wall around himself to prevent her from seeing his bizarre inner life. Whenever he considered breaching this wall, he was quickly discouraged by her behavior.

By the time Jung was eleven, his mother had made him her confidant and once told him something about his father that disturbed him greatly. (He never revealed the details of her story.) Jung decided to seek the advice of a friend of his father's, an influential man in the village, but he was not at home. A short while later, his mother told a different version, omitting the damaging remarks that had so upset Jung. This angered the boy because he had nearly repeated the tale to his father's friend.

"From then on," he said, "I decided to divide everything my mother said to me by two. My confidence in her was strictly limited."

Despite his reservations about his mother's reliability, Jung believed she was good to him. He praised her "hearty animal warmth" and her cooking and described her as a pleasant companion when she was in a stable mood. Then she would listen attentively to her son. He also enjoyed her talk. "Her chatter was like the gay plashing of a fountain. She had a decided literary gift, as well as taste and depth." He saw her as a "kindly, fat old woman, extremely hospitable, and possessor of a great sense of humor."

But Jung was often caught in the middle of his parents' unhappy marriage, compelled to choose sides in their continuous arguments and temperamental clashes. Usually he favored his mother, but that gave rise to conflicts. To deal with the situation, he set himself up as an arbitrator, a role that served to enhance his imagined feelings of self-worth and assurance. In reality, those feelings were fragile.

Jung's childhood could not be described as happy, nor did it furnish an emotionally secure foundation. His mother's unreliability, his father's rigidity, their frequent bickering, and Jung's disappointment in them combined to force him into a secret world of fantasies, dreams, and visions. Out of this unwholesome mixture he fashioned his adult personality and his unique explanation of human nature, which would ultimately place him in opposition to Freud.

Jung's parents provided him with a different social and emotional context than Freud's parents had given their son. Freud's mother was young, beautiful, warm, and devoted to Sigmund, who adored her in return. Freud's father was loving and kind, but also stern and authoritarian—a commanding, patriarchal figure.

Jung found the Oedipal theme to be unacceptable. He had no

intense and passionate attachment to his mother, no urge as a child to lust after that kindly, fat old woman, as he called her, and certainly no need to compete with his father for his mother's love. The suggestion that every young boy was in love with his mother and jealous of his father was "absurd" to Jung, "for it clearly did not reflect his own childhood experience."

Jung's childhood also differed from Freud's in terms of the variety of people who had the potential to shape his character. Whereas Freud contended with siblings, adult stepbrothers, and others in the household, Jung was virtually alone during the crucial years of his development. By the time his sister was born he had already retreated so completely into the fortress of his imagination that no one else could enter.

Another influence on Jung's development can be found in religion, which helped to shape his character and the system of psychology he proposed. He reported being struck by the religious doubts that would precipitate the break with his father as early as age three. Jungian analysts suggest that Jung's view of human nature stems from his attempt to find a substitute for his father's orthodox faith, the system of beliefs against which he rebelled at such a young age. Freud did not experience this problem because his parents were not devoutly religious and offered him no dogma against which to revolt.

Jung's initial fears grew out of his father's employment as a village pastor. The boy noticed that people from the village disappeared, often drowned in the nearby Rhine falls. Shortly after each disappearance, a hole would be dug in the cemetery near the vicarage. A ceremony followed, and a large black box was carried into the cemetery by men in long black coats. Jung's father spoke in a deep, solemn voice, people cried, and the box was lowered into the ground and covered with dirt.

When Jung asked about these rites he was told that people were buried in the hole because Jesus wanted them with him. Jung's mother had taught him to recite a nightly prayer in which Jesus was asked to take "thy child" unto him to keep Satan from devouring him. Jung connected these events in his mind and concluded that when Jesus took people, he buried them in a hole. "I began to distrust Lord Jesus," Jung wrote, associating him with the "gloomy black men in frock coats, top hats, and shiny black boots who busied themselves with the black box."

To compound the confusion, he overheard his father discussing the Jesuits with a colleague. His father sounded annoyed, leading Jung to conclude that the Jesuits were dangerous. Although he did not know what a Jesuit was, the word was sufficiently similar to *Jesus* to make him uncomfortable.

One day when Jung was playing in front of the house, he noticed a man in a long black robe. He assumed that the figure was a Jesuit, and he ran in terror to hide in the attic. For days he refused to leave the house, and when he finally did venture outside, he maintained an uneasy vigilance. Only many years later did he accept the fact that the man in black had been, as he put it, "a harmless Catholic priest."

Shortly after this experience Jung had a dream that haunted him for many years. Although it occurred when he was barely four years old, he was unable to speak of it until well into his sixties. In his dream he discovered a huge hole in the ground with stone steps leading into the darkness. He walked down the steps, passed through a green curtain, and entered a large, dimly lit room with an arched stone ceiling. A golden throne sat in the center of the room, and on it was an object about fifteen feet high and two feet in diameter.

At first Jung mistook the object for the trunk of a tree, but then he saw that it was composed of "skin and naked flesh, and on top there was something like a rounded head with no face and no hair. On the very top of the head was a single eye, gazing motionlessly upward. The thing did not move," Jung said, "yet I had the feeling that it might at any moment crawl off the throne like a worm and creep toward me. I was paralyzed with terror. At that moment I heard from outside and above me my mother's voice. She called out, 'Yes, just look at him. That is the man-eater!' That intensified my terror still more, and I awoke sweating and scared to death."

For a long time afterward he expected the nightmare to recur. It presented him with mysteries for which he was not equipped to cope. Who was the man-eater? Was it Jesus, or was it this worm-like creature, this phallus? Perhaps they were the same. He knew that he could not ask his parents about these riddles. His father was too committed to his own beliefs, and his mother was some-how allied with the man-eater and could not be trusted. Jung kept the matter to himself, another instance of the isolation, secrecy, and furtiveness that had become part of his character—a terrible burden for a child of four.

The conflicts deepened as he got older. Two years later, while on an excursion with his mother, they walked past a Cath-olic church. Jung felt both horror and curiosity, and he slipped away to peer inside. He saw the altar and some tall candles, and suddenly he tripped and fell, cutting his chin. He screamed as the blood ran down his neck and immediately felt guilty for having looked at what obviously was dangerous and forbidden. A chain of associations formed in his mind: Jesuits—green curtain—se-cret of the man-eater. "So that is the Catholic Church which has to do with Jesuits," he wrote. "It is their fault that I stumbled and screamed."

For thirty years Jung was unable to enter a Catholic church without being reminded of his fall and his childhood dread of the Jesuits. He did not overcome this fear until he entered Vienna's St. Stephen's Cathedral in the company of Sigmund Freud.

Jung's hostility toward Jesus festered, but at the age of eleven he became interested in God. Although pictures and likenesses of Jesus were familiar, God was not depicted at all. He was unique and secret, not unlike Jung's fantasy world. Jung's affection for God became an obsession, culminating in a psychotic hallucina-tion. It began at noon in Basel's cathedral square. The church roof had recently been retiled, and the sun sparkled on its fresh surface. Jung gazed at the roof, overcome by its beauty. "The world is beautiful," he wrote later, recording that extraordinary moment, "and the church is beautiful, and God made all this and sits above it far away in the blue sky on a golden throne and —"

Jung's mind stopped. His thoughts were blocked, and he felt numb and breathless. Something was trying to force its way into his consciousness. "Don't go on thinking now," he warned himself. "Something terrible is coming, something I do not want to think, something I dare not even approach. Why not? Because I would be committing the most frightful of sins."

For three days and nights his torment continued while the terrible, forbidden thought kept trying to claim his attention. On the third night he bolted upright in bed, his body soaked with sweat, wondering who was trying to force him to think this awful thought. He decided that it was God, and instantly he felt better. But why would God want him to sin? Because God was testing him to see if he would obey God's will even if it meant committing the sin. Finally, persuaded that God would want him to show courage, Jung opened his mind to the forbidden thought. "I saw before me the cathedral, the blue sky. God sits in his golden throne, high above the world—and from under the throne an enormous turd falls upon the sparkling new roof, shatters it, and breaks the walls of the cathedral asunder."

Jung's agony was over. The relief was indescribable, and with it came an exalted level of happiness. He believed that in some mysterious way, all God's wisdom and goodness had been revealed to him. He had directly experienced the miracle of grace that would heal "and make all comprehensible."

After this event Jung believed that he would be able to understand many things that previously had been unclear, such as what was troubling his father. Obviously the man had never directly known God's will. His father knew the Lord only indirectly, through the Bible and the teachings of the church. And so the son came to feel pity and compassion for the father, who had only dogma and unexamined belief but no personal experience. Being one of God's chosen few, however, was not without its emotional cost. The revelation filled Jung with shame. He realized that he must be depraved for having such blasphemous thoughts and for seeing God's dark side.

Although he told no one about his vision, he tried to find

evidence to support it. He listened to the theological discussions of his eight clergyman uncles and concluded that none of them understood the secret of grace any more than his father did. Nor did he find help in religious books.

Jung's dilemmas, his visions and dreams, had a profound and lasting effect on his life. His belief in his personal experience of divine grace and his dream of the underground man-eater drove him to a lonely existence. "The pattern of my relationship to the world was already prefigured," he wrote in his autobiography. "I am a solitary, because I know things and must hint at things which other people do not know, and usually do not even want to know."

At fifteen Jung prepared for confirmation in his father's church. Although the formal religious instruction bored him, he was curious about the Trinity. The idea that a oneness could at the same time be a threeness fascinated him, but when the lessons reached that topic, Jung's father announced that he would skip it because he did not understand it himself. The boy was bitterly disappointed. Here was additional proof that men like his father believed blindly in teachings they did not comprehend. Nevertheless, he tried to accept his father's attitude.

He was also intrigued by the idea that eating bread and drinking wine during the Communion service would allow him to symbolically incorporate the spirit of Jesus. Literally, the notion seemed so preposterous that he was sure some mystery was attached to it, some truth that would be unveiled during the service. When the big day arrived, Jung, dressed in a new black suit and black hat, listened to the prayers, ate the bread, and drank the wine. Nothing happened. No wisdom was revealed; no sense of communion with God resulted. He felt wretched, hollow, and empty.

He never attended another Communion service and began to miss regular church services. His search for a new faith that would favor thought and experience over the automatic acceptance of dogmatic beliefs would occupy the rest of his life.

In this way the personality of Carl Jung was shaped by his

parents and by his mystical experiences. In self-imposed solitude
he grew up amid dreams, fantasies, and visions. Apprehensive
about his mother and disappointed in his father, he had only
himself to rely on. He shut out the external world and directed
his view inward to his unconscious feelings. His entire intellectual and emotional life had been foretold in an early dream.
When Jung descended into the hole, passed through the green
curtain, and found a new world in the vault beneath the surface,
he uncovered the symbolism for his life's work. He would explore
that vast underground cavern of human existence, the residue and
storehouse of experience that lies beneath the surface of the conscious mind.

Jung's early years were spent in Laufen, a remote village near the
Rhine falls in northern Switzerland. From his home he could
hear the sound of the falling water and see the alpine peaks. The
setting was picturesque but lonely. The vicarage stood near the
church and the Laufen castle, but in the vicinity there was only
one other castle and the sexton's farm.

The proximity to the waterfall provided Jung with an early
exposure to death. The funerals conducted for drowning victims
spawned the boy's religious confusions. He recalled one victim
being laid out in a storage shed next to the house. He tried to get
inside to see the corpse, but the door was locked. He went
around to the rear of the building and saw blood and water
running out of the open drain and down the slope of the hill. "I
found this extraordinarily interesting," he said.

He once came close to drowning in the falls. While crossing
the bridge high above the roaring water he slipped and fell. By
the time his nursemaid caught him, he already had one leg under
the railing.

When he was four, the family moved to Klein-Hüningen, a
village on the outskirts of Basel, and his experience with death
continued. A dam collapsed and a torrent of water toppled a

bridge, drowning fourteen people. When the floodwaters receded, the townspeople gathered to search for bodies. Jung found a man dressed in a black frock coat half buried in the sand.

A vulnerable child, sensitive and isolated from his parents, he had no one else for companionship. Yet when friendship was offered, he rejected it, ignoring the children of family friends who came to visit. If they pursued him, he would insult them or hit them until they left him alone. An acquaintance from that time remembers him as an "asocial monster."

Jung amused himself with games and massive construction projects. Using bricks and wooden blocks, he built whole towns and other elaborate structures and destroyed them with imaginary earthquakes. He drew pictures of battles, sieges, bombardments, and naval engagements. He played the popular Swiss children's game called *Klecksography*, in which a blot of ink was placed on a piece of paper that was folded symmetrically to produce a fanciful shape. Jung interpreted the shapes to suit his own fantasies.*

He carved a small figure from a wooden ruler to serve as an imaginary companion. He colored the figure black and adorned it with a long coat, top hat, and boots. He put this manikin in a yellow pencil box, along with a smooth stone he painted in several colors, and hid the box in the attic. "I knew that not a soul would ever find it there. No one could discover my secret and destroy it. I felt safe."

When he was unhappy or felt threatened by his parents' quarrels, he would retreat to the attic to play with his stone and manikin. Sometimes he would place a piece of paper in the pencil box with great ceremony. The paper would contain some revelation, written in a secret code of Jung's devising.

His childhood loneliness is reflected in the theory of the human personality he later espoused. Unlike other theorists, Jung was not concerned with social relationships such as that between parent and child. He focused instead on the developments within

---

*Years later, a Swiss boy by the name of Hermann Rorschach became fascinated with the same game.

each person's mind, emphasizing inner growth, whereas Freud's theory stressed outer growth—the person's developing relationships with other people. But then Freud did not have a lonely childhood.

Jung attended the village school, found the work easy, and was always the best in his class. Beatings were not uncommon. After the teacher had written a lesson on the blackboard, "a whiplash was applied to [our] backs just to impress the lesson upon [us]." Jung said this was the best memory aid he knew of.

He got along well with the other students and enjoyed some status because he was the parson's son. He joined in his classmates' pranks and games and led them in forms of mischief. The exposure to the company of other children disturbed him, however, because he noticed that he was changing. The other people in his life were alienating him from his private self, and this increased his suspicion of the outside world. As Jung recalled in his autobiography, the events of his school years persuaded him more and more of the wisdom and goodness of the world he had created within his own mind.

When he was eleven he was enrolled in the *Gymnasium* in Basel and found himself in the company of the sons of wealthy and powerful families. His new schoolmates had traveled widely, spoke a refined German dialect, and rode about town in handsome carriages. They had generous allowances and exuded an air of sophistication that the son of a village parson lacked. "For the first time I became aware of how poor we were, that my father was a poor country parson and I a still poorer parson's son who had holes in his shoes." He felt humiliated by the contrast.

Not only a social misfit, Jung was also an intellectual outcast. Because he was forced to compete with brighter students than there were in the village school and to take more difficult courses, his academic performance declined. His worst subject was mathematics. "I didn't even know what numbers really were," he said. Divinity classes were boring. Drawing gave him so much trouble that he was excused. And, being unable to bear other people telling him how to move, he hated gymnastics. He was taunted by his schoolmates and grew to dread each day.

During his second year Jung was offered a temporary respite. One day after classes he was standing in the cathedral square when another boy shoved him to the ground. His head struck the curb and he nearly lost consciousness, remaining on the pavement longer than his condition warranted to make his assailant feel guilty. The liberating thought flashed through his mind that he would no longer have to go to school.

Jung remained at home for the next six months. Whenever his parents urged him to return to school or to do his homework, he fainted. Free to indulge his fantasies without interference, he returned to his solitary hobbies, making war paintings and roaming the countryside.

His parents consulted a variety of medical specialists. One diagnosis was epilepsy; Jung laughed at the idea. Curiously, however, although he was enjoying the freedom to live his own way, he found that he was no happier. He sensed that he was not so much escaping from school and the outside world as from himself. It was then that he overheard a conversation between his father and a friend who was commiserating about the boy's health. "It would be dreadful if he were incurable," Jung's father said. "What will become of the boy if he cannot earn his own living?"

The words jolted Jung. "I had seen how poor we were compared to other families," he remembered. "I must work to relieve my father's worries and save myself from becoming even poorer. Poverty suddenly seemed like a haunting ogre to me." He resolved to return to school and went immediately to his father's study to work on his Latin. After ten minutes he felt faint, but he continued on. He had several more dizzy episodes, but after an hour they ceased. He never fainted again.

"The whole bag of tricks was over and done with," he wrote. "That was when I learned what a neurosis is." He recognized that he had arranged the entire situation to suit himself, and this realization made him angry and ashamed.

Jung became a diligent and conscientious student, arising at five o'clock every morning to study. His grades improved—even in mathematics—although his social standing remained low. Unpopular with both students and teachers, Jung wondered what repulsive characteristics he possessed that caused others to shun him.

His fellow students considered him odd because he talked about things they thought he could not possibly know. He liked to discuss philosophy and paleontology, subjects that had not yet been taught in the classroom. Eventually he learned to stop speaking about such things, adding them to his list of secrets.

He was once attacked by seven classmates on the way home from school. Large for his age and physically strong, he grabbed one boy by the arms and swung him around like a club, knocking the others down. The teachers blamed Jung for the incident. They considered him to be crafty and suspected him of nearly every prank perpetrated at the school. He was singled out for punishment so frequently that he began to believe he might actually be responsible, although he knew that was not the case. He prepared alibis, expecting to be falsely accused, and became highly sensitive to criticism.

The teachers began to question his academic achievements. In discussing papers submitted in a literature class, the instructor announced that Jung's composition was the best, but it had to be a fraud. He accused Jung of plagiarism, and when Jung objected, the teacher called him a liar.

Jung turned for solace to the only reliable support he knew—his inner world—but a bewildering change was occurring in his repository of dreams and fantasies. Two distinct parts were forming within his personality, not unlike the two selves he suspected his mother of having. He believed this development was triggered by the sight of an ancient green carriage rolling past his house. He was struck by the thought that the carriage had come from an era in which he must once have lived. He had the feeling that he had ridden in that same kind of coach sometime in the last century, and he was overcome with nostalgia.

Shortly thereafter, while vacationing with friends of his parents, Jung was reprimanded by his host. The man thought Jung

was handling a small boat improperly. Jung was furious and in-
sulted because he thought of himself as someone of importance
and dignity, a person worthy of respect. In a moment he realized
that his feelings were ridiculous. He was, after all, a twelve-year-
old schoolboy.

"It occurred to me," he wrote, "that I was actually two
different persons. One of them was a schoolboy who could not
grasp algebra and was far from sure of himself; the other was
important, a high authority, a man not to be trifled with, powerful and influential." He spent many hours reflecting on this
dichotomy and gradually defined the essence of his different
beings. He called them his Number One and Number Two personalities.

Number One encompassed the conscious ego and the objective world of reality in which it operated. Number Two was
the unconscious, the all-important repository of fantasies and
dreams, offering not only escape from the harsh, everyday world
but also insight into God, nature, and the self. The Number Two
personality alone provided solitude and peace, but this personality was also the source of conflict and depression, of personal
and religious questions.

Toward the end of Jung's adolescent years, his turmoil
lessened as his Number One personality became clearer. He immersed himself in the study of philosophy as well as in school
activities and city life. His subjective world of intuitions and
premonitions became submerged, and his periods of depression
abated.

One reason for the ascendance of the conscious, reality-
oriented side of Jung's personality was related to his graduation
from the *Gymnasium* in 1895, which signaled his entry into adult
society. Faced with the decision about a career, he knew he had
to suppress the unconscious side of his nature because it would
be of little help in achieving success in the real world. Increasingly he identified with his Number One personality and
reduced his ties to Number Two.

Jung was interested in the sciences and the humanities, in

zoology and geology at one extreme and comparative religion and Egyptian civilization at the other. His clergyman uncles urged him toward theology, but his father advised him to be anything but a theologian. As happened so often in Jung's life, the voice of his unconscious made the choice for him. Two dreams eliminated all confusion.

In the first dream Jung found himself digging in a forest along the banks of the Rhine River. He uncovered bones of prehistoric animals and knew that his goal was to study the world of nature. In the second dream this desire was reinforced; in the woods he discovered a strange and wonderful animal in a pool of water. Taken together, the dreams told Jung to study science, but which science? His fascination with animals and with nature inclined him toward zoology, but his conscious mind insisted that he would be unable to support himself in that field. The compromise was medicine. Here he could pursue his interest in science and earn a good income. Many years later, when asked why he had become a doctor, Jung answered, simply, "Opportunism."

Other practical considerations were expressed in his dreams. In one he was visiting an unfamiliar place where a strong wind was blowing, and he could walk forward only with difficulty. Fog surrounded him, and he cupped his hands around a tiny light that the wind threatened to extinguish. He believed it was vital to keep the light alive. A huge, dark figure was following him. Terror-stricken, Jung realized that he had to protect the light, regardless of any danger.

When he awoke, he knew at once the dream's significance. The dark figure was his own shadow, outlined by the light he carried. The light was his conscious being, his Number One personality, and he understood that it was the only light he had. The light of his consciousness was tiny and fragile compared to the shadow of his unconscious. He decided his life's task must be to continue to shield the light of consciousness, to keep it burning and preserve it from being extinguished by darker forces. To do this he would have to extend himself more into the outside world. His future lay outward rather than inward; his goals should be study, financial security, and the assumption of adult responsibilities.

Although Jung's Number Two personality did not disappear, the conflict between the two personalities ceased. In the coming years he devoted his energies to worldly tasks, and it was not until middle age that his unconscious personality reasserted itself.

The most pressing problem facing Jung as he began his medical studies was money for his education. His father applied for a scholarship for him, but the idea embarrassed Jung because he thought that he would benefit only from his father's kindness and good name. When his father died in early 1896, Jung did not know if he could afford to continue his schooling. Responsible for his mother and sister, he asked an uncle for help. The older man advised Jung to leave school and find a job. Other uncles were more forthcoming with financial aid. Jung found part-time work at the medical school and also earned a commission for selling some antiques for one of his aunts.

Jung's social life at the University of Basel was far different than it had been at the *Gymnasium*. He formed several friendships and was initiated into a student fraternity. Nicknamed the Barrel, apparently because of his size and shape, he became a good dancer and took to carrying a revolver. He was remembered as an "exceedingly cheerful fellow who was always in a willing mood for any kind of fun." The dominance of his Number One personality seemed complete. He was a leading participant in debates and often held an audience spellbound with his observations on philosophy, psychology, and the occult.

Jung completed the medical-school curriculum in five years. Surgery was his first choice for a specialty, but his shaky financial condition ruled that out. He needed to earn a salary immediately after graduation and could not afford the extra years of training such a choice would demand.

He planned to take a job as an assistant in a district hospital, but shortly before taking his examinations two events altered his prospects. First, his professor of internal medicine accepted a position in Munich and offered Jung a job as assistant. Jung had almost decided to accept the offer when the second incident occurred.

One of the required university examinations was in psychiatry, a field Jung found boring, even disgusting. But on the evening before the exam, he boned up on the psychiatry textbook of the great neurologist Richard von Krafft-Ebing. Jung shared the prevailing medical establishment view that held psychiatry in contempt. In the few minutes it took to read the preface of Krafft-Ebing's book, however, Jung's outlook changed.

Krafft-Ebing described psychoses as "diseases of the personality." Abruptly, emotionally, Jung reached a decision. "My heart began to pound. I had to stand up and draw a deep breath. My excitement was intense, for it had become clear to me, in a flash of illumination, that for me the only possible goal was psychiatry."

Only in psychiatry could Jung combine his interests in science and in the world of the spirit. In psychiatry lay the possibility of reconciling the outer world with the inner world, his Number One and Number Two personalities.

When he announced his plan to enter this forsaken field, his professors and friends were astounded. They expressed amazement that he would sacrifice the Munich opportunity for that psychiatric nonsense. Undaunted, Jung applied for a residency at the Burghölzli Hospital in Zurich. He chose it not only because of its reputation but also because it would take him away from his mother. He needed the freedom to begin his professional life on his own terms, away from her disturbing influence. Jung was ready to shape his own identity.

CHAPTER FOUR

The Future Belongs to Us: 1907

At ten o'clock on the cold Sunday morning of March 3, 1907, Sigmund Freud and Carl Jung met for the first time. It was an epochal event in the lives of both men, and one they had eagerly anticipated. Yet even in this first joyous encounter there were harbingers of the coming tragedy, previews of the tension and anger that would develop in the years ahead. They first surfaced in the planning for the momentous meeting. Jung's truculence was spelled out in a series of letters through which he set the date. His indelicate and inconsiderate handling of these arrangements may have been an attempt to establish some measure of independence from his symbolic father at the outset, despite the fact that it was Jung who had expressed the stronger desire for the meeting.

In his first letter to Freud, dated January 8, 1907, Jung wrote of his long-felt desire to meet Freud and announced that he would come to Vienna in April, during the Easter holiday. Jung did not ask Freud if that would be convenient but simply stated in a straightforward fashion that *this* is when he would come.

Freud replied on January 13, asking for the exact dates of the visit so that he could reschedule his patients. Five weeks passed before Freud heard from Jung. Jung wrote on February 20 that he could not come in April after all but would be arriving in just ten days. This left Freud insufficient time to change his patients' appointments. He expressed dismay that Jung could not come at Easter, when Freud would have a holiday, and asked Jung to arrange his visit to encompass a Sunday, the only day Freud did not see patients. But Jung was even more peremptory in his next letter, announcing that he would come to Vienna in five days. "I much regret arriving at a time that doesn't suit you," Jung wrote. "Unfortunately, it can't be managed otherwise."

Freud-the-father adjusted to the demands of Jung-the-son and appeared at Jung's hotel with a bouquet of flowers for Jung's wife, Emma. They talked briefly, and Freud said, apologetically, "I am sorry that I can give you no real hospitality. I have nothing at home but an elderly wife." The remark embarrassed Emma and alerted Jung to the possibility of some disturbance in the Freud marriage, a suspicion he confirmed that evening and again a few days later.

At dinner at the Freud home later that day, Jung talked about psychoanalysis and discovered that Martha Freud knew nothing about her husband's work. Jung concluded that the marital relationship was superficial, and perhaps for that reason he rarely attempted to converse with Martha or the Freud children during that and subsequent visits. Freud's son Martin recalled that Jung ignored everyone else at the table and continued "the debate which had been interrupted by the call to dinner. Jung on those occasions did all the talking, and father with unconcealed delight did all the listening."

And talk Jung did. He had so much he wanted to tell Freud and so many questions to ask of him. Exhibiting his vitality, passion, and imagination in words and gestures, Jung spoke virtually nonstop for three hours. Finally, after listening so patiently for so long, Freud interrupted Jung's monologue to suggest that their discussions would be more profitable if they approached the many topics Jung had rambled about in a more systematic fashion. To Jung's amazement, Freud proceeded to summarize precisely all that Jung had said and to organize it coherently into discrete topics. Jung was impressed. "I found [Freud] extremely intelligent, shrewd, and altogether remarkable," Jung wrote later.

For ten more hours their conversation continued as they walked the streets of Vienna and returned to Freud's study for coffee and cigars. Their mutual respect and admiration grew by the hour, as each saw his expectations of the other confirmed. But there were also doubts among the certainties, reservations with the acceptance. "My first impressions of him remained somewhat tangled," Jung said. "I could not make him out." The primary reason for his confusion pertained to the central aspect of Freudian theory: the role of sexuality.

Jung understood and appreciated Freud's explanations of his sexual theory, yet his doubts persisted. Several times he mentioned his difficulties with the primacy of sexuality, but Freud insisted they could be explained by Jung's lack of clinical experience. Freud pointed out that he had analyzed many more patients than Jung and had observed ample proof of his theory in his patients' reports of their early lives. Jung agreed about the sparseness of his clinical work to date, and he could offer no alternative to account for neuroses. Nevertheless, his skepticism about the central role of sexuality in the formation of mental illness nagged at him.

Something else about his first encounter with Freud troubled Jung, a component not of Freud's theory but of his personality. "There was one characteristic of his that preoccupied me above all: his bitterness." And it would preoccupy Jung throughout the next six years. But those reflections came later. On that Sunday, March 3, Jung considered Sigmund Freud to be the most important person he had ever met. The trip to Vienna was an event of major magnitude in his life.

Carl and Emma Jung remained in Vienna for a week, during which time Jung recorded one additional warning about his relationship with Freud. On the night of their first encounter, Jung dreamed that he and Freud were walking the streets of Vienna, as they had done earlier in the evening. But in Jung's dream, Freud looked different. He appeared to be elderly, frail, and in delicate health, as though he did not have long to live.

In the morning Jung told Freud about the dream and asked

for his interpretation. Freud had the answer right away; after all, he had been the first to document the symbolism of such a dream. He said that it revealed an unconscious death wish toward Freud. Jung desired to dethrone Freud so that Jung could take his place. (About six months later, Jung wrote to Freud rejecting this interpretation of the dream, but the meaning of Jung's reply is unclear.)

Inadvertently, Jung found himself involved in Freud's private life. According to Jung's version of events, Freud's sister-in-law, Minna Bernays, asked to speak to him about a personal matter. Jung liked Minna because she understood psychoanalysis and talked intelligently about Freud's work, but she told Jung something that disturbed him. She said that Freud was in love with her and described their relationship as intimate. She also said that they both felt guilty about the situation.

"It was a shocking discovery to me," Jung wrote many years later, "and even now I can recall the agony I felt at the time." Perhaps one reason the revelation pained Jung was that he was having his own marital difficulties and was about to embark on an affair.

Jung attended the next meeting of the Wednesday Psychological Society and was introduced to the small band of Freud's Viennese loyalists. The following week the Jungs left for Budapest, then journeyed to a Yugoslavian port to continue their holiday by boat, crossing the Adriatic Sea to the Italian resort of Abbazia. There Jung was overcome by an infatuation for a woman who happened to be Jewish, something that came to have great significance for him.

Despite Jung's doubts, which he recorded many years after the event, there is no denying the personal and professional significance of his first meeting with Freud. The emotional effect of his association with this new father figure was revealed in Jung's first letter to Freud after he returned home, a letter that took him almost three weeks to write. Freud, a stickler for promptness in correspondence, must have chafed over the delay, wondering if Jung's reaction to him was as favorable as his to Jung.

When Jung finally wrote, on March 31, he invited Freud to apply his analytic skills to explain the procrastination. "You will doubtless have drawn your own conclusions from the prolongation of my reaction time," Jung wrote. He described his "complexes aroused in Vienna" without elaborating on their nature, but they probably revolved around what Jung referred to as his father complex and his previous disappointments in finding and keeping a mentor. Although it was difficult for Jung to decide to invest his emotional needs in Freud, he committed himself in the letter.

Any doubts Freud may have had about Jung's impression of him were dissolved by Jung's reverential attitude. Jung no longer questioned the correctness of Freud's theory. "The last shreds were dispelled by my stay in Vienna," Jung wrote. "I hope my work for your cause will show you the depths of my gratitude and veneration. I hope and even dream that we may welcome you in Zurich next summer or autumn. A visit from you would be seventh heaven for me personally. The few hours I was permitted to spend with you were all too fleeting."

Freud replied on April 7, indicating clearly his fond hopes for his newfound son and heir. He told Jung that he could not imagine anyone better qualified to replace him one day as head of the psychoanalytic movement, to carry on and complete his work. But if there was praise and confidence in Freud's words, there was also an urgent plea that Jung not abandon psychoanalysis. Freud believed that Jung's objections about sexuality lingered and needed to be overcome. "You have gone into it too deeply," Freud wrote, "and seen for yourself how exciting, how far-reaching, and how beautiful our subject is." Freud's campaign to win Jung's complete and undivided allegiance was under way.

Throughout 1907 Freud repeatedly demonstrated his growing need of Jung. Even before his expectations for Jung were confirmed by their Vienna meeting in March, he had lavishly praised

Jung, actively currying his favor. In a letter written early that year he called Jung the most competent helper to join him so far and added that none of the Viennese disciples was so capable of advancing the psychoanalytic system. Of Jung's book on dementia praecox Freud wrote that it was the most important contribution to psychoanalysis he had ever read.

By the time a month had passed after their meeting, Freud was openly admitting his dependence on Jung, noting that their correspondence and exchange of views were necessary to him. The letters show that Freud's growing attachment to Jung was at least as much emotional as it was intellectual and professional. When their communication was interrupted for several weeks because of Freud's summer travels, he noted that his personality had become impoverished.

Jung's veneration of Freud was just as evident. "I rejoice every day in *your* riches," Jung wrote, "and live from the crumbs that fall from the rich man's table." When he was late in responding to Freud's letter, Jung admitted to being scared of Freud's reaction.

In September, in a tone of fawning worship, Jung told Freud of his "long-cherished and constantly repressed wish. I would dearly love to have a photograph of you, not as you used to look but as you did when I first got to know you. Would you have the great kindness to grant this wish of mine sometime? I would be ever so grateful because again and again I feel the want of your picture."

Jung's request prompted Freud to ask for a snapshot of Jung in return. He said that for fifteen years he had not wanted to have his photograph taken for reasons of vanity, being unwilling to accept the physical deterioration that accompanies aging. He agreed, however, to send a picture to Jung. He also included the most flattering picture he had, the profile portrait that appeared on the medallion presented on his fiftieth birthday the year before. Jung was overjoyed; now he had two likenesses of Freud. "Heartiest thanks," he wrote. In a mood of abject humility, befitting his self-perceived role as son to a mighty father, Jung said he would forward his own picture to Freud immediately, "although such an exchange seems absurd."

In October 1907 Jung's feelings reached new heights of passion when he confessed that his adoration of Freud had "something of the character of a 'religious' crush." He recognized the erotic nature of these feelings and called them disgusting. They reminded him of his childhood worship of an older man who, Jung wrote, had sexually assaulted him.*

Jung was afraid of the sensual component of his attraction to Freud and to other men. He repeatedly used the word *disgusting* to describe his attitude toward colleagues who demonstrated a strong emotional transference to him.** He was concerned that Freud would react similarly and call Jung's feelings disgusting. "Consequently, I skirt round such things as much as possible," Jung wrote to Freud, "for, to my feeling at any rate, every intimate relationship turns out after a while to be sentimental and banal or exhibitionistic, as with [Bleuler], whose confidences are offensive."

It was a none too subtle warning and prophecy about their relationship, to which Freud, in his zeal to bind Jung to his cause, paid no heed. Jung's confession of such intimate feelings was traumatic, and before Freud could reply to his letter, Jung wrote again, describing his anguish about Freud's response. He reminded Freud of the dream in which Freud appeared to Jung as a frail old man. The dream had been preying on Jung's mind. Rejecting Freud's death-wish interpretation, Jung arrived at his own conclusion. In an enigmatic statement he wrote, "The dream sets my mind at rest about your + + + dangerousness!"†

---

*Jung did not identify the man or the nature of the assault; therefore we do not know whether the incident was real or a fantasy.

**In psychoanalytic therapy, transference is said to occur when patients transfer their childhood feelings about their parents to their therapist.

†The three crosses were markings "chalked on the inside of doors in peasant houses to ward off danger." Their use in this letter indicates Jung's superstitious nature.

Freud made little of Jung's confession and his analysis of the dream, but he warned Jung of the dangers of transference based on a religious crush. It could lead only to Jung's defection, Freud said. He added that he would do his best to demonstrate that he was not suited to being someone Jung should worship.

Although the emotional side of their relationship grew deeper and more convoluted, the intellectual side did not keep pace. Jung assured Freud that their Vienna meeting had removed his doubts about psychoanalysis, but that remark was not altogether truthful. The demon of sexuality plagued Jung, and he was really no closer to accepting Freud's view. He cited two reasons for his concern about the primacy of sexuality in neuroses. First, he suspected but could not confirm that other forces in the unconscious mind could cause neurotic behavior. Second, he believed that psychoanalysis could be made more acceptable to its critics if the emphasis on sex was minimized.

Freud denied the first point. His evaluation of his patients' problems supported in case after case the accuracy of his sexual theories. As for the second point, Freud opposed the idea of de-emphasizing sex in an attempt to pander to the opposition. He urged Jung not to be concerned about the orthodox medical establishment. "The 'leading lights' of psychiatry really don't amount to much. The future belongs to us and our view."

Freud scorned all such opposition, as befitted a key characteristic of his personality formed in his early years—his defiance. He took no small pleasure in playing the outsider and advocating an unpopular position. Jung, however, was bothered by public disapproval. He was ambitious and eager to advance his career. If he could diminish the role of sexuality in psychoanalytic theory, the system might become more successful. And if psychoanalysis won wider acceptance, this would enhance his professional stature. Thus Jung was more sensitive than Freud to criticism of psychoanalysis. Having publicly affiliated himself early in his career with the Freudian movement, he was vulnerable to attacks on it, and he tended to take those attacks personally. The fate of psychoanalysis would be his fate.

Jung tried to explain to Freud that the opposition to psychoanalysis would affect his future in psychiatry. He agreed that Freud might be correct in urging him to pay less attention to their detractors, "but I am still young, and now and then one has one's quirks in the matter of recognition and scientific standing."

Jung persisted in his efforts to make the sexual theory of neurosis more palatable. He suggested limiting the concept of sexuality to the most extreme aspects of *libido* and selecting a term that would be less offensive to describe other manifestations of sexual energy.

Freud quashed this attempt to "sweeten the sour apple. Even if we do not call the driving force in the broadened conception of sexuality 'libido,' it will still be libido." He added, "We cannot avoid resistances.* Why not face up to them from the start? In my opinion, attack is the best form of defense. Perhaps you are underestimating the intensity of these resistances if you hope to disarm them with small concessions. We are being asked neither more nor less than to abjure our belief in the sexual drive. The only answer is to profess it openly."

However much Jung was concerned about his personal risk in facing up to the vocal opposition to sexuality in psychoanalytic theory, it did not prevent him from courageously defending Freud in public. His role as spokesman for the movement was put to its most severe test at the First International Congress of Psychiatry and Neurology, held in Amsterdam in early September 1907. Freud's most spirited critic, Gustav Aschaffenburg from Heidelberg, would also be attending.

Freud declined an invitation to participate in the conference. "I detest gladiatorial fights in front of the noble rabble and cannot easily bring myself to put my findings to the vote of an indifferent crowd," he wrote to Jung. Also, the meeting coincided with his annual holiday. He was pleased to learn that Jung would be defending psychoanalysis in a debate with Aschaffen-

---

*The tendency to resist revealing repressed material; that is, material that is threatening to the individual's ego.

burg. "I recommend ruthlessness," Freud advised. "Our opponents are pachyderms. You must reckon with their thick hides."

Jung understood that it would be difficult for Freud to be involved in such a debate, but it was different for him. "Since I am not so deeply committed and am not defending my own brain-children, it sometimes tickles me to venture into the arena. The identification with you will later prove to be very flattering. Now it is *honor cum onere* [honor with burden]."

As the date of the meeting approached, Jung became less eager. In mid-August, the secretary of the congress asked Jung for the manuscript of his lecture, but he had not yet written it. "It's a hard nut!" he told Freud. "Often I want to give up in sheer despair." He thought that most of the participants would not understand his paper anyway. Its importance lay only in the fact that something favorable would be said about Freudian theory at an influential meeting.

Freud warned Jung against despair, reminding him that it was not so vital to persuade prominent psychiatrists to accept psychoanalysis. The younger attendees would understand. "Your lecture in Amsterdam will be a milestone in history, and after all it is largely for history that we work." Freud offered an analysis of Jung's despair, suggesting that ambition was the cause.

Jung hastened to agree. "As usual, you have hit the nail on the head. All the same I have unpleasant presentiments, for it is no small thing to be defending *such* a position before *such* a public."

Jung completed his paper within the week. He alerted Freud that he intended to be uncompromising at the congress, the position Freud often recommended to him. In truth, Jung added, there was no other stand he could take if he wanted to be intellectually honest.

On September 2, when the congress convened, Freud was enjoying his holiday on Lake Ossiacher in Carinthia, in southern Austria. He felt guilty about deliberately avoiding the public confrontation and sending his young friend to do battle for him. He wrote to Jung, eloquently expressing his feelings:

I know you are now in Amsterdam, just before or after your perilous lecture, engaged in the defense of my cause, and it strikes me as almost cowardly that I should meanwhile be looking for mushrooms in the woods or bathing in this peaceful Carinthian lake instead of fighting for my own cause or at least standing by your side. I take comfort by telling myself that it is better for the cause this way. You are better fitted for propaganda, for I have always felt that there is something about my personality, my ideas and manner of speaking, that people find strange and repellent, whereas all hearts open to you.

Now of all times I wish I were with you, taking pleasure in no longer being alone and, if you are in need of encouragement, telling you about my long years of honorable but painful solitude, which began after I cast my first glance into the new world, about the indifference and incomprehension of my closest friends, about the terrifying moments when I myself thought I had gone astray, about my slowly growing conviction which fastened itself to the interpretation of my dreams as to a rock in a stormy sea, and about the serene certainty which finally took possession of me and bade me wait until a voice from the unknown multitude should answer mine. That voice was yours. Don't let anything shake your confidence. You will witness our triumph and share in it.

Whatever triumph there was to be for psychoanalysis, it was not evident at the Amsterdam congress. The orderly processes of formal debate disintegrated, partly because of Aschaffenburg's vehemence, but also because of Jung's inexcusably poor planning.

Aschaffenburg's paper was a bold frontal attack on Freud and Jung. He argued that they so strongly emphasized sexuality that they actively encouraged their patients to discuss sexual material. It was no wonder that they found evidence of sexuality where none actually existed! To interpret everything a patient said in sexual terms was wrong, he charged, and it was harmful to the patient. Aschaffenburg self-righteously thumped his chest and told his audience that in his psychiatric practice he did not permit patients to mention sex.

During his lecture, Aschaffenburg made two meaningful verbal errors, saying "facts" when he meant "no facts," and referring to a book published by "Breuer and me" when the book in question had been published by Breuer and *Freud*. Jung believed that these psychopathological slips of the tongue indicated Aschaffenburg was unconsciously "infected" with psychoanalysis but was resisting the theory for personal and emotional reasons.

In the audience for the lectures was a young British physician, Ernest Jones, who had recently become interested in psychoanalysis. He would later join Freud's band of followers and write the great man's first major biography. Jones reported that he and Jung were the only ones present to notice Aschaffenburg's mistakes and to appreciate their significance. They smiled at each incident and nodded to each other. (After the sessions, Jung wrote to apprise Freud of his meeting with Jones, noting that Jones seemed intelligent and might be an asset to the movement.)

Jung's turn to speak followed Aschaffenburg's. He began with an overview of the development of psychoanalysis and described the influence of Pierre Janet, who was in attendance. He then discussed Freud's therapeutic techniques and noted how his own research supported Freud's conclusions.

After thirty minutes Jung showed no signs of stopping, although he knew that was the maximum time allotted to each speaker. The chairman of the session signaled that Jung's time was up, but Jung ignored him. He continued to talk while the chairman's gestures grew more agitated. Finally he was forced to stop. Red-faced, he stalked from the room. Ernest Jones recalled that Jung's behavior made a poor impression on the "impatient and already prejudiced audience, so that there could be no doubt about the issue of the debate."

Jung was furious and poured out his anger to Freud: "What a gang of cutthroats we have here! A ghastly crowd, reeking of vanity, Janet the worst of the lot. I constantly feel the urgent need of a bath. What a morass of nonsense and stupidity!" He felt "contempt bordering on nausea" for them all.

The congress was not yet over. The next day brought a lively and sometimes bitter discussion of the lectures. Many of the participants delivered diatribes against Freud and Jung—greeted, Jung said, by applause—but others spoke in favor of psychoanalysis.

Not all those who criticized Freud and Jung did so because of the explosive issue of sex. Some protested against certain aspects of Freudian technique and theory while praising other parts of the system. Some supporters objected to the messianic fervor with which Freudian disciples claimed that their leader could do no wrong. One participant faulted the "manner in which Freud's disciples compared their master to Galileo and refused to listen to any opinion that did not correspond to Freud's theories."

Another objection was to a point Jung made (and one that Freud had demanded): that anyone who did not subscribe to psychoanalysis had no right to question it. This attitude was considered high-handed and inconsistent with the basic tenets of science, more appropriate for a religious faith than for a doctrine that claimed to be based on objective evidence.

After receiving Jung's report on the Amsterdam congress, Freud wrote that his opponents

> don't want to be enlightened. That is why they are incapable right now of understanding the simplest things. There is nothing for it but to go on working and to argue as little as possible. . . . We know that they are poor devils, who on the one hand are afraid of giving offense, because that might jeopardize their careers, and on the other hand are paralyzed by fear of their own repressed material. We must wait until they die out or gradually shrink to a minority. All the young fresh blood, after all, is on our side.

Although Freud cautioned Jung to ignore the attacks that were made at the congress and published in the professional journals, he nevertheless referred to them frequently in his letters. His message to Jung was the same: we must forge ahead with the development of psychoanalysis and not waste time and energy on useless refutation. He never admitted that anyone outside the psychoanalytic circle could offer valid criticism. All objections were ridiculous and absurd and indicated only the opponents' ignorance.

By this stage of his career Freud was accustomed to scorn, but he recognized that Jung, because of his youth and ambition, might be troubled by it. He attempted to promote in Jung a belief in their eventual success. "As we know," Freud wrote, "others before us have had to wait for the world to understand what they were saying. Every time we are ridiculed, I become more convinced than ever that we are in possession of a great idea."

Jung did not permit the controversy to dim his resolve to support and promote psychoanalysis. His ambition was an advantage because it spurred him to take the lead in helping Freud formalize psychoanalysis into a legitimate scientific movement. It had been an informal organization up to that time, centered on weekly meetings of the apostles in Freud's study and at the Burghölzli under Bleuler. Jung recognized that formal trappings were required—a society, a journal, an annual meeting—to draw together like-minded individuals in a cohesive band that would strengthen the movement. Such a structure, Jung knew, would lend greater credibility to Freudian theory in the minds of adherents and opponents.

Jung took the necessary steps. In September 1907 he organized the Freudian Society of Physicians in Zurich, which had twelve participants at its first meeting. They presented papers on various aspects of psychoanalysis and enjoyed a lively discussion. At the Burghölzli, under Bleuler's direction, the Society for Freudian Researches was established.

Jung proposed to publish what he called an "amusing picture book" to illustrate case histories in psychoanalysis. Freud liked the idea but had already tried something similar without success. He suggested a different sort of publication, but he did so in such a way as to dare Jung to undertake it. He directly challenged Jung's commitment to psychoanalysis by asking if he was serious about fighting for its acceptance. If so, it was Freud's recommendation that they start a journal. He knew that Jung was the only choice for its editor, and he said that he would try to persuade Bleuler to be codirector with himself.

Freud expected that his followers would submit many more articles than could possibly be published and that a great deal of care in selecting and editing the contributions would be necessary. He thought he and Jung could easily fill one volume each year with their own case material. "Doesn't it tempt you?" he asked Jung. "Think it over!"

Surprisingly, the idea did not tempt Jung initially. He was not receptive to the notion and did not believe the journal would be a success because of the medical establishment's opposition to psychoanalysis. He also had personal reservations because he was working on the second volume of his word-association studies and needed more time to complete it.

Freud wrote that Jung could surely see the need for the journal and insisted that it would have a broad audience. He proposed that the first issue be published in the autumn of 1908. He said no more about it for three months, but after the Amsterdam congress he broached the topic again. "Let's go ahead with our journal," he suggested. "People will abuse us, buy it, and read it." He added, perhaps as much for himself as for Jung, "Someday you will remember the years of struggle as the best."

Although Jung liked the idea of a psychoanalytic journal, he continued to plead that the pressure of other work would prevent his involvement. Finally he consented but said that he could not undertake the project until the end of the following year. In December he changed his mind and announced to Freud that he was negotiating with a publisher for the journal; he would tell Freud more as soon as he had something tangible to report. Gratified, Freud reminded Jung that the journal was a matter of the highest priority for the visibility and success of the movement.

Although Jung showed reluctance about starting the journal, he was enthusiastic about another aspect of the formalization of psychoanalysis: an international congress. This was the result of two highly successful professional meetings.

Toward the end of 1907 Jung delivered a lecture to the Zurich Medical Society on the importance of psychoanalysis to the fields of neurology and psychiatry. The audience of more than one hundred physicians greeted his remarks with applause. At the next gathering of his Freudian Society of Physicians, twenty-five people were in attendance, twice the number at the original meeting. Ernest Jones, who was visiting Jung to discuss psychoanalysis, was there, and Jung had high praise for him. "He will be a staunch supporter of our cause," he wrote to Freud, "for besides his intellectual gifts he is full of enthusiasm."

After these well-attended meetings, and buoyed by Jones's support, Jung proposed convening a "congress of Freudian followers" in Innsbruck or Salzburg during 1908. Freud replied that such an event would make him proud, but he added, curiously, "I suppose I should be in the way and that you will not invite me." As expected of a dutiful son, Jung protested that Freud would indeed be welcome at the congress. "You deceive yourself mightily if you think we are going to let you off. On the contrary, we hope and expect to meet under your chairmanship."

"What magnificent plans!" Freud wrote. "You certainly are not lacking in energy." He recommended Salzburg for the site and repeated that he would stay away if Jung thought the meetings would go better without him. He was also explicit in stating his opinion that the people in Zurich, not Vienna, should take the lead in this most important attempt to formalize and promote his work. Jung and Bleuler, he insisted, must spearhead the movement. Freud's dependence on Jung was complete.

That dependence, and the intimacy and trust allied with it, were the keynotes of their relationship in 1907. Thanks to Freud, Jung had assumed a personal and professional identity and had found both a religion and a father figure to provide the support he craved and the stability his life had lacked. Thanks to Jung, Freud's work was evolving into a formal movement, and he no longer felt alone. He had an aggressive, ambitious, and competent son and heir. That Jung would prove too ambitious to linger in Freud's shadow, and that he would not remain content as a bishop but would want to be pope, was inevitable.

CHAPTER FIVE

My Own Fatherhood Will Not Be a Burden: 1908

The enchanting baroque city of Salzburg, Austria, lies in a narrow valley lined by graceful hills and towering mountains. The fast-flowing Salzach River divides the city into the old quarter—a warren of twisting streets—and the new quarter with its wide boulevards, grand hotels, and concert halls, bordered by the elegant Mirabell Palace and its exquisite gardens.

Dominating the city is the Hohensalzburg Fortress, an eleventh-century citadel of walls, towers, and gun ports overlooking the valley. In April 1908, this gloomy stronghold brooded over an event of historic significance, the Congress of Freudian Psychology, the first international meeting devoted to psychoanalysis.

On Sunday, April 26, forty-two men and women gathered in Salzburg from Austria, England, Germany, Hungary, Switzerland, and the United States, a tangible indication of how widespread the interest had grown in Freud's teachings only eight years after the publication of *The Interpretation of Dreams*. Fully half the participants were practicing psychoanalysts or in training to become analysts. The others were intrigued by Freud's revolutionary approach to neurosis and had come to meet the master in person and learn more about his work.

The congress was held in the Hotel Bristol on the Markart-platz in the new quarter. From the hotel's large front rooms with their fancifully painted milk-glass chandeliers, visitors could look across the square to the house in which Mozart was born and up to the dark outline of Hohensalzburg.

The conference opened at eight o'clock the next morning, with Freud presenting the first paper. In the audience was virtually everyone who would figure prominently in the further development of psychoanalysis. From his chair at the end of a long table, Freud regarded his disciples and his future dissenters and enemies. From Vienna had come Alfred Adler, Wilhelm Stekel, Paul Federn, Otto Gross, Max Kahane, Otto Rank, and Fritz Wittels. Jung and Bleuler led the six-man Swiss contingent. Sandor Ferenczi had arrived from Budapest, Karl Abraham from Berlin, Ernest Jones from London, and A. A. Brill from New York.

Promptly at eight, Freud began to speak while the others listened with attentive reverence. For the first time in his career Freud was lecturing to people who were sympathetic to his views. They had come prepared to learn from him and to applaud and affirm the path he had chosen.

Freud spoke without pause for three hours, although the program called for only thirty minutes. No one interrupted. He held them spellbound, delivering a fascinating account of the case of the Rat Man, so called because rats figured prominently in his delusions and dreams. The patient, a Viennese lawyer in his late twenties, was deeply troubled by neurotic obsessions, which Freud traced to a time when, as a child, he had seen his parents engaging in sexual intercourse. Freud described to his audience the conflicting emotions of love and hate one may feel toward the same person. (The situation was reminiscent of his childhood tie to his nephew, John, and it foreshadowed his relationships with Jung and Adler.)

Freud concluded his remarks at eleven o'clock, suggesting to the group that they certainly must have had enough. They protested and urged him to continue. As Ernest Jones recalled, "We begged him to go on, and he did so for another hour. I had never before been so oblivious of the passage of time."

Following lunch, Jones delivered a paper, as did Jung, Abraham, Stekel, Ferenczi, and two others, and their remarks were met by an enthusiastic discussion. In the evening they adjourned to the hotel dining room to offer friendly and spirited toasts. Among those paying tribute to Freud was the gifted and highly neurotic psychiatrist Otto Gross. He compared Freud to Nietzsche and "hailed him as a destroyer of old prejudices, an enlarger of psychological horizons, and a scientific revolutionary."

It was a day of overwhelming success and joy for Freud, and he reveled in the adoration. "The congress is a great success," he wrote to his wife, "and I think it has left a good impression on all those who took part in it."

After the evening presentations Freud met with six of the participants to discuss the publication of a journal that would become the official organ of the psychoanalytic movement. They agreed to lend their support to the efforts Freud and Jung had already begun. But there was something significant and prophetic about this group. Aside from Freud's, not a single Viennese accent was heard in the room. Those who decided on the founding of the journal included Bleuler, Abraham, Jones, Ferenczi, and Brill. Although more than half the analysts at the congress were from Vienna, and many of them had been devoted to Freud from the earliest days of the movement, none was asked to share in the discussion of the journal.

When the Vienna contingent learned of this private meeting they were offended, jealous at being passed over in favor of the foreigners. Freud had not solicited their opinions or even notified them that the issue was being considered. Now, when they would finally have a formal outlet for their papers and case studies, they were to have no control over it. The Swiss—Jung and Bleuler— had been given the authority to decide what would be published and in what form. The loyal Viennese were being eased out of the center of power and responsibility for the movement that they thought belonged to them.

In their eyes, the outsiders, the latecomers, were taking over, and, what was worse, they were not Jewish. Ernest Jones noted that the increasingly hostile attitude of the Viennese was "accentuated by their Jewish suspicion of Gentiles in general, with its rarely failing expectation of anti-Semitism. The Viennese predicted even at that early date that Jung would not long remain in the psychoanalytic camp. Whether they at that time had any justification for this is another matter, but the Germans have a good saying, *der Hass sieht scharf* [hate has a keen eye]." More and more that keen eye was focusing on the tall, rough-hewn figure of Carl Jung, the "blond Siegfried," as the Viennese came to call him.

But if the Viennese group grumbled about the situation, they did so among themselves. Freud was not aware of their complaints, although he should have been able to anticipate them. He was basking in the light of the international recognition from his new admirers at the congress. In time, the Viennese would make their feelings known, but on that April day in Salzburg in 1908, there was for Freud only happiness.

One evening at the congress, midway through dinner, Freud glanced through the door and into the hallway. He was momentarily stunned, thinking that he saw a familiar figure. He excused himself and went out into the corridor, to be greeted by his seventy-five-year-old half brother, Emanuel, who had come from England to surprise him. They spent the next day together, touring Salzburg, reminiscing, and drinking beer. Emanuel consumed most of the beer, or so Freud assured his wife.

The Congress of Freudian Psychology was a triumph for Freud personally and a success for the movement as a whole. Freud knew that this attempt to reach a wider audience with his ideas was a result of the work of Carl Jung. Without Jung's efforts over the previous months, there might not have been such a conference. Even the title of the meeting, which had focused on Freud rather than on psychoanalysis, had been Jung's choice, to which Freud raised no objection. Jung had suggested the designation in January, when he sent Freud copies of the "impudent invitations," which he hoped Freud would approve. "From many quarters," the printed circular began, "the followers of Freud's teachings have expressed a desire for an annual meeting which would afford them an opportunity to discuss their practical experiences and to exchange ideas."

Jung also had requested, in the name of his friends, that Freud speak at the meeting. He added that Freud was not to go to a lot of trouble. "Nothing special," Jung said. Something "quite ordinary" would do nicely.

Freud replied that he might find something suitable on which to speak, and he accepted the chairmanship of the congress, but only because Jung insisted. He immediately tried to foist the job on Bleuler, Jung's superior at the Burghölzli. Explaining that he wanted to honor Bleuler in some way, Freud asked Jung to intercede by telling Bleuler that Freud personally requested that he chair the meeting. It would be more dignified, Freud believed, if Bleuler presided. Because of Bleuler's authority and reputation, his appearance as head of the first international Congress of Freudian Psychology would be a public-relations coup, bringing it prestige, recognition, and stature in the eyes of the psychiatric establishment. Jung was so certain that Bleuler would refuse that he did not even ask him. Bleuler, Jung said, was "above all that," a man who abominated all forms of recognition.

Prior to the congress, Freud had also made a number of disparaging comments to Jung about the Viennese followers, comparing them unfavorably with Jung's colleagues in Zurich. Freud even expressed the hope that some of his Vienna disciples who planned to present papers would change their minds and withdraw. "They are not all fit to exhibit," Freud wrote. He urged Jung to use his influence to keep their contributions to a minimum. Restrict their speaking time, he suggested, or reject their papers; otherwise "we shall all drown in the torrent of words." Freud was concerned that the Vienna group would make a poor impression on the others, but he would not intervene by editing their papers himself. "These people are so dreadfully sensitive," he explained to Jung.

As the date of the congress approached, he continued to denigrate the Viennese loyalists while increasing his flattery of Jung, saying that Jung was the only person capable of making an original contribution. Freud urged Jung to give his paper last; that way, the others would hurry through their talks in their eagerness to hear what Jung had to say.

It was Jung's turn to exude compliments when he prepared the final program. Each speaker would be allotted thirty minutes, except for Freud. He told Freud that all that mattered was to hear him, not the Viennese. Jung begged Freud to talk about one of his cases rather than the theory of neurosis itself. This may have reflected Jung's lingering resistance to psychoanalysis, which prevented him from accepting it unconditionally. Concerned that he had overstepped his authority, however, Jung added that it was not for him to pressure Freud about his topic. Undoubtedly, Freud's judgment was more sound than his.

Two days after the congress, when Jung had returned home, he wrote to Freud that he was still "under the reverberating impact of your lecture, which seemed to me perfection itself. All the rest was simply padding, sterile twaddle in the darkness of inanity." Fine words of devotion from a faithful follower. Yet in the same letter, Jung expressed another sentiment. He said that he had been devoting too much time to his students and too little time to his patients. He begged Freud to bear with him and to have confidence in what he had achieved thus far. "I always have a little more to do than be just a faithful follower," he wrote. "You have no lack of those anyway. But they do not advance the cause, for by faith alone nothing prospers in the long run." Was this a belated warning to his own father, a reminder to himself, or a plea to his newly adopted mentor?

Freud ignored both the warning and Jung's concern about how time-consuming his pupils were, saying only that the problem could be easily overcome. It had been more important to Freud to see Jung again: "Every suspicion of resentment melted away when I saw you again and understood you. I am quite certain that after having moved a few steps away from me you will find your way back, and then go far with me. I can't give you any reason for this certainty. It probably springs from a feeling I have when I look at you. But I am satisfied to feel at one with you and no longer feel that we might be torn apart."

One reason for Freud's concern was that he and Jung had had a minor spat two weeks before the congress. Jung had sent Freud three recently published papers. The first, in collaboration with Bleuler, was on dementia praecox, and the second was Jung's speech from the Amsterdam conference, the one he had not finished delivering because it was too long. The third, on psychoses, was written for a lay audience. Freud liked the last but was displeased with the others. They were too tentative, he thought, too full of concern for the prejudices and ignorance of those arrayed in opposition to psychoanalysis. Jung was not defending the faith vigorously enough. Further, Freud believed, Jung seemed to be more in agreement with Bleuler on certain issues than with him. He expressed the hope that he and Jung could have a private talk in Salzburg about paranoia—presumably Jung's.

Jung was devastated by Freud's letter. "I have done bad work," he wrote. He was eager to learn from his mistakes and said that they would surely reach agreement when they met.

Freud responded by wishing Jung a happy Easter and urging him not to nurse hard feelings. He admitted to having been "cranky" in his last letter, a condition brought on by overwork. He was not angry with Jung, and he pointed out how it was his habit to be pleased with Jung's support rather than reproachful about their differences. He hoped to find Jung "unruffled" when they met in Salzburg. And when they did finally get together, their relationship seemed once again secure.

The depth of their personal commitment to each other intensified over the course of 1908, after a rocky start. At the beginning of the year, after Freud requested that Jung write more often, Jung said he was afraid of boring Freud with too-frequent letters. Freud wrote back to ask how Jung could imagine that he would ever complain about receiving too many letters from Jung. Calling him the "spirit of my spirit," Freud expressed dissatisfaction at not hearing from him for several weeks.

One of the most emotional moments for Jung in their relationship resulted from Freud's letter of February 17, in which, for the first time, he addressed Jung simply as "dear friend" instead of "colleague." Jung was ecstatic: "I thank you with all my heart for this token of your confidence. The undeserved gift of your friendship is one of the high points in my life which I cannot celebrate with big words. Let me enjoy your friendship not as one between equals but as that of father and son. This distance appears to me fitting and natural." He signed the letter "Jung and *Jünger*," the latter word meaning "younger" or "disciple."

The spiral of mutual need and dependence deepened. "I need you," Freud wrote, "the cause cannot do without you. . . . I must persuade you to continue and complete my work by applying to psychoses what I have begun with neuroses. With your strong and independent character, with your Germanic blood, which enables you to command the sympathies of the public more readily than I, you seem more fitted than anyone else I know to carry out this mission. Besides, I'm fond of you, but I have learned to subordinate that factor."

A letter Freud wrote in the fall of the year began with the salutation, "My dear friend and heir." Jung wrote that he had a sin to confess. "I have had your photograph enlarged. It looks marvelous."

A dispute was brewing between Jung and Karl Abraham, a Freudian loyalist working in Berlin. It had to do in part with the touchy subject of priority in science, but the manner in which Freud handled the situation revealed much about his dependence on Jung. Abraham had once studied with Jung at the Burghölzli but left within a year, frustrated and unhappy with Jung's interest in the occult, astrology, and mysticism.

According to Ernest Jones, Abraham was hostile toward Jung even before the international congress in Salzburg, a feeling that derived from their relationship in Zurich coupled with Abraham's jealousy over Freud's obvious favoring of Jung. The Salzburg incident smacks of the behavior of two brothers vying for the favor of their father.

It was Freud, the symbolic father, who set the stage for this sibling rivalry. Months before, in separate conversations with Jung and Abraham, Freud stated his belief that dementia praecox was caused by the same factors that produced neuroses. Thus he was suggesting that psychoses were psychological in origin and not attributable to physiological causes, in contrast to the prevailing view of medical science. At the Salzburg congress, Abraham incorporated Freud's idea in his presentation, but Jung did not. Instead, Jung extolled the teachings of Bleuler, who thought that dementia praecox—indeed, all psychoses—were induced by organic factors such as a toxin in the brain. Jung explained to Freud, however, that he was considering Freud's notion and planned to develop it but that Abraham had beat him to it.

Freud was disappointed because he knew that he was still waging a battle with Bleuler for Jung's allegiance. But what increased the antagonism between Jung and Abraham resulted from a curious omission in Abraham's presentation. In his paper—a copy of which Jung, as organizer of the congress, had received in advance—Abraham gave credit to Jung and Bleuler for their extensive research on dementia praecox, but when Abraham read the paper at Salzburg, he omitted all mention of them!

Of course, all psychoanalysts know that any such misstatement has a cause, either conscious or unconscious. Abraham defended the omission by telling Freud that he had left out mention of Jung and Bleuler to save time, to make sure he did not exceed his allotted thirty minutes. But his real and unconscious motivation, Abraham confessed, was animosity because the Swiss were deviating from Freud's sexual theory. Because Jung and Bleuler were not being true to Freud's views, Abraham felt justified in refusing to cite their work.

Jung was furious, and he wasted no time in telling Freud that Abraham was not a gentleman. He exchanged angry words with Abraham, leaving Freud with the task of reconciling them. Freud pleaded with each man for harmony on the grounds that there were too few members of the psychoanalytic family to tolerate warring factions.

To Jung he wrote that Abraham was a valuable follower he did not want to lose, but he assured Jung that Abraham could never replace Jung in his esteem. He asked Jung to be helpful if Abraham submitted his Salzburg paper to the new psychoanalytic journal. Abraham espoused the Freudian view of the psychological origin of psychoses, Freud reminded Jung, whereas Jung did not.

Freud told Abraham that Jung was overly sensitive because his loyalties wavered between Freud and Bleuler, but it was vital for psychoanalysis that Jung return to the fold and accept Freud's views. Freud asked Abraham to make a friendly gesture by asking Jung to discuss his position with Abraham before Abraham submitted his Salzburg paper to the journal. "Be tolerant," Freud urged Abraham, "and don't forget that really it is easier for you to follow my thoughts than for Jung, since to begin with you are completely independent, and then racial relationship brings you closer to my intellectual constitution, whereas he, being a Christian and the son of a pastor, can only find his way to me against great inner resistances. His adherence is therefore all the more valuable."

Abraham made the friendly gesture that Freud requested, but Jung never responded. Abraham wrote to Freud criticizing Jung, and Freud countered by praising his Swiss son and interpreting the impasse in terms of anti-Semitism: "I surmise that the repressed anti-Semitism of the Swiss, from which I am to be spared, has been directed against you in increased force. But my opinion is that we Jews, if we want to cooperate with other people, have to develop a little masochism and be prepared to endure a certain amount of injustice. There is no other way of working together."

For a while, the hostility between Jung and Abraham was smoothed over, but months later it resurfaced. Abraham sent Jung some reviews he had written for the first issue of the journal, but Jung said they could not be published until the next issue because of lack of space.

Abraham interpreted this as a personal insult and reported it to Freud, who rebuked him and supported Jung's decision. It was, Freud said, within Jung's province as editor of the psychoanalytic journal, and no one had the right to interfere with or question Jung's judgment. Freud reemphasized the importance of Jung to the advancement of the cause. "Our Aryan comrades are quite indispensable to us; otherwise psychoanalysis would fall victim to anti-Semitism."

The year 1908 also brought the strange and tragic case of Otto Gross, which was both a personal failure for Jung and a professional failure for psychoanalysis in the area in which Freud most wanted to be successful—the application of his ideas to the treatment of dementia praecox. If psychoanalysis could cure someone suffering from this psychotic disorder, that success was sure to influence Jung's views on psychoses and accelerate the transfer of his loyalty from Bleuler's organic theory to Freud's psychological one. And, by extension, from the person of Bleuler to the person of Freud.

Otto Gross, who at the Salzburg congress had compared Freud with Nietzsche, was a talented analyst to whom Freud had paid the supreme compliment. He said that Gross and Jung were the "only truly original minds" in the movement. But Gross was also emotionally disturbed and addicted to opium and cocaine.

Freud was greatly concerned about Gross's health and arranged for him to be committed to the Burghölzli under Jung's care. Freud wanted Jung to treat Gross from May until October and supervise his withdrawal from the drugs. After that, Freud would undertake Gross's psychoanalysis himself.

Jung diagnosed Gross as an obsessional neurotic and pro-

ceeded to treat him on that basis. At first, Gross showed rapid
progress. It was a bizarre situation in that therapist and patient
sometimes switched roles. Whenever Jung reached an impasse,
Gross would analyze *him*. Jung's own mental health improved as
a result, so he reported to Freud, and after just two weeks—with
marathon sessions of many hours—Jung decided his method had
been successful. Further, Gross was maintaining his own program to withdraw from the drugs. Although the case had all the
signs of an amazing cure, Freud cautioned Jung that he could not
have brought about such a profound change in so short a time.

A month later Freud received disturbing news. Jung said that
his initial diagnosis of Gross had been incorrect. He now believed that Gross was suffering from dementia praecox. He was a
schizophrenic. In desperation, Jung was willing to try something
new—treating a schizophrenic using the psychoanalytic approach. Whereas all of Freud's patients were neurotics (he had
never worked with a psychotic), Jung's patients at the Burghölzli
were psychotics. In the past, Jung had used his own eclectic
brand of therapy with them rather than the orthodox Freudian
approach.

Jung resumed his sessions with Gross, once working twenty-
four hours without a break until they both were exhausted, but
nothing proved effective. Gross fled from the hospital by climb-
ing over a wall. The following day he sent a note praising Jung
for curing him and asking for money to pay his hotel bill. A week
later Gross's wife informed Jung that Gross had left the Zurich
hotel because someone was spying on him. Gross returned to his
home in Munich, where he reported that voices were calling to
him and someone was pounding on the walls and ceiling.

Jung was greatly upset by this therapeutic failure and called
it one of the worst experiences of his life. He liked Gross and saw
much of himself reflected in Gross's personality. Except for the
psychosis, he and Gross seemed like brothers, but now he knew
that Gross was doomed, despite his best efforts. Nevertheless,
Jung admitted to Freud, he was grateful for the experience because it gave him new insight into the mind of the insane. It also

suggested to him that Freud's view of the psychological origin of schizophrenia might be correct.

Freud took this confession as a victory. He told Jung that the Gross case had been good for him—a rare opportunity to learn much from a patient. An additional benefit, of course, was that it brought Jung's views in line with Freud's own. Freud said he was convinced that any differences between them could be attributed to Bleuler's influence. "I was not entirely pleased with Bleuler," Freud wrote, referring to the Salzburg congress. "He sometimes made me feel rather creepy, but after a while I felt sure that I would not lose you to him."

As for Gross, Freud dismissed him abruptly and cruelly. "There is nothing to be said of him. He is addicted and can only do great harm to our cause." Nothing more was heard of Gross for three years. In April 1911, then a patient at the Steinhof sanatorium near Vienna, he wrote to Freud and to Jung. The letters were scribbled in pencil and accused Bleuler of stealing the word *dementia* from him. He also charged that Jung had stolen various ideas that Gross had mentioned during his analysis. The charges angered Freud, and he called Gross a "complete nut." Gross was never able to free himself of his drug addictions, and he died a few years later under mysterious circumstances, possibly a suicide.

Under Jung's aggressive editorship, the first journal of psychoanalysis, the *Yearbook for Psychoanalysis and Research in Psychopathology*, was taking shape. There was no dearth of papers. Almost everyone who had attended the Salzburg congress wanted to be published in the first issue.

Jung's contribution dealt with the father complex: "The Meaning of the Father for the Destiny of the Individual." He described it to Freud as "no great shakes" but hoped Freud would like it. "In any event," Jung said, "its staunchness to the cause leaves nothing to be desired."

Jung's assessment of his own paper is questionable. It was not very supportive of Freud's views, particularly with regard to the Oedipus complex, which Jung never completely accepted. So in the first issue of the *Yearbook* Jung described the behaviors and feelings that Freud said derived from the resolution of the Oedipus complex and attributed them to a cause that was more social than sexual; that is, to the unconscious assimilation of family attitudes. In a footnote to the paper Jung disputed Freud's definition of *libido* as sexual energy. Jung wrote that a proper psychiatric definition of *libido* would be simply "will" or "striving."

Quibbling arose about the order of names on the title page of the first issue. Bleuler argued that his contribution to the journal was so modest that his name should not appear on the same line as Freud's. Jung was concerned lest his own name be too prominent, which he thought would work to the disadvantage of the movement. He was too young for such a conspicuous display, he argued, and it might be too hard for others to forgive.

The version finally agreed on listed Bleuler and Freud on the same line, with Jung's name below. It distressed Jung to place Bleuler's name first, and he explained to Freud that he did so only because Bleuler held the academic rank of full professor. Freud insisted that he also be listed as professor although his own rank carried no academic standing. He suggested that it would be obvious to everyone that Bleuler's name was first merely to conform to alphabetical order.

Freud was delighted with the first issue of the *Yearbook* when it appeared early the next year. "Jung has done a splendid job," he wrote to Sandor Ferenczi in Budapest. "It is something to be proud of."

In September 1908 Freud paid a four-day visit to Zurich as part of his extended summer travels. Since mid-July he had been vacationing with his family near Berchtesgaden. On September 1

he went to The Hague to see the Rembrandt paintings, and from there traveled to England to stay with Emanuel and Philipp in Manchester and Blackpool. He spent a week in London, which he enjoyed immensely.

He then went on to Zurich to stay with the Jungs in their quarters on the grounds of the Burghölzli Hospital. Emma Jung found Freud to be a "delightful man—on the gloomy side perhaps. I talked to him once about my own troubles."

Freud and Jung talked for hours and strolled the institution's grounds. Jung took him to see a patient, and they also found time for a drive in the mountains. The visit left Freud in "high good humor," and it did Jung so much good that he planned to go to Vienna to see Freud the following spring. Refreshed and happy, Freud departed Zurich on September 21 to join his sister-in-law Minna for a few days on Lake Garda in Italy. Never again would Freud and Jung meet in such harmony. Never again would they achieve such closeness.

One reason for Freud's satisfaction after his stay in Zurich was his pleasure over Jung's announcement that he had decided to break with Bleuler and leave his position at the Burghölzli. The Jungs were having a house built on the shore of Lake Zurich near the village of Küsnacht. Jung planned to devote himself to study, writing, and perhaps treating a few private patients. Jung's departure from the hospital meant that Freud had won. Surely now Jung's loyalty would be undivided.

Jung was harsh in his criticism of Bleuler, a former mentor and father surrogate, calling him difficult and intolerably infantile, someone ruthlessly acting out his complexes. Working under Bleuler, Jung said, had restricted his intellectual freedom. Leaving Bleuler would be a turning point in his life and would free him of that father complex. The loss would not grieve him, Jung claimed, because the tie was much stronger on Bleuler's side than on his.

Freud responded that Jung's decision was "an answer to my heartfelt wishes. You will see what a blessing it is to have no master over you. My own fatherhood will not be a burden to you."

Another significant event marked Jung's life toward the end of 1908: the birth of a son. To Freud he wrote that he regretted being no longer a peasant. If he were, he could succumb to the peasant belief that he could die in peace because he had a son. "A great deal more could be said on this complex theme." Perhaps he was recalling his mother's remark when his father died. "He died in time for you," she had said—in time to get out of your way. Freud replied that Jung's regret at not playing the "ideal hero-father" by dying at the moment of his son's birth was a bit premature. "The child will find you indispensable for many many years, first in a positive, then in a negative sense."

At Christmas, Jung sent Freud a cheese. Apparently it was pungent because Freud wrote that he had it all to himself; the rest of the family "rejected it with indignation." Freud received another Christmas gift as well—an invitation to deliver a series of lectures in the United States in July. The American psychologist G. Stanley Hall, professor of psychology and president of Clark University in Worcester, Massachusetts, asked Freud to participate in the twentieth-anniversary celebration of the school's founding. Hall offered Freud $400 plus travel expenses.

Although Freud was highly flattered, he declined the invitation, claiming that he would lose too much money by being away from his practice for three weeks. Four hundred dollars was insufficient to compensate for the loss. "America," he wrote to Ferenczi, "should bring in money, not cost money." Hall persisted, however, and Freud agreed in the end to make the trip. Jung would go with him.

———— ·◦∞◦· ————

CHAPTER SIX

The Peat-Bog Corpses: 1909

*T*he peat-bog corpses are a macabre residue of human history found in the far reaches of northern Germany. Thousands of years old, the corpses have been preserved in grotesque fashion by the high humic-acid content of the marshy soil in which they were either buried or drowned. The corpses have no skeletons. The bones were long ago eaten away by the acid. But the skin and the hair of the bodies remain intact, mummified by nature. The corpses are two-dimensional. They have been pressed flat under the centuries-old buildup of peat. Nothing remains beneath the surface of the skin.

In the early afternoon hours of Friday, August 20, 1909, the peat-bog corpses were the subject of a lively but increasingly irritating discussion among three friends—Sigmund Freud, Carl Jung, and Sandor Ferenczi. They were eating lunch at the Essighaus in Bremen, amid the 300-year-old restaurant's ornate Hanseatic woodwork. Located at 19–20 Langenstrasse, it was then, and remains today, one of the city's finest restaurants.

The meal began on a celebratory note. The men were sailing the next day for America on the North German Lloyd liner *George Washington*. They, and psychoanalysis, were to be honored at Clark University in Massachusetts. But the joyful mood was fading as Jung talked compulsively about the peat-bog corpses. His animated monologue was bordering on incoherence. He spoke louder and more rapidly than usual, and his powerful hands sliced the air abruptly, punctuating his speech. Freud was growing uncomfortable, but Jung did not seem to notice.

Jung's confused manner was partly Freud's fault. After much effort, he had persuaded Jung to take a glass of wine with lunch. That was quite a concession on Jung's part because since joining the staff of the Burghölzli, he had followed Bleuler's example and abstained from alcohol. But now he was violating Bleuler's proscription, and Freud savored the victory, further proof of Jung's shifting allegiance.

However, as Jung droned on about the peat-bog corpses, Freud's pleasure paled. His interpretation of Jung's obsession with death and corpses chilled him. He understood the symbolism of Jung's conversation, and it was not the first time he had sensed such unconscious longings on Jung's part. Suddenly Jung made a mistake, confirming Freud's analysis of the meaning of Jung's words.

The peat-bog corpses had been discovered some distance north of Bremen, but Jung talked of them as though they were in the city, confusing them with the five-hundred-year-old remains of archbishops locked in the lead crypt beneath St. Peter's Cathedral, a few blocks from the restaurant. Freud believed that Jung, unconsciously, had "transported" the peat-bog corpses to Bremen because that was where *Freud* was.

Freud interrupted Jung several times to question him about this fixation on corpses. Jung did not respond, but Freud already knew the answer: Jung harbored an unconscious death wish toward Freud and wanted to take Freud's place. When Freud suggested this, Jung quickly denied it, saying that Freud made that interpretation only because it fit his theory. Freud's anger overwhelmed him. The room began to spin before his eyes, and he keeled over in a faint.*

---

*Discussing the episode many years later, Jung said, "Why should I want him to die? I had come to learn. He was not standing in my way. He was in Vienna, I was in Zurich." Freud made no more mention of the death wish, although he did purchase traveler's insurance for the trip to America in the amount of twenty thousand marks. Ferenczi, perhaps feeling less threatened, insured his life for ten thousand marks.

Freud's invitation to visit the United States was another sign of recognition for psychoanalysis on an international scale and a visible indication of the widespread interest in his theories. When Jung learned of the trip, he congratulated Freud on the triumph but suggested that he go at a time that might be more convenient in terms of his patients.

He also urged Freud to consider the financial advantages of such a trip. Lectures in America could attract a rich clientele. He told Freud that the German psychiatrist Emil Kraepelin had received $12,000 for a single consultation in California. "I think this side of things should also be taken into account," Jung wrote.

Freud replied that he was not optimistic about getting lucrative consultations or about psychoanalysis being accepted in the United States. He believed that American society was too prudish and would abandon the Freudian system once its sexual basis became apparent.

In early March 1909, Freud heard again from G. Stanley Hall. The enterprising American psychologist issued another invitation to Freud, one more to his liking. Hall had arranged to postpone the twentieth-anniversary celebration at Clark University until the week of September 6, during the vacation period when Freud ordinarily did not see patients. In this way, he would not lose fees by making the trip. Hall raised the promised stipend to $750. It was an offer Freud could not refuse, and he told Jung that nothing in the last few years had thrilled him so much. Indeed, he could think of little else.

Freud reminisced about the last time he had considered crossing the Atlantic—in 1886, when he was just starting his private practice. If he did not attract enough patients to provide a sufficient income, he intended to ask his fiancée to accompany him to the United States. But things worked out in Vienna, "unfortunately," he remarked to Jung, "and now, twenty-three years later, I am to go to America after all, not, to be sure, to make money, but in response to an honorable call."

Freud wanted a companion for the trip, someone with whom he could talk easily and pass the time pleasantly. He chose Sandor Ferenczi, who, at thirty-six, retained the round, boyish face that reflected the inner man. Ferenczi possessed "a good deal of the simplicity and a still greater amount of the imagination of the child." Sensitive, honest, and likable, Ferenczi was totally committed to Freud and his teachings. There was no question of divided loyalty on his part.

He was also an enthusiastic traveler. As soon as Freud invited him, Ferenczi bought travel books and threw himself into the study of the English language. Freud declined to read the guidebooks. All he wanted to see was Niagara Falls. Analyzing this behavior later, Ernest Jones thought that Freud deliberately suppressed his initial excitement about the trip to reduce his apprehension about his forthcoming lectures.

"The thought of America," Freud wrote to Ferenczi, "does not seem to matter to me, but I am looking forward very much to our journey together." Ferenczi asked if he should pack a silk top hat to wear during the ceremonies at the university. Freud joked that he would buy one in the United States and toss it overboard on the voyage home.

Freud was uncertain about topics for his American lectures. He asked Jung for suggestions and lamented the fact that he would have to speak in German. Jung felt that the interpretation of dreams would be a suitable subject. As for the language problem, Jung dismissed it. There was nothing the Americans could do about it anyway.

Several weeks later Jung informed Freud that he too had been invited to Clark University. "Isn't it splendid about America?" Jung wrote. He booked passage on the same ship and mentioned twice to Freud that he had had to take an expensive cabin because all the cheaper ones were reserved.

At that point, Jung became less cavalier about the selection of a lecture topic because he was faced with the same decision.

"What am I to say? What can one say of all this in three lectures? I'd be grateful for advice."

Freud expressed delight that Jung would be traveling with them. (It is strange that Freud had not originally asked Jung to accompany him.) He told Jung that the invitation conveyed remarkable recognition considering his relatively young age. Freud may have been feeling a hint of jealousy, perhaps slighted that Jung was being accorded a similar honor, despite being nearly twenty years younger. Was the father reluctant to share the stage with the son?

On the nagging question of their lectures, Freud suggested that they decide during the voyage while taking long walks around the ship's deck. The invitation was the important thing. "The audience is now at our mercy, under obligation to applaud whatever we bring them."

When the three men boarded the *George Washington*, Freud was met with a pleasant surprise. He found his cabin steward reading *The Psychopathology of Everyday Life* and for the first time realized that he might be famous.

They all enjoyed the six-day crossing. The weather was good, and Freud proclaimed himself the heartiest sailor of the trio. They passed the time in conversation and the analysis of one another's dreams. Most of Freud's dreams centered around his anxiety about the future of his six children and the future of his system of psychoanalysis. What would become of them when he was no longer there to guide and support them? Who would take his place?

He also reported a long, disturbing dream with a different theme. Jung interpreted as much of the dream's symbolism as he could but found himself unable to proceed without asking about Freud's private life. Would Freud free-associate to various aspects of the dream? This was the accepted—indeed necessary—way to conduct a dream analysis, as Freud himself had developed the technique. But Freud balked, refusing to reveal anything further about the dream or to describe his associations to it. "He looked at me with bitterness," Jung wrote, "and said, 'I could tell you more, but I cannot risk my authority.' In that moment something snapped in me. I knew that if a man cared more for his authority than for the truth I could no longer go down the same road with him."

The experience was shattering for Jung, reminding him all too vividly of his disappointment with his father almost two decades earlier. When Jung had turned to his father for guidance in dealing with his religious doubts, all he had received was the exhortation to believe, to refrain from questioning or thinking. His father had insisted on dogmatic loyalty; the emphasis was on authority, not truth. And now Freud was behaving in a similar way. The parallel was cruel.

Sixty years passed before Jung revealed the circumstances of Freud's dream. In an interview in 1969 he spoke about that trip to America. The dream dealt with the alleged romantic triangle involving Freud, his wife Martha, and his sister-in-law Minna, who lived with the family and often traveled with Freud on his summer holidays.

Jung also recalled in that interview that Freud developed severe neurotic symptoms on the voyage to America, including unspecified psychosomatic disorders and problems with bladder control. Jung had urged Freud to undergo a complete analysis, which he volunteered to conduct, but Freud refused. "If Freud would have tried to understand consciously the triangle," Jung said, "he would have been much, much better off."

The story of Freud, Martha, and Minna arose yet another time on the trip. This time Jung used his own knowledge of the triangle in an act of willful deception. The conflict about Freud's dream and his unwillingness to divulge personal details for fear of losing his authority had already shown Jung that he and Freud would one day have to part company. The new incident, in which Freud analyzed a dream of Jung's, revealed the direction of Jung's work and how far it would ultimately diverge from Freud's.

Jung described a dream in which he was in an unfamiliar house. He had never seen the house before, yet he knew it belonged to him, not to Freud or anyone else. He wandered around the top floor into a room he described as a salon, furnished in rococo style with fine old paintings on the walls. He realized that he had never seen the first floor, so he walked down the steps and found that everything there was much older than in the upper story. The floors were paved with red brick and the furniture was medieval. He dated this part of the house as fifteenth or sixteenth century. He descended a stone stairway into the cellar and discovered an even older room. The walls were of brick and stone blocks, and Jung was convinced they had been built during the Roman era.

He noticed a ring in one of the stone slabs of the floor. He tugged on it and lifted the slab to reveal another staircase. He walked down narrow stone steps into a cave carved out of rock. It was thick with dust. The ceiling was low, and scattered over the floor were skeletons and bits of broken pottery, remnants of a primitive people. Among the artifacts Jung discovered two ancient and partially disintegrated human skulls. Then he awoke; the dream was over.

Freud showed little interest in Jung's narration of the dream until he mentioned the skulls. Freud seized upon these symbols, questioning Jung repeatedly, pressuring him to reveal the wishes that must be associated with them. Whose skulls did Jung think they were?

"I knew perfectly well, of course, what he was driving at," Jung wrote in his autobiography, "that secret death wishes were concealed in the dream." Obviously Freud believed that the skulls, those images of death, were additional evidence of Jung's unconscious death wish toward Freud. The second skull might have been Ferenczi's, a man whose faith in Freud's teachings was more absolute than Jung's.

Jung listened dutifully to Freud's interpretation. He was caught in a dilemma about how to respond to Freud's questions. He resisted the death-wish interpretation because he had his own idea about the dream's meaning, but he was pulled by his need for Freud's approval and did not yet trust his own interpretation.

The thought of losing Freud's friendship was intolerable to Jung, despite his growing doubts about the man and his theories.

Jung decided that he could not offer Freud his own analysis of the dream. It varied so strongly from the psychoanalytic view that Freud would surely resist it. Jung resolved, instead, to tell a lie, to see how Freud would interpret an answer deliberately slanted to suit Freudian theory. Mindful of Freud's romantic-triangle dream and of the problems in his own marriage, Jung said that the two skulls represented his own wife and sister-in-law.

Freud was relieved. Jung decided that Freud's reaction was additional evidence that Freud could not see beyond his own doctrines. To Jung, psychoanalysis could not make sense of his dream; he would have to find the meaning on his own.

On Sunday evening, August 29, the *George Washington* sailed into New York harbor. The passengers lined the rail to gaze at the dramatic skyline. Jung was fascinated by the sights, but Freud seemed lost in thought. Finally he said what was on his mind. "Won't they get a surprise when they hear what we have to say to them?"

Jung, startled, said, "How ambitious you are!"

"Me?" Freud said. "I'm the most humble of men and the only man who isn't ambitious."

"That's a big thing," Jung said, "to be the only one."

Their arrival in New York caused little comment. The only mention in the newspapers misspelled Freud's name, referring to Professor "Freund" of Vienna. A. A. Brill, the Austrian-born American psychoanalyst, was at the dock to greet them and to act as their host and guide for their week in the city. Ernest Jones, then living in Toronto, joined them a few days later.

The tour of New York was both exhausting and exhilarating. Brill and Jones took them sightseeing in Central Park, China-town, Harlem, and Coney Island. The collection of Greek antiquities at the Metropolitan Museum of Art was Freud's favorite stop. They dined at Hammerstein's Roof Garden and saw their first motion picture, one that featured several frantic chase scenes. Ferenczi found it exciting, but Freud was only "quietly amused." By the fourth day the abundance of rich American food had made them ill, and they resolved to fast.

According to Jones, Freud was bothered by prostate problems, which was probably what Jung later called bladder difficulties. Because of his discomfort and frequent need to urinate, Freud became annoyed by the inaccessibility of most public toilets. "They escort you along miles of corridors," he complained to Jones, "and ultimately you are taken to the very basement where a marble palace awaits you, only just in time."

On Saturday, September 4, the party boarded an overnight steamer for Fall River, Massachusetts. The European visitors were still suffering the effects of the food. "All three of us were afflicted with diarrhea and had pretty bad stomach aches," Jung wrote to his wife. By noon the next day, after a train ride from Fall River to Boston and Worcester, they checked into the Standish Hotel. After a few hours' rest, they called on Professor G. Stanley Hall, whose refined, distinguished manner and warm hospitality cheered them. Jung was attracted to Hall's wife, whom he described as "plump, jolly, good-natured, and extremely ugly." She was an outstanding cook and most solicitous of her guests. Jung wrote, "She promptly took over Freud and me as her 'boys' and plied us with delicious nourishment and noble wine, so that we began visibly to recover."

In the morning they moved from the hotel into the Halls' spacious house but found it difficult to adjust to the American lack of privacy. A friend wrote that "Jung used to say that every door was wide open in America and that it was all but impossible to get five minutes alone. Once he found himself in a spare room with a door open to the double room occupied by his host and hostess, and any attempt to shut it [while he was dressing] was immediately frustrated." Jung said that the Halls "evidently regarded me as their baby and felt they had every right to look after me all the time. In fact, they clearly regarded it as their sacred duty."

The visitors were so well cared for that Freud regained his sense of humor, which Hall did not appear to appreciate. Hall had described the case of a friend who could not hold a job because of severe agoraphobia, a fear of going out in public places. Freud talked to the man briefly and reported back to Hall that the man was unable to overcome a desire to be supported by his authoritarian father.

Hall asked Freud what could be done.

"Kill his father," Freud said.

Hall gasped, and Freud hastened to assure him that he had not suggested this course of action to the patient.

Although Freud felt physically stronger than he had in New York, thanks to the ministrations of Mrs. Hall, he did have trouble sleeping. When he joined Jung for breakfast one morning he complained, "I haven't been able to sleep since I came to America. I continue to dream of prostitutes."

"Well," Jung said, "why don't you do something about it?"

Freud was appalled. "I'm a married man," he said.

Freud had not yet settled on the topic for his Worcester lectures, which were due to begin two days after the men's arrival. Five talks had been scheduled from Tuesday through Saturday at eleven o'clock each morning. Jung would give three lectures. Freud asked Ernest Jones for advice, and Jones urged him to talk about something broader than dreams. The Americans might consider dream analysis impractical, even frivolous. Freud agreed to give a more inclusive description of psychoanalysis, but as the time for the first lecture approached, he had nothing definite prepared. He composed each speech in his mind during a half-hour walk with Ferenczi, shortly before his talk. He did not use notes or papers, yet his presentations were models of organization and clarity.

Freud "received great applause," Jung wrote to his wife on the afternoon of Freud's first lecture. As for himself, he told Emma, "Tomorrow comes my first lecture. All my dread of it has vanished since the audience is harmless and merely eager to hear new things, which is certainly what we can supply them with." He added that he had been a popular fellow at a garden party, at which he surrounded himself "with five ladies."

Jung reveled in the attention the group was receiving, particularly from a Boston newspaper reporter. "We are the men of the hour here," he told his wife. Actually, the reporter, Adelbert Albrecht, was interested only in Freud. His article in the September 11, 1909, edition of the *Boston Evening Transcript* was headlined, "Prof. Sigmund Freud, The Eminent Vienna Psycho-Therapeutist Now in America."

The piece was highly flattering. Albrecht wrote:

> One sees at a glance that [Freud] is a man of great refinement, of intellect, and of a many-sided education. His sharp, yet kind, clear eyes suggest at once the doctor. His high forehead . . . and his beautiful, energetic hands are very striking. Students of Dr. Freud's book on Psychic Analysis have doubtless fancied him as a cold and cheerless person, but that prepossession vanishes when one confronts the man, bent and grey, but wearing the kindly face that age could never stiffen, and hears his own stories of his patients.

Jung's talks were also well received. He spoke primarily about his word-association experiments and how he used the technique to reveal previously unknown causes of illnesses and to detect criminal behavior by assessing a thief's emotional responses to the stimulus words.

The anniversary celebrations for Clark University attracted well-known scholars from many disciplines. Lectures were offered in biology, mathematics, physics, education, and experimental psychology. The English psychologist Edward Bradford Titchener, then at Cornell University, spoke on the structure of consciousness, and the German psychologist William Stern, a professor at the University of Breslau, talked about the fallibility of eyewitness testimony in courtroom trials. The week also included discussion groups, parties, and a protest demonstration. The anarchist Emma Goldman tried to disrupt a conference on education.

Honorary doctorates were conferred on Freud and Jung. "There was a tremendous amount of ceremony and fancy dress," Jung wrote to his wife, "with all sorts of red and black gowns and gold-tasseled square caps. In a grand and festive assemblage I was appointed Doctor of Laws and Freud likewise. Now I may place an L.L.D. after my name. Impressive, what? Freud is in seventh heaven, and I am glad with all my heart to see him so."

Freud was moved by the recognition bestowed on him. "In Europe," he wrote, "I felt as though I were despised, but [in America] I found myself received by the foremost men as an equal. It seemed like the realization of some incredible daydream: psychoanalysis was no longer a product of delusion; it had become a valuable part of reality."

For several days after the ceremonies, Freud, Jung, and Ferenczi toured more of the United States. Their first stop was Niagara Falls, which Freud found more dramatic and exciting than expected. They boarded the steamer *Maid of the Mists* for a cruise below the falls and crossed the wooden catwalk in the Cave of the Winds. As they prepared to enter the cave, their guide pushed the other tourists aside and shouted, "Let the old fellow go first," gesturing to Freud. The words rankled in Freud's mind, and his bitterness over this incident lingered.

They visited a rustic retreat called Sugar Maple Camp in the Adirondack Mountains near Lake Placid. The camp, a group of primitive huts in a clearing in the woods, was owned by a Harvard neurology professor, James Jackson Putnam, who befriended Freud at Worcester.* About three dozen men were in residence for four days. Jung entertained them by singing German songs around the evening campfire.

*Two years later Putnam founded the American Psychoanalytic Association and became its first president.

The single glass of wine Freud had persuaded Jung to drink at the Bremen restaurant before the trip signaled a change in Jung's life; he never again professed abstinence from liquor. "As far as abstinence goes," he wrote to Emma, "I've arrived on very shaky ground indeed, in point of principle, so that I am honorably withdrawing from my various teetotal societies. I confess myself an honest sinner and only hope that I can endure the sight of a glass of wine without emotion—an undrunk glass, of course. That is always so; only the forbidden attracts. I think I must not forbid myself too much."

Freud's stay at the Putnam camp was overshadowed by a mild case of appendicitis. He endured the physical discomfort stoically, telling no one of his distress. He knew it would upset Ferenczi, make his host uncomfortable, and dampen the festivities. He was enjoying himself in spite of it. He had even seen a wild porcupine.

When Freud was experiencing anxiety about something, such as presenting lectures to a group of foreigners, he would focus on some secondary goal. Channeling his emotions in this way seemed to ease his fears. Before departing for the United States, Freud told himself and others that he was making the trip "in the hope of catching sight of a wild porcupine *and* to give some lectures." Having achieved both goals, Freud was satisfied to return home.

On Sunday, September 19, the three weary travelers returned to New York and two days later boarded the *Kaiser Wilhelm der Grosse* for the eight-day voyage to Bremen. The crossing was rough. Fierce storms and gale-force winds buffeted the ship, sending Freud and Jung to their beds early. They carried with them quite different impressions of the United States. Jung returned several times for lectures and consultations with wealthy American patients. Freud never again set foot on American soil.

Although not lacking in criticism of what he had seen, Jung was nevertheless impressed with much of what the United States had to offer, not the least of which were money and an increasingly receptive attitude toward his ideas. In America, he wrote to his wife, "an ideal potentiality of life has become reality. We have seen things here that inspire enthusiastic admiration and things that make one ponder. As far as technological culture is concerned, we lag miles behind America. But all that is frightfully costly and already carries the germ of the end in itself."

Two months later Jung told Freud that America was characterized by a mother complex. "The mother is decidedly the dominant member of the family. American culture really is a bottomless abyss; the men have become a flock of sheep and the women play the ravening wolves." He doubted if such a situation had existed anywhere else at any time, yet he praised the United States as a "wonderland" with an ideal way of life.

Freud remained unsympathetic. Ernest Jones said that Freud was "obviously unfair" in his prejudice about America. Freud took pleasure in claiming that he disliked the United States because of its bad cooking, which, he said, had brought about his chronic intestinal discomfort.

However, Freud had been bothered by similar complaints for years before his American visit. Appendicitis and prostate problems caused him embarrassment on the trip, but they were not unique to his few weeks abroad. He nevertheless blamed a host of physical ailments on America and even told Jones that since the trip his handwriting had deteriorated.

Freud was also sensitive about his imperfect command of the English language. In conversation he was concerned about grasping the meaning of what others were saying and making sure that he was understood. When he overheard one American ask another to repeat a remark, Freud exclaimed to Jones, "These people cannot even understand each other." Thus it was Freud's judgment that the United States was "a mistake—a gigantic mistake, it is true, but nonetheless a mistake."

The journey to America was the longest period Freud and Jung spent in each other's company. For Freud, the experience increased his affection and need for Jung. Writing to Jung five days after the ship docked in Bremen, Freud said that the day after they parted, "an incredible number of people looked amazingly like you. Wherever I went in Hamburg, your light hat with the dark band kept turning up."

Jung did not reply for almost a month. The waiting was intolerable. Freud chastised him, saying that it was not nice to be kept waiting for a letter. Evidently Freud had not sensed that Jung, in his disappointment, had begun to withdraw from him after the dream incidents aboard ship. Jung had kept his feelings under control because he was not prepared to sacrifice Freud's friendship. His expressed need for Freud remained strong, although his letters were beginning to indicate that the dependence might be diminishing.

"Occasionally," Jung wrote, "a spasm of homesickness for you comes over me, but only occasionally." More than three weeks later he wrote that it was scandalous to have kept Freud waiting so long for a letter, but he offered no word of apology, no plea for forgiveness.

Earlier in the year, when Jung failed to write for two weeks, Freud had sent him a telegram. Jung said it had thrown him into a "fluster." At some length he detailed the reasons he had not written, and in a postscript he implored Freud not to scold him for his negligence. This contrasts sharply with Jung's later behavior.

Their correspondence shows, then, that after the trip to America, Freud's need for Jung was greater than Jung's need for Freud. Freud believed that his dream indicated his worry about who would promote psychoanalysis after his death. It had to be Jung; there was no one else. "If I am Moses," Freud wrote to Jung, "then you are Joshua and will take possession of the promised land of psychiatry, which I shall only be able to glimpse from afar."

In March 1909 Carl and Emma Jung spent five days in Vienna. Jung had just resigned his position at the Burghölzli, and his feeling of freedom lent the trip a festive air. He celebrated the break with one father surrogate—Bleuler—by coming to visit Bleuler's replacement.

The men spent their evenings in Freud's study, in relaxed conversation. Jung regaled Freud with stories of his experiences with occult phenomena. Long fascinated by the supernatural, Jung may have developed this interest from his mother's uncanny and witchlike behaviors, which had so amazed and frightened him as a child. His own dreams and visions, which had tormented and perplexed him throughout his early years, fostered this attraction to the occult. During his first year at the university, he read a book on spiritualism and instantly was hooked.

Jung claimed that initially he was skeptical but soon became convinced of the reality of such odd events. "Why, after all," he asked, "should there not be ghosts?" Supernatural phenomena were not uncommon in the countryside where he had grown up. Everyone knew stories of dreams that foretold calamities, of images of the dead that reappeared, of glass that shattered at significant moments. Who was to say these things did not happen? Jung had witnessed them himself.

Toward the end of Jung's college years, two bizarre events in his mother's house left a lasting impression on his character, and he described them to Freud during the visit. The first occurred one summer afternoon. Jung was studying in his room when he heard a sharp cracking sound from the room next door. He rushed in and found his mother staring at their seventy-year-old dining table. The solid walnut top had split from the edge to the center. "I was thunderstruck," Jung said. "How could such a thing happen?"

"That means something," his mother said.

Two weeks later Jung came home one evening to find his mother, sister, and the maid visibly upset. They had heard a noise like a pistol shot coming from the sideboard in the dining room. They examined the piece carefully but found no sign of a crack or split in the wood. Jung noticed then that the bread knife had snapped in several places. He took the pieces to a repairman who inspected them under a magnifying glass. He pronounced the steel to be perfectly sound and said that someone must have broken it apart piece by piece; good steel does not explode spontaneously.

Jung knew that the knife had shattered on its own. He told Freud of his annoyance at being unable to find a rational explanation for the damage to the knife and the table. It could not be attributed to coincidence or to some form of trickery or hallucination. He had seen them with his own eyes and touched them with his fingers.

Jung told Freud of attending séances conducted by his fourteen-year-old cousin, Helene Preiswerk. Jung's attraction to Helene may not have been due entirely to her alleged supernatural powers. Many years later a relative described the "deep bond that united Jung with his little fourteen-year-old cousin, suggesting that it was very close, albeit unconsciously, to love." Helene had dark hair and liked to say she was Jewish, which was not the case. Her self-characterization, and her youth, physical appearance, and hysterical nature were similar to those of the young woman with whom Jung conducted his first known extramarital affair. Helene Preiswerk served as a prototype for that woman and others to follow.

Whatever his other interests in Helene may have been, Jung was entranced by her mastery of the occult. She was proficient at table turning and other dramatic feats. She used a wine glass held upside down to spell out messages from the dead, calling it her "psychograph."

She claimed to have made contact with their grandfather, a man also given to visions, and had reached the German poet Goethe and other notable figures. "Pale as a ghost, her eyes closed, hardly breathing, she would slowly sink into a chair and stiffen. Then she would begin to speak: spirit messages from people long dead, using her cataleptic body as a channel, flowed easily from her almost motionless lips. Gradually, these trances evolved into full-fledged psychodrama. She began to orchestrate her utterances with bold gestures, throwing herself into attitudes of rapt prayer, rising to dizzy heights of rhetoric."

Playing the devil's advocate, Jung taunted her, suggesting that she was suffering from delusions. Helene denied it. The spirits were real. She could see them, touch them, and talk with them as naturally as she could with him. These were no hallucinations, Helene insisted—and Jung agreed.

Jung accepted the reality of supernatural phenomena even when Helene was caught in an act of deception. Although he could no longer believe in her, he continued to have faith in the mysterious experiences to which she had introduced him. He referred to her séances as the "great experience which superseded my whole early philosophy." For his doctoral thesis he conducted a psychological analysis of Helene, dealing with the changes in her character that occurred during her trances.

When Jung delivered his first formal lecture to a student association during his fourth semester in medical school, he spoke about the limitations of science. He criticized its emphasis on the material world, the belief that all things—including mental experiences—could be described only in the language of physics and understood only in terms of the physical properties of matter and energy. Jung argued that such nonmaterial phenomena as hypnotism and spiritualism could also be studied objectively and should not be ignored by scientists.

As Jung described all these events to Freud, he was his usual animated self. Freud, however, did not share his friend's enthusiasm for or belief in the supernatural. Freud was a materialist and a positivist in science, firmly believing that science must be based exclusively on facts that were immediately observable and undebatable. All else—all that could not be seen or heard or touched, all speculation, all inference—he considered to be illusory. As for ghosts and spirits, turning tables, and communicating with the dead, they were not proper subjects for science.

Freud did not deny the possibility that supernatural phenomena could occur, however. In the 1907 edition of *The Psychopathology of Everyday Life*, he noted that he was "far from meaning to pass so sweeping a condemnation of these phenomena." He admitted that he had never had any such experiences himself, to his regret. "I must confess that I am one of those unworthy people in whose presence spirits suspend their activity and the supernatural vanishes away, so that I have never been in a position to experience anything myself which might arouse a belief in the miraculous. Like every human being, I have had presentiments and experienced trouble, but the two failed to coincide with one another, so that nothing followed the presentiments, and the trouble came upon me unannounced."

In a lecture delivered later Freud said, "If such things exist at all, they are physiological and not psychological. Besides, it seems that, subjectively, the impulses to cheat must always be present." In subsequent years, perhaps because of the influence of Ferenczi, an ardent believer in the occult, Freud's attitude softened. In the 1924 edition of *The Psychopathology of Everyday Life*, he added, "In the last few years I have had a few remarkable experiences which might easily have been explained on the hypothesis of telepathic thought transference." And in a letter to a correspondent in New York he wrote, "If I had my life to live over again, I should devote myself to psychical research rather than to psychoanalysis."

But with Jung sitting in his study in Vienna describing the weird events of his college years, Freud was not at all supportive of any interest in occult phenomena. He dismissed Jung's experiences as nonsense and rejected their existence on the grounds of what Jung termed a shallow positivist philosophy. Jung was angry but kept his emotions reined in, forcing himself not to respond to Freud's disparaging comments.

Freud went on the attack against the credibility of occult phenomena. He did not relish the idea that his son and heir was enamored of the supernatural. Freud could not risk having psychoanalysis confused with parapsychology or psychical dabblings. And of course he did not want psychoanalysis shunted in the direction of some pseudoscience by the very man he had chosen to carry on the work after his death. He had to dissuade Jung from maintaining an interest in the occult.

While Freud was trying to reason with him, Jung felt a strange sensation. "It was as if my diaphragm were made of iron and were becoming red hot—a glowing vault." A noise like a gunshot rang out from the tall bookcase next to their chairs. They jumped to their feet, fearing that it would topple over and crush them. After a moment of reflection, Jung realized what had caused the sound. The wood in the bookcase had been affected by his own mental state. He explained this to Freud, describing it as an "example of a so-called catalytic exteriorization phenomenon."

"Oh come," Freud said. "That is sheer bosh."

"It is not," Jung said. "You are mistaken, Herr Professor. And to prove my point I now predict that in a moment there will be another such loud report."

Jung did not know why he was so certain of this, but he believed beyond all doubt that a cracking sound would come from the bookcase again. No sooner had he made that prediction than the bookcase seemed to explode.

Freud was speechless. He stared at the piece of furniture in amazement. "I do not know what was in his mind," Jung wrote later, "or what his look meant. In any case, this incident aroused his mistrust of me, and I had the feeling that I had done something against him."

Jung returned to Zurich after his visit with Freud, and they exchanged letters about the curious incident with the bookcase. Jung wrote first to describe a case he was treating that involved a "first-rate spiritualistic phenomenon." He came straight to the point in his letter. "It seemed to me that my spookery struck you as altogether too stupid and perhaps unpleasant." Yet, he went on, his experiences with this patient lent credence to the notion that some people have the ability to affect or create events. Jung called this ability "psychosynthesis," the opposite of "psychoanalysis."

Injecting a personal note, Jung mentioned the effect on him of the events in Freud's study. "That last evening with you has, most happily, freed me inwardly from the oppressive sense of your paternal authority. My unconscious celebrated this impression with a great dream which has preoccupied me for some days and which I have just finished analyzing. I hope I am now rid of all unnecessary encumbrances. Your cause must and will prosper."

Jung clearly sounded pleased to have suddenly freed himself from Freud's fatherhood, from the paternal authority he now called a burden. And when he referred to psychoanalysis as *your* cause, was he divorcing himself from Freud?

Freud responded to Jung's letter at once while the feelings it aroused were fresh in his mind. It seemed peculiar to him that Jung should divest him of his "paternal dignity" on the same evening Freud had designated Jung as "successor and crown prince." Jung was apparently taking as much pleasure in the divesting as Freud had derived from the vesting. Freud expressed concern about exerting his parental authority to tell Jung how he interpreted their conversation about the occult, but there was no avoiding it now.

Jung's stories about supernatural phenomena and the incident with the bookcase had so affected Freud that he pursued the matter after Jung left. He occasionally heard the same sound from the bookcase but observed that it had no connection with his thoughts, even when he was thinking about Jung and the occult. Nor did the noise occur when Freud was writing to Jung. Freud found that there was no premonition involved, no linkage of thought or will with the cracking noise.

There was another consideration, Freud wrote. "My credulity, or at least my willingness to believe, vanished with the magic of your personal presence. Once again, for some inward reasons that I can't put my finger on, it strikes me as quite unlikely that such phenomena should exist."

It was time, Freud believed, to put the errant son in his place. "I put my fatherly horned-rimmed spectacles on again and warn my dear son to keep a cool head. I also shake my wise head over psychosynthesis and think: Yes, that's how the young people are, the only places they really enjoy visiting are those they can visit without us, to which we with our short breath and weary legs cannot follow them."

Jung was silent for almost a month, and when he did react to Freud's fatherly lecture he had little to say about the matter. He reminded Freud not to get carried away by his first impression of the incident. "The trouble," Jung said, "is that one is eager to discover something." He promised to guard against putting his trust in mystical happenings.

Jung's reply seemed satisfactory on the surface, but Freud recorded a warning to himself. "Beware of this brilliant young man. You have just chosen him as your successor, but he is already after your crown."

Another subject discussed during Jung's visit to Freud was the sexual basis of Freudian theory.* Jung remarked, not for the first time, how intensely and emotionally involved Freud was in that aspect of the work. When Freud spoke about sexuality, Jung wrote, "his tone became urgent, almost anxious, and all signs of his normally critical and skeptical manner vanished. A strange, deeply moved expression came over his face, the cause of which I was at a loss to understand."

Freud's manner seemed most unsettled. "My dear Jung," he said, "promise me never to abandon the sexual theory. That is the most essential thing of all. You see, we must make a dogma of it, an unshakable bulwark." To Jung, such words and sentiments echoed his father: "Promise me this one thing, my dear son: that you will go to church every Sunday."

"A bulwark—against what?" he asked Freud.

"Against the black tide of mud . . ."

Freud paused.

---

*Jung's autobiography dates this conversation as occurring in 1910, but this is almost surely an error.

". . . of occultism."

Images from Jung's past flooded over him. Here again was his father's insistence on dogma and the insensitive dismissal of Jung's doubts. It "struck at the heart of our friendship," Jung wrote. He saw that Freud was linking parapsychology and the supernatural with philosophy and religion and placing them all in the category of the occult—something psychoanalysis had to defend itself against by invoking the doctrine of the primacy of sexuality. "To me," Jung added, "the sexual theory was just as occult," by which he meant speculative, a hypothesis still unproven. To Freud, however, the sexual basis of his theory was "something to be religiously observed." In light of Freud's views on religion, his attitude was most perplexing. It was clear to Jung that Freud, "who had always made much of his irreligiosity, had now constructed a dogma. In the place of a jealous God whom he had lost, he had substituted another compelling image, that of sexuality." That new god was just as persistent, domineering, and threatening as the old. Jung may have been reminded of a favorite quotation, inscribed over the shrine of the oracle at Delphi: "Called or not called, God will be there."

Between Jung's visit to Freud in Vienna and the trip to America, he made an important change in his personal life. That summer he moved his family into a splendid lakeside villa built on land he had purchased in the Zurich suburb of Küsnacht. He was fulfilling a childhood resolution he had made when his mother had once taken him to Lake Constance. Jung found that he liked the water. "The idea became fixed in my mind that I must live near a lake." The change also satisfied his belief that one became an adult only when one attained a certain degree of material comfort and stability, which was represented by owning one's home.

Another reason for Jung's move had to do with Freud. While on the staff of the Burghölzli Jung developed a large private practice, which, combined with his hospital duties, did not allow him sufficient time to do all the necessary work for the psycho-analytic movement, such as editing the *Yearbook* and planning the annual congresses. By resigning from the Burghölzli and moving some distance from Zurich, Jung hoped to be rid not only of Bleuler but also of most of his private patients, who, he assumed, would find other psychiatrists at the hospital.

Jung expected to concentrate on his research, writing, and lecturing at the University of Zurich and his organizational activities for Freud, free of the daily hospital routine. Although he had made no provision for doing therapy at home, before long he had acquired a thriving practice. He converted a storage room for household linens and a small study with stained-glass windows into makeshift reception and consultation rooms.

The house was designed in the style of an eighteenth-century patrician mansion. Surrounded by beautiful gardens, it was separated from the main road by a long driveway flanked with pear, cherry, and apple trees. Jutting into the lake was a boathouse for Jung's sailboat, and close by was a pavilion overlooking the lake and the Alps. Palatial inside and out, the house reflected Jung's desired level of comfort for his scholarly life. Carved in Gothic script on the stone lintel above the doorway were several inscriptions. One, in Latin, translates as "Called or not called, God will be there."

The first area of research on which Jung embarked, once settled in his new house, derived from his recurrent dream about the multilevel house in which each story was older than the one above it. The symbolism he detected in this dream led him to revive a dormant interest in archeology and mythology. The desire to understand ancient cultures and to decipher their rituals and symbols preyed on his mind. He nurtured the vague suspicion that he might find answers in the past that would help him in the present.

"I read like mad," Jung wrote, "and worked with feverish interest through a mountain of mythological material." He described his progress to Freud. "Archeology or rather mythology has got me in its grip; it's a mine of marvelous material."

Freud was gratified by the direction of Jung's study but reminded Jung of his own interest in the field. "I am glad you share my belief that we must conquer the whole field of mythology," Freud wrote, appropriating Jung's new interest. Freud also pointed out that Karl Abraham and Otto Rank were mining the same vein. If Jung harbored the idea that he had found a niche in which to work alone and make important discoveries, he was mistaken. Freud welcomed him as a longtime resident might greet a new neighbor and told him that now the study of mythology would be less lonely.

Jung persisted. After a month of reading he announced to Freud that he no longer had doubts about his interpretation of the oldest myths. They revealed, Jung said, the sexual origin of most neuroses. Phallic symbols were rampant; the Oedipal theme was dominant. Freud must have taken comfort in Jung's opinion, thinking that Jung's explorations in mythology had finally answered his questions about the primacy of sexuality. The study of the ancient myths was obviously accomplishing what Freud himself had not—persuading Jung that Freud's theories were correct.

Freud wrote that he was delighted with Jung's conclusions, but in fewer than two weeks Jung showed signs of veering down another path, using myths as primary evidence rather than as corroboration for the revelations of their patients. He wrote to Freud that he was becoming more convinced that the only way to understand the human psyche was through the study of history. "For this reason antiquity now appears to me in a new and significant light. What we now find in the individual psyche—in compressed, stunted, or one-sidedly differentiated forms—may be seen spread out in all its fullness in times past. Happy the man who can read these signs."

Jung criticized previous work in psychology as "hopelessly inept" in interpreting the meanings of legends and myths. It was clear to him that there was a universal heritage that was repeated or represented in the mind of each individual. He implied that psychoanalysis was incapable of revealing this heritage because it focused too much on the person and too little on the collective history of the human species. This evolutionary heritage, the accumulated experiences of human and prehuman species, is represented, according to Jung, in the mind of each individual in every generation. He later called this concept the "collective unconscious."

Jung staked his claim and was ready to build on his new territory. "I have the most marvelous visions," he wrote to Freud, "glimpses of far-ranging interconnections which I am at present incapable of grasping, for the subject really is too big and I hate impotent bungling. Who then is to do the work? Surely it must be someone who knows the psyche and has the passion for it."

He soon answered his own question. *He* was to do the work. Only two months after rediscovering mythology Jung announced to Freud that he had a follower, a student, someone who he hoped would one day carry on his research. The disciple's name was Johann Honegger, Jr., a twenty-four-year-old Swiss psychiatrist who worked at the Burghölzli. Ernest Jones called him the most promising of the Swiss analysts. Jung may have forced this mentor-disciple relationship on Honegger to make Freud jealous and to re-create his early situation with Freud. A biographer of Jung's later noted that "the potent blend of despotism and masochism that Jung found so irritating in Freud he was to display himself toward a protégé of his own." Jung explained to Freud that Honegger would assist him "with great understanding, and I shall entrust to him everything I know so that something good may come of it." Jung would learn, as did Freud, that disciples, like sons, are not always content to accept the mentor's ways.

One final indication of the trouble between Freud and Jung surfaced in 1909. It started in December, in a long letter from Jung about his studies in mythology. He mused on how often he wished Freud lived nearby because there were so many things Jung wanted to discuss with him. For example, did Freud have a good definition of *libido?* So far, Jung said, he had not found any that was satisfactory.

A definition of *libido!* Freud thought. Jung had not found anything satisfactory? Libido was a cornerstone of psychoanalysis. Freud had defined it explicitly in his book *Three Essays on the Theory of Sexuality*, and there was nothing ambiguous about it. His definition was straightforward and, Freud believed, correct. He wrote angrily to Jung, referring him to the book. The definition of *libido* was clear, and he saw no reason to change it.

Jung's difficulty in defining *libido*, he responded to Freud, was "obviously due to the fact that I have not yet adjusted my attitude sufficiently to yours." As it turned out, that was something he would never do.

CHAPTER SEVEN

A Brutal Reality:
Wives and Other Women

*F*our and a half years ago Dr. Jung was my doctor, then he became my friend and finally my 'poet,' that is, my beloved. Eventually he came to me and things went as they usually do with 'poetry.' He preached polygamy; his wife was supposed to have no objection."

On June 11, 1909, twenty-four-year-old Sabina Spielrein, a medical student in Zurich, wrote to Sigmund Freud about her love affair with Carl Jung. She followed this note with a series of emotional letters. Those letters—along with Freud's replies, her diary, and her letters to Jung—were found some seventy years later in the basement of a house in Geneva. Translated into English and published in 1982, they tell a fascinating and familiar tale.

Sabina was born into a wealthy Russian Jewish family in Rostov-on-Don in 1885. From a young age she displayed a rich fantasy life, which, in time, yielded to bizarre hallucinations and equally unusual behaviors. At the age of three she began deliberately to retain her feces, refusing to have a bowel movement for up to two weeks. At seven she masturbated frequently but maintained her preoccupation with defecation. In her imagination, everyone she saw was defecating.

By the time she was eighteen, she could not bear to look at other people and would turn away if anyone approached her. She also suffered periodic bouts of depression that alternated with fits of weeping, laughing, and screaming. The following year, in 1904, her parents sent her to the famous Burghölzli Hospital in Zurich, where she was treated for ten months by Jung. After her release she enrolled as a medical student at the University of Zurich, continuing her analysis with Jung as a private patient.

In 1906 Jung mentioned in a letter to Freud that he was treating a twenty-year-old Russian girl. A year later he presented her case to the First International Congress of Psychiatry and Neurology in Amsterdam, diagnosing her condition as psychotic hysteria and his treatment of her as an example of the Freudian approach. In 1908 he fell in love with her.

"I was still a baby," Sabina wrote, "and ran around in very simple dresses and with a long, dangling braid, since I wanted to elevate my soul above my body." She was intelligent, attractive, sensitive, innocent, and vulnerable, particularly to the attentions of the man who saved her from madness. Jung, then thirty-three and unhappily married, was himself highly susceptible. In a letter to Sabina he disclosed his defenselessness before her charms. He abandoned himself to what he called his overwhelming experience of love. "It is my misfortune," he confessed, "that my life means nothing to me without the joy of love, of tempestuous, eternally changing love," the kind of love he no longer felt for Emma, who was expecting their third child. "Return to me," Jung begged Sabina, "in this moment of my need, some of the love and guilt and altruism I was able to give you at the time of your illness. Now it is I who am ill."

Sabina recorded the development of their affair in her diary, revealing the all-consuming character of her love for Jung and his need for her. "He admitted to me that so far he knew no female who could replace me. It was as if he had a necklace in which all his other admirers were pearls, and I, the medallion." Jung permitted her to read his diary and told her that no one understood him the way she did. "He told me that he loved Jewish women, that he wanted to love a dark Jewish girl." And he loved her for her proud character, the parallel nature of their thoughts, and her ability to foretell his thoughts.

At the same time, Jung set limits on the relationship. He had no intention of leaving his wife, no matter how unhappy he claimed to be with her. He told Sabina that he would never marry her. "He already has a wife" was the plaint Sabina repeated in her diary. Emma's existence was the ultimate barrier to the fulfillment of their love. Sabina found that she could be with Jung more in her daydreams than in person, and she retained no hope of being more than his companion—and that, mostly in a spiritual sense. "Allow me to be his guardian angel, his spirit of inspiration, always spurring him to new and greater things." At that, she wondered if she was asking too much.

"Why can't I be happy?" she wrote in her diary. Why couldn't she be content with their friendship, satisfied with their "pure and noble" relationship? "His wife is protected by the law, respected by all, and I, who wanted to give him everything I possessed, without the slightest regard for myself, I am called immoral in the language of society. He can appear anywhere in public with his wife, and I have to skulk around in dark corners."

Fantasies, dreams, and memories were all Sabina had. She wanted to bear Jung a son. She wrote poems for him, composed songs about him, and thought of no one else night after night. "My love for my friend overwhelmed me with a mad glow," she wrote. "At some moments I resisted violently, at others I let him kiss every one of my little fingers and clung to his lips, swooning with love. How foolish to talk about it! So this is I, usually the soul of pure, clear reason, allowing myself such fantasies."

One day in June 1909 the fantasies came to an end, and Sabina Spielrein turned in desperation to the only person she could think of who might help. She wrote to Sigmund Freud. Freud had suspected that Jung was involved with a woman who was or had been a patient. He did not know who she was, and for a while he held a misleading view of the situation. He knew only Jung's version, and Jung had lied to him.

Jung first mentioned the incident about three months before Sabina wrote to Freud. On March 7, 1909, Jung described to Freud a patient he had cured through unstinting effort but who had violated their friendship and confidence. "She has kicked up a vile scandal solely because I denied myself the pleasure of giving her a child," Jung said. "I have always acted the gentleman toward her, but before the bar of my rather too-sensitive conscience I nevertheless don't feel clean, and that is what hurts the most because my intentions were always honorable."

Even good and kind acts, Jung added, could be used to manufacture filth. He claimed to have learned "an unspeakable amount of marital wisdom" from the experience and had finally come to recognize his basically polygamous nature. The experience endowed him with certain moral qualities—which he did not identify to Freud—and he said it had deepened his relationship with his wife.

The messy situation also had a positive practical outcome. Jung had accepted a new American patient, the Chicago philanthropist Harold McCormick, "a friend of Roosevelt and Taft," Jung bragged. McCormick was undergoing the same conflict Jung had just resolved, and Jung believed that his successful handling of his troublesome woman patient would help him in treating McCormick.

Freud answered Jung's letter two days later with the news that a visitor from Basel had told an interesting story about Jung. The visitor said he had met an unidentified woman who claimed to be Jung's mistress. Freud placed no credence in the story, he assured Jung. Obviously the woman was neurotic. "To be slandered and scorched by the love with which we operate—such are the perils of our trade."

Jung was indignant. "I've never really had a mistress," he wrote to Freud, "and am the most innocent of spouses. Hence my terrific moral reaction." He could not identify the woman, but he doubted that it was the patient he had mentioned in his letter. Jung did not believe that Sabina would tell anyone she was his mistress, and he may have been correct. The woman in the Basel story was likely someone who, in fact or in fantasy, had had an affair with Jung. "Such stories give me the horrors," Jung said, but the real horror—the truth—was yet to emerge.

In early June Freud received a brief letter, the first of many, from Sabina Spielrein, asking for an appointment. He had no idea who she was. Her reason for seeing him had to do with "something of greatest importance to me which you would probably be interested in hearing about." It was all a mystery to Freud. The only possible clue was the woman's address: Platterstrasse 33 in Zurich. From that, Freud associated her with Jung. "What is she?" Freud asked. "A busybody, a chatterbox, or a paranoiac?" He communicated his sense of urgency to Jung by requesting that he reply by telegram if he knew anything about this Spielrein woman. Jung cabled Freud and followed it up with a letter in which he heaped all the blame on Sabina. Jung declared that Sabina would suffer a sudden relapse if he ever withdrew his emotional support. Therefore, he had "prolonged the relationship over the years and in the end found myself morally obliged, as it were, to devote a large measure of friendship to her, until I saw that an unintended wheel had started turning, whereupon I finally broke with her. She was, of course, systematically planning my seduction, which I considered inopportune."

According to Jung, Sabina was spreading the rumor that Jung planned to divorce his wife and marry a student. He told Freud that he had never bestowed so much friendship on any patient as he had given Sabina. He had treated her without charge and with "untold tons of patience." In return he received untold grief and sorrow. The unfairness of it all!

Jung's letter to Freud revealed a good and sincere man, a kindly analyst and faithful husband who had been wronged by a vengeful, spiteful woman. When Freud read Jung's words, he was convinced of his friend's innocence. The experience Jung described was painful and difficult to prevent. "I myself have never been taken in quite so badly," Freud replied, "but I have come very close to it a number of times and had a *narrow escape*." Freud believed he had been spared only by the necessities of his work and by the fact that he was ten years older than Jung when the similar incident occurred. To reassure Jung that he understood, Freud also held Sabina responsible: "The way these women manage to charm us with every conceivable psychic perfection until they have attained their purpose is one of nature's great spectacles."

Jung was relieved and grateful for Freud's understanding. He had expected Freud to chastise him, as a father would a son, for behaving stupidly. A scandal would have played into the hands of the enemies of psychoanalysis, and Jung, of all people, should not have placed the movement and its founder in such a vulnerable position.

The Spielrein matter appeared to be settled as far as Jung was concerned, but he shortly found out that it was not. Sabina's mother received an anonymous letter describing her daughter's affair with Jung and urging her to save Sabina from the ruin she would undoubtedly suffer at Jung's hands. Madame Spielrein wrote to Jung, imploring him not to jeopardize all he had accomplished in restoring Sabina's mental health by exceeding the bounds of propriety and friendship.

Jung hastily dispatched three letters to Sabina's mother, none of them expressing contrition, apology, or even embarrassment. In one he wrote:

I moved from being her doctor to being her friend when I ceased to push my own feelings into the background. I could drop my role as doctor the more easily because I did not feel professionally obligated, for I never charged a fee. This latter clearly establishes the limits imposed upon a doctor. You do understand, of course, that a man and a girl cannot possibly continue indefinitely to have friendship dealings with one another without the likelihood that something may enter into the relationship. For what would restrain the two from drawing the consequences of their love? A *doctor* and his *patient*, on the other hand, can talk of the most intimate matters for as long as they like, and the patient may expect her doctor to give her all the love and concern she requires. But the doctor knows his

limits and will never cross them, for he is *paid* for his trouble.
That imposes the necessary restraint on him.

Therefore I would suggest that if you wish me to adhere
strictly to my role as doctor, you should pay me a fee as
suitable recompense for my trouble. In that way you may be
absolutely certain that I will respect my duty as a doctor *under
all circumstances*. My fee is ten francs per consultation.

Jung told Madame Spielrein that he had made it clear to
Sabina initially that there was no question of a sexual relationship
between them. "My actions were intended to express my feelings
of friendship. When this occurred, I happened to be in a very
gentle and compassionate mood, and I wanted to give your
daughter convincing proof of my trust, my friendship, in order to
liberate her inwardly. That turned out to be a grave mistake,
which I greatly regret."

Jung does not sound so blameless in these letters as he did in
his letter to Freud. He seems to admit, obliquely, that he and
Sabina were lovers, but only as proof of his friendship. Further,
he implies that his actions were not improper or unprofessional.
He was not formally Sabina's doctor because he was not receiving a fee.

Sabina wrote to Freud to inform him of Jung's letters to her
mother. She said she was heartbroken at the way Jung was treating her, refusing to see her anymore as a private patient. She had
pleaded with Jung until he relented and agreed to see her for one
hour each week, but at their first appointment he delivered a
sermon about everything he had done for her.

Jung acknowledged he had committed a folly that may have
harmed her, Sabina told Freud, but that was because she expected too much of him. Jung had been too good to her, and it
was because of his excessive kindness that she wanted to have sex
with him. He insisted that was something he never desired. On
hearing this from the man who used to weep in her presence,
with whom she had been able to sit in "speechless ecstasy" for
hours, Sabina became unhinged.

"You can form a picture," she wrote to Freud, and continued:

> My ideal personage was completely destroyed; I was done for;
> I thought I wanted to kiss him and had no will to resist, since I
> no longer respected either him or myself. I stood there with a
> knife in my left hand and do not know what I intended to do
> with it; he grabbed my hand, I resisted; I have no idea of what
> happened then. Suddenly he went very pale and clapped his
> hand to his left temple: "You struck me!" I had no notion of
> what I had done, found myself sitting in the trolley with my
> hands over my face and weeping in torrents. I did wonder why
> people asked me if I were injured. I rushed over to a cluster of
> women colleagues, and the first thing I heard was, "Look,
> you're bleeding!" And sure enough my left hand and forearm
> were covered with blood. "That's not my blood, that's his: I
> murdered him!" I babbled, and other such rubbish.

Sabina had struck Jung on the side of the head with her fists,
but she did not stab him. Nevertheless, Jung was properly impressed by her anger. He sent a curt note to say that he would be
out of town on the day of their next scheduled session. It was best
that they not see each other; that would make it easier to put this
painful business behind them.

Sabina confided to Freud an "infinitude of thoughts." There
were certain things she wanted Freud to know. First, that Jung
was involved with many other women, although his relationships
with them were minor affairs. Second, that their souls were "profoundly akin." When discussing Wagner's music with Jung she
had mentioned her fondness for the opera *Das Rheingold*. Jung's
eyes had filled with tears, and he said he had just been writing
the same thing. He told her that Freud could also move him to
tears when he found that they were thinking along the same lines.
"He found your face enormously likable," Sabina told Freud,
"particularly around the ears."

She also wanted Freud to know that Jung thought she was

intelligent and sensitive, much more so than his wife was. He urged her to enroll in medical school to become a psychiatrist. He complained that his wife was ordinary and had no personal interests. Finally, Sabina quoted to Freud from one of Jung's letters: "When love for a woman awakens within me, the first thing I feel is regret, pity for the poor woman who dreams of eternal faithfulness and other impossibilities and is slated for a rude awakening."

This gave Freud quite a different picture of the situation than the one Jung had painted for him. Jung no longer seemed so innocent, but could Freud believe what this stranger was telling him? Not only was she unknown to him, but she was also in therapy, and Freud well knew how powerful transference could be. It had led more than one patient to imagine that she was in love with her analyst.

Surely that must be the explanation. Jung was his friend, his son and heir. He had explained the situation to Freud by telegram and by letter. Perhaps this woman was fabricating the whole story, firing off letter after letter to Freud as fast as her warped imagination could conjure up the tales.

On June 18 Freud wrote to Jung, but the letter dealt with many things, especially the trip to America. Compared with that, little else mattered, certainly not the ravings of a neurotic woman. Freud advised Jung not to be overly contrite. "In view of the kind of matter we work with, it will never be possible to avoid little laboratory explosions."

Jung was pleased by Freud's reaction. It showed that Freud was not disturbed by the sordid business, which was merely something to be expected in the course of treating patients. This would be the end of it, if only Sabina would stop writing letters.

On June 19 Sabina spent an hour and a half with Jung—the "miscreant," she called him—and described the session in another letter to Freud. She said that Jung had excused his passion for her by explaining that he was really in love with Freud's daughter Mathilde, who had dark hair and eyes, and had transferred those feelings to Sabina.

Sabina did not believe him. She wrote to Freud that Jung had "betrayed himself, that he was looking to you for support, that he wanted your love and therefore in his own defense grasped at the first plausible thing that entered his conscious mind upon hasty reflection, and which also appeared suitable to him in that particular situation because it would be pleasing to you." What better way, she suggested, for Jung to obtain Freud's approval than to attribute his passion to a love for one of Freud's daughters?

Two days after the session with Sabina, Jung provided Freud with another version of the relationship. He began his letter with good news. He and Sabina had had a nice talk, and Jung had learned that she was not the source of the rumor that Jung was about to divorce his wife and marry a student. He said that she was free of her transference to him and had suffered no ill effects except for a crying spell. (That may have been the time when she hit him, but Jung did not tell Freud of that.) Jung believed that Sabina was now fine.

As for himself, although he felt little remorse, "I nevertheless deplore the sins I have committed, for I am largely to blame for the high-flying hopes of my former patient. When the situation had become so tense that the continued perseveration of the relationship could be rounded out only by sexual acts, I defended myself in a manner that cannot be justified morally."

And here Jung told Freud a strange tale. Jung was convinced that he was the victim of Sabina's sexual trickery to ensnare him. Therefore, he had written to Sabina's mother to say that he would not gratify her daughter's sexual longings. Jung was her doctor, nothing more. Further, he had implored Madame Spielrein to free him from her daughter's clutches. Jung also told Freud that he felt contrite about writing to Sabina's mother. "In view of the fact that the patient had shortly before been my friend and enjoyed my full confidence, my action was a piece of knavery which I very reluctantly confess to you as my father."

Having made his confession, Jung asked Freud to write to Madame Spielrein and apologize on Jung's behalf. "I would like to give my patient at least this satisfaction: That you and she know of my 'perfect honesty.' I ask your pardon many times, for it was my stupidity that drew you into this imbroglio."

Freud did as Jung requested. He told Jung that his letter would have "reconciled me to greater misdeeds on your part; perhaps I am already too biased in your favor." Madame Spielrein answered Freud's note, but her reply was difficult to fathom. Freud urged Jung not to blame himself for involving him in the matter. That was Sabina's fault; she was the one who had written to Freud first. Freud had persuaded himself that everyone was satisfied. He as the father had extricated the son from an awkward state of affairs, and he may have derived considerable pleasure from having done so.

Sabina Spielrein went on to receive her medical degree in 1911, and she became a psychiatrist and a follower of psychoanalysis. Freud later told Jung that he found "the little girl" very nice and understood Jung's attraction to her. She wrote several scholarly papers on psychoanalysis, and it has been suggested that Freud derived the idea of a death instinct from her work. She married in 1913 but was determined to maintain a relationship with Jung. Between 1910 and 1919 they exchanged many letters, mostly dealing with professional issues. In one letter Jung resumed the role of therapist and alluded to their past intimacy. "I allow myself to write to you so frankly and admonish you because after long reflection I have eliminated from my heart all the bitterness against you which it still harbored."

Sabina worked as an analyst in several European cities— among her patients was the noted child psychologist Jean Piaget—before returning to her native Russia. She became a lecturer at the North Caucasus University in Rostov-on-Don. Casualties of World War II, Sabina and her two daughters were shot to death by German soldiers in 1942.

During the time Jung was ending his relationship with Sabina, he began to treat a shy, attractive twenty-one-year-old woman who had been diagnosed as schizophrenic. She "radiated the nymphlike sensuality often found in girls living at the edge of madness."

A disciple of Jung's recalled that she "carried herself with natural elegance, had a formidable intelligence and generally a great air of something select and special about her. But I myself remember above all those wide-open dark eyes." Her name was Toni Wolff.

When Jung first undertook Toni's therapy, she was extremely depressed and disoriented, a condition aggravated by the recent death of her father. Jung believed that she needed something to reawaken her interest in life, so he made her his research assistant, putting her to work on his book about mythology and the libido. Before long, with a meaningful job and a new relationship with an older, vital, stimulating man, Toni Wolff blossomed.

Toni and Jung were strongly attracted to each other, a fact that did not escape Emma Jung's attention. Unlike the situation with Sabina Spielrein, Jung made no effort to hide his involvement with Toni. Quite the opposite. He forced the family to accept her. She traveled with them, helped care for them, and became Aunt Toni to the children. Jung insisted that she join them for dinner every Sunday.

Emma was greatly upset. Jung's reaction to her anger was to insist on his need—and his right—to enlarge his life by seeing another woman. In his view there were two types of women: one was like Emma, the wife, mother, and homemaker; the other was like Toni, destined to be the mistress and source of inspiration to a creative man. As a man of genius, Jung told Emma, he required both types.

Further, he explained, he had become involved with Toni for the sake of the children. He knew from his clinical experience that a daughter suffers when her father does not fulfill his erotic life. A father's sexual frustrations will be displaced unconsciously to his daughter, which inhibits her sexual development. This fear troubled Jung and "kept him awake a whole night, a night during which he slowly realized that if he refused to live the outside attraction that had come to him entirely from the unconscious against his will, he would inevitably ruin his daughters' eros." As a concerned father, Jung could do no less.

Jung maintained the romantic triangle for more than thirty years. Both Emma and Toni eventually became analysts and followers of Jungian psychology. They each served as president of the Jungian Psychological Club, published papers on their work, and even analyzed each other.

Jung reserved Wednesday afternoons for Toni, which he spent at her house. He was proud of managing two devoted women and apparently was able to persuade them that their status was ideal. "What saved the situation," a friend wrote, "was that there was no 'lack of love' in any of the three. Jung was able to give both his wife and Toni a most satisfactory amount, and *both* women *really* loved him. Emma Jung even said years later: 'You see, he never took anything from me to give to Toni, but the more he gave her, the more he seemed to be able to give me.'"

Jung liked to think of himself as a skilled lover, and he was concerned that his biographers would be unaware of that aspect of his life. He need not have worried; everyone connected with him soon became aware of it.

Toni Wolff's later years were unhappy. She rebelled, demanding that Jung marry her, and interfered in his home life, upsetting what Jung considered the natural order of things. Even Jung's children turned against her. Her insistence on marriage came at a time when Jung had less need of her. He had won the admiration and devotion of many younger women and was at an age where he was even more reluctant to give up the comforts of home and family.

Toni was forced to abandon her campaign and to settle for being a spiritual companion, a role she increasingly had to share with others. Heartbroken, she drank to excess and had several affairs, but she found little satisfaction in them. She died of a heart attack in 1953 at the age of sixty-four. After her death, her letters from Jung were returned to him. He burned them all, along with her letters to him.

After Emma died two years later, Jung carved stone tablets as memorials to signify what each woman meant to him. For Emma he chose Chinese symbols meaning "She was the foundation of my house." Toni's stone read "She was the fragrance of my house."

"A brutal reality"—that was how Jung characterized not only his own marriage but the married state in general. It was not, of course, the way he described it when he wooed and won Emma Rauschenbach. As with all major decisions in Jung's life, his choice of a wife was impulsive and based on memories, visions, and other products of his unconscious mind. One of his biographers, a psychotherapist, wrote, "To know how Jung first caught sight of and, on the spot, 'recognized' his future wife is to know Jung at his most authentic. It was an instant enchantment, fateful, preordained, inevitable: the stuff of legend."

The story began when Jung was five years old. Even as an old man he retained a sharp memory of the event that occurred while he lived in Laufen, at the vicarage above the Rhine Falls. His mother was hospitalized, and the boy was feeling rejected and alone. One day he was taken for a walk along the riverbank by a family friend, a pretty young woman with blue eyes and blond hair. Jung remembered bright sunlight playing on fallen leaves and shining through the branches of the maple and chestnut trees, but mostly he recalled the woman, an admirer of his father, who soon married a man named Rauschenbach. She named the first of her two daughters Emma.

Another young woman figured vividly in Jung's memories of that same unhappy period—a maid who helped look after him while his mother was away. "I still remember her picking me up and laying her head against my shoulder. She had black hair and an olive complexion. I can see her even now, her hairline, her throat with its darkly pigmented skin, and her ear."

He sensed that being with her was both familiar and exotic. He felt that she belonged to him, not to his parents, and was somehow linked with obscure and enigmatic things he could not understand. So strong was her impact on his childhood that she came to symbolize for him the intrinsic qualities and character of all women.

It may have been her image in his unconscious mind that drove him to seek out women who looked so different from his pale, blond, blue-eyed wife. The significant women in his later years—his cousin Helene Preiswerk, Sabina Spielrein, and Toni Wolff—all had dark hair and eyes. Yet it was the opposite image, his memory of Emma's mother as a young woman, that accounted for his choice of a wife.

The first time Jung saw Emma was about a year after his father died. He was taking a brief holiday from his medical studies and went with a friend to Schaffhausen. His mother asked him to call on an old family friend, a woman married to the wealthy industrialist Rauschenbach. When Jung entered their home, Emma was standing on the stairway. Just fourteen, she wore her hair in braids and appeared innocent, charming, and nymphlike. Jung was instantly struck with the "absolute certainty" that he would marry her. He told his traveling companion of that feeling and was ridiculed for it. Jung was twenty-one, with poor prospects and little to offer a girl used to immense wealth, but he remained convinced that he would win her.

Little is known about their courtship, which probably did not begin seriously until Jung completed medical school and joined the staff of the Burghölzli Hospital. The job paid only a small salary, and it would be years before Jung could think of establishing a lucrative private practice. He asked Emma to marry him anyway, but she said no. Crestfallen, he was reminded of his grandfather's similar dilemma.

An eccentric figure—who was rumored to be Goethe's illegitimate son and who walked a pet pig on a leash—Professor Doctor Carl Gustav Jung was a respected physician and a rector of the University of Basel. When his first wife died, he asked for the hand of the mayor's daughter, who was eighteen years younger than he. She turned him down. Immediately he went to his favorite tavern and asked the barmaid to marry him. She agreed, and when she died a few years later he asked the mayor's daughter again. This time she said yes.

Jung did not have to follow his grandfather's example; he had a friend in Emma's mother. The reason Emma had rejected his proposal was that she had kissed another man and assumed she would have to marry him. Her mother persuaded her otherwise. When Frau Rauschenbach was Emma's age she had been in love with Jung's father and had lost him to another woman, but she played a major role in arranging for Emma's marriage to Jung in February 1903. Carl was twenty-seven, Emma twenty.

They spent their honeymoon at Lake Como. Years later Jung said, "Honeymoons are tricky things. I was lucky. My wife was apprehensive—but all went well." The only note of discord resulted from an argument about money. Because Jung had little of his own, they were really discussing the distribution of Emma's funds. "Trust a Swiss bank account to break into a honeymoon in Italy," Jung remarked.

Emma was a shy and lonely girl whose childhood, in that respect, was very much like Jung's. Herr Rauschenbach was a tyrannical father, embittered by the blindness that had struck him when Emma was twelve. As an adolescent Emma was not permitted a normal social life, nor was she allowed to attend college. She grew up with little in the way of social and intellectual stimulation. "Carl, oddly eloquent, overflowing with bold ideas, provided both. Her timidity made him expansive. He played the seasoned man of the world . . . fascinating her with his put-on swagger and gauche charm."

So marriage for Emma was initially a liberation from an oppressive home. She and Carl appeared content, but the more perceptive of their friends predicted that he would tire of her and seek satisfaction elsewhere. She was highly dependent on him in the early years of their marriage, clinging to him for emotional sustenance. In time they would reverse roles, but until that happened, her married life became increasingly difficult.

Like so many women in their circle, Emma became Jung's pupil and disciple, poring over every thought he committed to paper as if it were scripture. She reared five children and studied mathematics, Latin, and Greek, but despite her diligent efforts she could not keep pace with Jung intellectually, and he became less tolerant of what he saw as her shortcomings.

Before long, Emma felt constrained, reminiscent of the atmosphere in her parents' home but with the additional pressures of being wife and mother. It did not help that Jung insisted on psychoanalyzing her, a process that released a depressive component of her nature.

After several years of marriage she revealed some of her unhappiness in letters to Sigmund Freud, telling him of her despondency. She begged him to keep her feelings secret from Jung because things were going badly enough already. She said she was

> tormented by the conflict about how I can hold my own against Carl. I find I have no friends. All the people who associate with us really only want to see Carl. Naturally the women are all in love with him, and with the men I am instantly cordoned off as the wife of the father or friend. Yet I have a strong need for people and Carl too says I should stop concentrating on him and the children, but what on earth am I to do? I can never compete with Carl. In order to emphasize this I usually have to talk extra stupidly when in company.

Freud was aware that the Jungs' marriage was not happy even before Emma wrote to him. In 1906, when Carl and Emma had been married only three years, Jung told Freud of a dream about her. He did not write about the dream except to say that it involved the "failure of the rich marriage," noting that although Emma was wealthy, he was pleased with her in every way. The dream nagged at Jung and may have been based on an "illegitimate sexual wish that had better not see the light of day."

Early in 1910 Jung told Freud of more dreams about Emma, which "revel in symbols that speak volumes, for instance, my wife had her right arm chopped off." Emma was displaying considerable jealousy—without any reason, Jung wrote. He was convinced that the "requisite for a good marriage, it seems to me, is the license to be unfaithful."

Jung used that license liberally. One of his biographers noted: "Jung's magnetism for female neurotics of all shades was remarkable. Part of Jung's secret was that he empathized strongly with the aspirations of women who were or felt misunderstood; undoubtedly, his extreme, almost 'feminine' sensitivity also contributed to this peculiar sex appeal. In any case, women were his first, most enthusiastic, and most fanatic disciples."

Despite the difficulties between Carl and Emma, the marriage endured. Emma outlasted his interests in other women, even Toni Wolff. Jung never seriously considered leaving Emma, and it turned out that she had a far richer and more nurturing personality than he did. To her wealth, which was the foundation of his economic stability, she added the strong and consistent emotional support and steadfastness that his mother had failed to provide in childhood. "Emma, benign and steady as his mother had never been, played her role flawlessly. Not once did she force Carl to confront the fact that he was her adopted sixth child."

"I am sorry that I can give you no real hospitality," Freud had said to Carl and Emma Jung. "I have nothing at home but an elderly wife." It was an awkward moment, that cold March day in 1907 when Freud and Jung met for the first time. The Jungs had been married four years; Emma was twenty-four. The Freuds had been married twenty-one years; Martha was forty-six.

The passion had fled from Freud's relationship with his "beloved Marty." He later told Emma that the joy in his marriage had been extinguished long ago. But those who knew Freud believed he got exactly what he wanted and needed from his wife, precisely what Jung eventually got from Emma. Freud would later write that a marriage cannot be made secure "until the wife has succeeded in making her husband her child as well and in acting as a mother to him." This was what Martha Freud, like Emma Jung, had done. Her "Sigi" became her adopted seventh child. She took exquisite care of him, selecting his clothes and putting the toothpaste on his toothbrush. She became the stereotypical hausfrau, cleaning and straightening and putting everything in order, including most of the details of her husband's life. "I always tried as much as possible," she said, "to remove the *misère* of everyday life from his path."

What Freud desired in a wife, one analyst wrote, was "a woman who would not share in the intellectual life which became his consuming passion; a woman who could free him completely, by taking superb care of his physical needs, to pursue his own ends in his own way. A woman, in short, whose functions resembled his mother's."

Another who knew Freud observed, "Freud was ardently in love before his marriage—because he had to prove his manliness by the conquest of the girl he had chosen. Once the conquest was sealed by the marriage, the 'adored darling' was transformed into the loving mother on whose care and love one could depend without an active, passionate love for her."

In 1897, when Freud was forty-one, his sex life apparently came to an end. "Sexual excitation is of no more use to a person like me," he wrote to his friend Wilhelm Fliess. Paradoxical as it may seem, the man who focused the world's attention on the importance of sex as a motivating force in life seemed to have little sex drive himself. "It is likely," wrote Ernest Jones, "that the more passionate side of life subsided with him earlier than it does with many men."

Much of Freud's sex life was characterized by frustration and by periods of abstinence. For four long years he and Martha carried on a chaste courtship, and during much of the first nine years of their marriage she was either pregnant or recovering from childbirth. By then Freud—and perhaps Martha, too—had decided not to have any more children. Anna, the youngest of the six, later said that "if any acceptable, safe means of contraception had been available" to her parents, she would not have been born.

The problem was how to prevent further pregnancies when

contraceptive devices were so unreliable. Jung had the same concern and once wrote to Freud, "All is well with us except for the worry (another false alarm, fortunately) about the blessing of too many children. One tries every conceivable trick to stem the tide of these little blessings, but without much confidence. One scrapes along, one might say, from one menstruation to the next. The life of civilized man does have its quaint side."

Freud commented that after "three, four, or five years, marriage ceases to furnish the satisfaction of the sexual needs that it promised, since all the contraceptives available hitherto impair sexual enjoyment, disturb the finer susceptibilities of both partners, or even act as a direct cause of illness."

One popular method of birth control, coitus interruptus, may have contributed to the neurotic episode that led to Freud's self-analysis through the interpretation of his dreams. He diagnosed his problem as an anxiety neurosis and determined that its major cause was the practice of coitus interruptus and the consequent accumulation of sexual tension. Further, he attributed his frequent and severe headaches to sexual deprivation.

It was during this period that Freud was formulating his sex-based theory of neurosis, developed in part from his own dreams and fantasies, many of which, he admitted, derived from the same sexual urges that his patients were revealing during therapy. Freud dreamed about incest, rape, homosexuality, and emasculation. He believed that his wife was depriving him of his sexual rights and that his children were turning his sex organs into useless relics.

But the cessation of Freud's sex life cannot be explained solely by his desire to have no more children and his dissatisfaction with thick lambskin condoms and the effects of coitus interruptus. There was also his basic puritanical attitude toward sex, evident in much of his writing. He termed the sex act degrading and said that it soiled and contaminated the mind. He believed that any sexual activity for pleasure and not procreation was perverse. He described the perils of sexuality and called it "one of the most dangerous activities of the human being." He wrote of the "hardship of sex" and suggested that anyone who could free the human race of this burden would be hailed as a hero.

Freud wanted to be that hero. His life's mission, the essence of his psychoanalysis, was to urge, to insist on, the control by the conscious ego of the unconscious forces of the id. Reason over passion in all things. The goal of human existence, in Freud's view, was the suppression of the sexual impulses, which was the only path to a life of refinement and culture. The id instincts must be sublimated for higher, nobler purposes. Civilized human beings could derive only a limited satisfaction from sex. Only by suppressing sexual impulses could individuals, and civilization as a whole, advance.

Freud believed that it was the responsibility, even the duty, of the intellectual elite to live in accordance with this principle, to sacrifice the baser instincts for finer purposes. As for the rest of mankind—the uncivilized mob, Freud called them—their psychology was different.

Long before Freud formulated his system of psychoanalysis he had written to Martha about a train of thought released in his mind while listening to Bizet's opera *Carmen*. "The mob give vent to its appetites, and we deprive ourselves. We must deprive ourselves in order to maintain our integrity; we economize in our health, our capacity for enjoyment, our emotions; we save ourselves for something, not knowing for what. And this habit of constant suppression of natural instincts gives us the quality of refinement." Given this attitude, and the wish to have no more children, it may not seem so surprising that Freud abandoned sex at the age of forty-one.

And yet the matter is not so straightforward as Freud's writings may at first suggest. He also made guarded, cryptic, and sometimes confusing references to his sex life in his letters and books. He may have suppressed the desire for sex, but he had not succeeded in eliminating it. In *The Interpretation of Dreams* he described his physical attraction to a young woman while he was in his forties. He touched her—accidentally, he said—and was surprised to find himself sexually aroused.

On another occasion Freud's response to a young woman was clearly apparent. Edward Hitschmann, a Viennese analyst who joined Freud's group in 1905, reported that Freud developed an erection that was visible through his trousers after talking with the woman for an hour.

In Freud's book *The Psychopathology of Everyday Life*, he recorded an incident that occurred when he was forty-five. He was visiting friends and met a woman "who aroused a feeling of pleasure in me which I had long thought was extinct. As a result I was in a jovial, talkative, and obliging mood."

At the age of fifty-two Freud told a meeting of the Vienna Psychoanalytic Society that he was preparing a paper on sexual perversion. He said, however, that he would delay it for "practical reasons . . . until the time when his own sexuality has been extinguished." While analyzing Ernest Jones's mistress, Loe Kann, Freud said that he would like to indulge his fantasies of her were she not his patient. She aroused his feelings "with full symptoms."

During the voyage to America Freud mentioned to Jung a revival of his sexual interest, which, however, did not last long. A few months later he wrote to Jung that "my Indian summer of eroticism that we spoke of on our trip has withered lamentably under the pressure of work. I am resigned to being old and no longer even think continually of growing old."

The link between the end of one's sex life and old age, between impotence and death, was invoked by Freud several times. Typical of his comments was a remark to Jung about his old-age complex, "whose erotic base is known to you." In *The Psychopathology of Everyday Life*, Freud connected impotence with death, citing the story of a colleague who said that when sex came to an end, life was of no more value. That belief, Freud wrote, was "intimately bound up with trains of thought which were in a state of repression within me. That this was really true at the time of the topic of 'death and sexuality' I have plenty of evidence, which I need not bring up here, derived from my own self-investigation."

Then there were his dreams of prostitutes during the trip to the United States. Jung had suggested doing something practical about it, but Freud could not. Years before, while traveling in Italy, Freud frequently found himself walking through red-light districts, drawn to them irresistibly without his awareness and against his will. He left hurriedly each time, he said.

Writing to the American psychoanalyst James Jackson Putnam, Freud left the matter of his sex life in a state of tantalizing ambiguity. "I stand for an infinitely freer sexual life, although I myself have made very little use of such freedom." But he added, "Only so far as I considered myself entitled to."

Was Minna Bernays, Freud's sister-in-law, an example of what he considered himself entitled to? Had he ceased having sex with Martha only to replace her with Minna? Speculation about Freud and Minna has raged for decades and was the subject of gossip and rumor among Freud's psychoanalytic family. He was aware of the talk, and there are indications that he was not entirely displeased by it. At least once he mentioned the matter to a patient.

"So you believe in my famous love affair with Minna?" he asked. When the patient said no, Freud "seemed a bit miffed, as much offended for Minna's sake as for his own."

The rumors gathered strength from the early 1900s but did not receive substantial support or credibility until the 1960s. In 1969, John Billinsky, an American disciple of Jung's, published an account of an interview he had conducted with Jung in 1957, when the latter revealed for the first time that in 1907 Minna had confided to him her concern about her relationship with Freud. Jung, himself on the verge of a lifetime of infidelity, said that he was so shaken by the revelation that he could still recall his discomfort.

The Harvard psychologist Henry Murray spent three weeks with Jung in 1927. In a 1965 interview he reported a different version of what Jung told Billinsky. Murray said that Jung had told him that Minna was upset because Freud was expressing affection for her and not because they were actually having a love affair.

Jung offered another version in the late 1950s, which was

published in a 1978 biography. According to this account Jung said, " 'But his wife's younger sister. She appreciated the old man.' Jung laughed mischievously and said more soberly: 'I don't know what happened. Once I think—I think he slept with her once.' "

In 1982 four popular publications—*The New York Times, The Sunday Times of London, Newsweek*, and *Psychology Today*—published articles about Freud and Minna Bernays, with headlines promising revelations about "The Secret Love Life of Sigmund Freud." What sparked so much interest was a magazine article arguing that in August 1900, Minna lost her virginity to Freud on a trip to Italy. Several weeks after this alleged incident, Freud left Minna at a spa in Merano and continued his travels alone. Some time later Freud had a dream in which he had to pay a considerable sum of money for a relative's hospital stay, an expenditure he regretted. These events were interpreted as evidence that Freud got Minna pregnant and that she had an abortion at Merano for which he paid.

Minna Bernays and her sister Martha were close, but they differed from each other in many ways. Minna was the more attractive of the two. Taller than Martha, statuesque and full figured, she wore a small, old-fashioned cap on her head. She reminded some people of Freud's mother, who was also large and wore the same kind of cap.

Intellectually the differences between the sisters were more pronounced. Minna was extremely well read and possessed a sharp, critical mind. Her intellectual interests were broader than her sister's. She understood and supported Freud's system of psychoanalysis, whereas Martha knew little about her husband's work.

Although Minna did not become an analyst or undergo analysis herself, Freud discussed his cases with her, and she responded with a genuine appreciation of the nature of his theories. During the years of Freud's self-analysis, when he was beginning to develop his ideas, he said that only two people helped sustain his faith in himself: Wilhelm Fliess and Minna. She was also

Freud's most frequent traveling companion, and at home, Freud preferred to spend time in the evening playing cards with her.

Minna never married, although she had been engaged at the age of sixteen to an impoverished student of Sanskrit who died before the marriage could take place. Her betrothal occurred not long after Freud and Martha announced their engagement, and during that period Freud wrote passionate letters to Minna, addressing her as "my treasure."

Minna came to live with the Freuds at a crucial point in Freud's life: the year 1896. Their sixth and last child was born the year before. Freud was in the grip of his neurotic crisis and soon announced that sexual relations with Martha had ceased. Minna was thirty-one, Freud forty. Martha, tired from childbearing, was thirty-five. Minna was given the bedroom next to Freud and Martha's and had to pass through their room to reach hers. She stayed with the family until her death in 1941.

History's judgment of their alleged affair remains inconclusive, the evidence incomplete. In the late 1980s Freud scholar Peter Gay became the first person to read the correspondence between Freud and Minna held at the Library of Congress in Washington, D.C. He reported in 1989 that the letters reveal no suggestion of an affair between them. However, sixty-five letters (the letters had been numbered at some previous time), written between 1893 and 1910, the years when such an affair would have occurred, are missing from the collection. Those lost letters might be taken as support for an affair, but if someone had destroyed them because they were incriminating, why did that person not renumber the rest of the letters to conceal the gap—or simply destroy them all to avoid later suspicion and speculation?

Other arguments support the conclusion that no sexual relations between them ever occurred. Freud's daughter Anna, his closest companion in his later years, was jealous of her Aunt Minna but never detected any indication of an affair. Also, Peter Gay suggested that Jung was not always a reliable reporter of events, and it is questionable whether Minna would have discussed her personal life with him, as he claimed, when she had only just met him and knew him to be a colleague of Freud's.

It is clear, however, that Minna occupied a central position in Freud's emotional life. Another Freud scholar wrote, "Freud seemed to have a split in his love life, his sexuality remaining with Martha and his spiritual involvement shifting to Minna. . . . Perhaps out of his feelings for Minna, Freud's sexual enthusiasm had waned; loss of potency could have been an unconscious device for preventing himself from being unfaithful to Martha."

When Freud learned of Jung's affair with Sabina Spielrein, discovering that Jung was doing what Freud only fantasized about, he responded with sympathy and understanding. Perhaps that was because he, too, was living with the desire for another woman but was prevented from acting to fulfill it. And perhaps much of Freud's focus on sex in his theory—what Jung called his obsession with sex—was an outgrowth of his own sexual frustration. When Jung later developed his own view of the human personality he made little mention of sex. To Jung, who freely and frequently satisfied his sexual needs, sex played a minimal role in human motivation. To Freud, beset by frustrations and anxious about his thwarted desires, sex played the central role.

At this time, the midpoint of their years together, they faced the brutal reality of their marriages but chose to react in very different ways.

CHAPTER EIGHT

The Swiss Will Save Us: 1910

Two dozen Viennese psychoanalysts crowded into Wilhelm Stekel's room in the Grand Hotel in Nuremberg, Germany. They were annoyed and felt resentful toward Carl Jung, but they were even more angry with Sigmund Freud. This time he had gone too far. His favoritism toward Jung and the Swiss analysts was too blatant to be ignored any longer. Cigar smoke filled the room—they were, after all, *Freudian* analysts—as they reviewed the disappointing events of the day. Together they formulated plans to deal with the intolerable situation Freud had created.

It was March 30, 1910. The Second International Psychoanalytic Congress had convened that morning. The scientific portion of the meeting was a success, beginning with Freud's paper, "The Future Prospects of Psychoanalytic Therapy." Everyone agreed that the papers, questions, and discussions were first-rate. But after the scientific session, when Sandor Ferenczi, the Hungarian (another outsider), got up to speak, the trouble began.

Ferenczi started out reasonably enough. He proposed the establishment of an international psychoanalytic association with branch societies in various countries. A fine idea, the Viennese said. It was time for a more formal structure. Of course the headquarters of the international organization would be in Freud's Vienna. It was, after all, the center of the movement.

But Ferenczi was not finished. He stunned the Viennese analysts with his derogatory comments about their abilities, suggesting that the quality of their contributions was not so high as that of the Swiss. Therefore, Ferenczi said, it was fitting that Zurich be the hub of the international psychoanalytic movement and that Jung be acclaimed lifetime president of the new association. The final insult came when Ferenczi recommended that all papers and lectures prepared by psychoanalysts be submitted to Jung for approval. He would have absolute censorship powers over everything written or spoken about psychoanalysis.

The plan had to be Freud's. Everyone knew that Ferenczi, the most loyal of acolytes, would never advance such ideas on his own. The Viennese felt betrayed. They had supported Freud from the beginning. Jung was a latecomer, a Gentile, and not to be trusted, and Freud wanted to turn everything over to him!

Stekel, a brilliant writer and an intuitive psychoanalyst who himself had been analyzed by Freud, jumped to his feet to protest. As he recalled in his autobiography, "I was against this motion. I insisted that our new science would go down if it were not absolutely free. I mentioned how difficult it had been to place our first papers in the medical journals. If a lifetime president had to be elected, no one but Freud had the right to hold this office. In this vein I spoke for almost half an hour."

As soon as Stekel finished, Alfred Adler took the floor. Waving his long, thin cigar, he echoed Stekel's objections, point by point. Others followed, and the discussion grew so bitter that it was decided to postpone the vote until the next day.

The Viennese were correct; the plan *was* Freud's. He had arranged with Ferenczi to deliver the proposals at the congress, and Ferenczi, eager to please, was only too willing to put them forth. He agreed with Freud's ideas and had said that the "psychoanalytic outlook does not lead to democratic equalizing: there should be an elite rather on the lines of Plato's rule of philosophers." Freud acknowledged the same thought. Jung, the son and heir, should constitute that elite.

Four years later, after Jung had gone his own way, Freud wrote *On the History of the Psychoanalytic Movement*, in which he presented his reasons for wanting Jung to lead the movement from Zurich. Vienna, Freud believed, was a handicap because so many people considered it to be on the fringe of Europe, more Eastern than Western. Zurich, on the other hand, was squarely at Europe's heart. Also, Zurich could claim established institutional support for psychoanalysis through its use at the Burghölzli and Jung's lectures at the University of Zurich. No clinic or university in Vienna sanctioned or supported Freud's ideas.

If Vienna was one handicap for psychoanalysis, Freud's continued leadership was another. Public and professional opinions about him were extreme. He was revered and reviled, hated and loved. He knew he had to withdraw so that acceptance of his theories would not be hostage to the sentiments held about him personally. There was also his age, fifty-four. The long struggle that lay ahead was a trial fit only for a younger man.

Freud wanted to establish a dictator for psychoanalysis, an authority "who would be prepared to instruct and admonish." As new and competing ideas surfaced, someone should be prepared to declare, "All this nonsense is nothing to do with psychoanalysis; this is not psychoanalysis." He wanted a judge to decree what was and what was not the official party line, the tenets of the faith.

He realized by the intensity of the debate that afternoon in Nuremberg that he had made a serious error. He had blundered in thinking that his Viennese followers would blithely agree to pass the torch to the Swiss. He later admitted this to Ferenczi, but he also handed him part of the blame. "We were both somewhat to blame," Freud wrote to Ferenczi, "in not reckoning with the effect [these changes] would have on the Viennese. It would have been easy for you to have entirely omitted the critical remarks and to have assured them of their scientific freedom. I believe that my long-pent-up aversion for the Viennese combined with your brother complex [toward Jung] to make us shortsighted."

Freud had, indeed, miscalculated, and he had to salvage the situation as best he could by persuading the Viennese to accept at least some of his suggestions. But he knew he would have to offer incentives in return.

The emotional protest meeting in Stekel's hotel room was meant to be a secret from Freud, but like an omniscient father who always knows what his children are doing, Freud soon learned of it. Stekel, who had summoned the group, recalled that moment in his autobiography: "Psychoanalysis, I said, had been founded in Vienna; for a long time we had been the only ones to fight for Freud. It would be preposterous if Vienna were deprived of the leadership. We had to stand for the independence of the new science. Were we to be dependent upon the mercy of Zurich?"

The door swung open and Freud burst into the room. His obvious distress alarmed them. "Most of you are Jews," he said, "and therefore you are incompetent to win friends for the new teaching. Jews must be content with the modest role of preparing the ground. It is absolutely essential that I should form ties in the world of general science. I am getting on in years and am weary of being perpetually attacked."

His words spilled out, faster and louder. "An official psychiatrist and a Gentile must be the leader of the movement!" Tears streamed down his cheeks. "We are all in danger."

He gripped his coat by the lapels and yanked it open. "They begrudge me the coat I am wearing. I don't know whether in the future I will earn my daily bread. The Swiss will save us—will save me, and all of you as well!"

They were shocked. No one had ever seen Freud in such a state, and for a long time no one could speak.

Freud's emotional outburst was effective. He was able to get some—though not all—of the concessions he wanted. The International Psychoanalytic Association was founded, and Jung was elected its first president for a two-year term. Zurich was designated not as the headquarters of the movement but simply the place of residence of the president. Jung was also appointed editor of a new publication, the *Bulletin*, which would be published monthly. It would contain news of general interest to members, such as notices of meetings and lectures.

To appease the Viennese and make them feel they had some independence from Jung, another publication, the *Central Jour-*

nal for Psychoanalysis, was established. Freud would be its director, Stekel and Adler the editors. Freud also announced that he would retire as president of the Vienna society and would no longer host meetings at his home. Adler would be the new president, and the meetings would take place in more neutral territory, at the Vienna Medical Society building.

In relinquishing the leadership of the Vienna branch of the International Psychoanalytic Association and entrusting it to Adler, Freud was trying to undermine the opposition. He suggested that Adler, as president, would then "feel an obligation to defend our common ground."

Freud expressed the opinion that his Viennese disciples would not be sorry to see him step down. "I had almost got into the painful role of the dissatisfied and unwanted old man," he wrote to Ferenczi. "That I certainly don't want, so I prefer to go before I need, but voluntarily." To Karl Abraham, his friend and associate in Berlin, he complained about the Viennese group, particularly Adler and Stekel. "I no longer get any pleasure from the Viennese. I have a heavy cross to bear with the older generation. They will soon be feeling that I am an obstacle and will treat me as such, but I can't believe that they have anyone better to substitute for me."

After the congress had concluded, Fritz Wittels, another Viennese analyst, observed what Freud was still incapable of seeing: "Freud does not think much of us, his Viennese pupils. If he knew the Swiss as well as he knows us, he would like them still less."*

---

*The preparations for the Nuremberg congress had been Jung's responsibility, but three weeks before its opening he left for America to cope with the sudden illness of his wealthy Chicago patient, Harold McCormick. Jung's plans called for him to arrive in Nuremberg at five o'clock on the morning of the congress's first day. Freud, with his long-standing anxiety about travel, was certain that Jung would miss the meeting. Bleuler had declined to attend for reasons of health, and Oskar Pfister, another Swiss analyst, would not be there. "I have not got over your not coming to Nuremberg," Freud wrote to Pfister. "Bleuler is not coming either, and Jung is in America, so that I am trembling about his return. What will happen if my Zurichers desert me?"

❖

Overall, Freud considered the Nuremberg congress to be a great success, notwithstanding the confrontation with his Viennese disciples. A few days after returning home he wrote to thank Ferenczi for his support and to note that they had "accomplished an important piece of work which will have a profound influence in shaping the future." After the close of the sessions, Freud and Jung spent the day touring Rothenburg, a picturesque medieval town. They had had an enjoyable time, Freud wrote to Ferenczi, and Jung was "at the top of his form, and it is to be hoped he will prove himself." Freud reiterated his dependence on his Swiss colleagues and said how much more satisfying his relations were with them than with the Viennese.

He closed the letter to Ferenczi by declaring that psychoanalysis had passed into a new stage of development. "With the Nuremberg *Reichstag* closes the childhood of our movement; that is my impression. I hope now for a rich and fair time of youth."

Neither of Freud's hopes was to be satisfied. Psychoanalysis did not enter into a rich and fair time, nor did Jung prove himself. Freud received the first inklings of Jung's failure as an administrator several weeks later when Jung wrote about the problems of organizing the Swiss branch of the International Psychoanalytic Association. It was a "painful affair," Jung said, and matters had gone far beyond his control.

Ludwig Binswanger, an analyst on the staff of the Burghölzli, was elected president of the Swiss group. He insisted that nonmembers be allowed to attend the meetings. Jung, at Freud's instigation, expected to hold only occasional public meetings, restricting the majority of the gatherings to members. He was unable to win acceptance of this point. The result was a small Zurich society open to a large audience of observers, people who could attend the meetings without joining, without publicly pledging their allegiance to Freud and psychoanalysis.

Jung was unhappy but was powerless to change the situation.

He suggested that the group ask Freud for his "fatherly advice," but they rejected the idea. Jung described these events to Freud in a letter and asked Freud to forgive him for his poor handling of the affair.

Freud was not in a forgiving mood. He was disappointed and did not hesitate to make his feelings plain. "Naturally I was very much dismayed not to see you take a firm stand in your first official function. I am amazed that you could not summon up the authority to forestall a decision which is quite untenable. In your place I should never have given in." Freud had never before expressed his anger so frankly.

Opening the meetings of the Zurich society to nonmembers was disturbing for several reasons. First, Freud wanted as large an official membership as possible for the sake of appearances. The larger the group, the greater the perceived support for psychoanalysis. Second, he knew that making the public commitment of affiliating with a group would bind members to the group's views. This would help to blunt criticism and dissidence. Third, there were factions—including a group under Bleuler at the Burghölzli—that followed Freud's teachings and techniques but were reluctant to join an organization in open support of Freud. Having them remain outside the official organization was visible evidence of cracks in the facade.

Freud cautioned Jung not to print the Swiss society's membership list in the *Bulletin*, because that would enable his enemies to rejoice over the small number of members and the factions that were not represented. He also urged Jung to make it clear to those who refused to join that they would be ineligible to attend the next congress or be involved in decisions regarding the future of the movement.

Jung offered no apologies in his next letter to Freud. There was no way, he said, that he could have prevented the outcome. He had to go along with the majority, but he hoped that others would change their minds and join the society.

Freud had no more to say about Jung's handling of the Zurich society, but two months later he criticized Jung again, this time for a greater disappointment. The problem was Jung's presidency of the International Psychoanalytic Association. In Freud's view, Jung was not devoting sufficient time and attention to his duties. Freud expected him to coordinate the activities of the movement worldwide. Jung was supposed to mediate among the various national societies, offering advice and assistance where needed. In addition, he was to manage the conferences and edit the publications. Freud hoped that Jung would relieve him of the burden of all these leadership chores.

As Ernest Jones observed:

> Freud would thus in this way be relieved from the active central position for which he had no taste. Unfortunately neither had Jung. Jung often said he was by nature a heretic, which was why he was drawn at first to Freud's very heretical work. But he worked best alone and had none of the special talent needed for cooperative or supervisory work with other colleagues. Nor had he much taste for business details, including regular correspondence. In short he was unsuited to the position Freud had planned for him as president of the association and leader of the movement.

Freud reached that disturbing conclusion for himself by the end of the summer of 1910. Only five months after he had forced such sweeping changes onto the organization of psychoanalysis, he admitted to having made a serious mistake. He wrote to Jung in August to suggest that he had acted hastily. He should not have been so eager to start an international organization. It was his impatience to see Jung in place as the leader of psychoanalysis and his own desire to abandon his responsibilities to the movement that had precipitated his actions. He admitted to Jung that he should have done nothing at all. He accused Jung of not taking his new duties seriously, of failing to act in a conscientious manner. He thought Jung was skillful in persuading and cultivating people, but he had misjudged him. "The first months of your reign, my dear son and successor," Freud wrote, "have not turned out brilliantly."

Jung agreed that his regency had not gotten off to a successful start, but that was because he had developed resistances to the Viennese, especially to Adler and Stekel. Their hostility in Nuremberg had affected him greatly. He explained in a letter to Freud that "the less than cordial reception in Nuremberg (I don't mean the election of the pope, but the purely personal aspect) has chilled me somewhat. I have never sought the presidency and therefore object to being looked at askance or envied because of it." He had tried to be amiable toward the others, but to be an effective administrator he would have to be tougher. He promised Freud that he would try to improve, but he also agreed that Freud had acted too quickly.

Something else was bothering Jung. He suggested to Freud that they listen to their opponents. "They are saying some very remarkable things which ought to open our eyes in several ways. All these mutterings about sectarianism, mysticism, arcane jargon, initiation, and so forth, mean something. Even the deep-rooted outrage, the moral indignation, can only be aimed at something gripping, that has all the trappings of a religion." He warned that the interest Swiss clergymen were showing in psychoanalysis was disturbing.

Jung was concerned that psychoanalysis was wrapping itself in the cloak of a religious faith with its creeds, societies, and members versus nonmembers. That all produced a negative response in Jung, the pastor's son, whose childhood and adolescence were torn by rebellion against his father's religious ideas. He would not permit himself to fall into that trap again.

Jung's administration of the Swiss society and the International Psychoanalytic Association became more frustrating as summer cooled to autumn. Bleuler, whose support Freud maintained was crucial to the cause, continued to vacillate in his formal commitment. He and some of his assistants at the Burghölzli remained aloof from the society. Freud and Jung tried to change his mind, but his public statements on psychoanalysis were sometimes so timid that Jung once called him a coward.

Increasingly Jung found the daily management chores distasteful. In October he wrote to Freud, "Sometimes it makes my gorge rise to think that I have to dirty my hands with all these machinations and cleaning up of messes. I am not a politician." He recommended that they simply let their opponents kill one another off and stick to self-defense.

Freud counseled a different approach. Because they had an organization and a movement to defend by then, they also had responsibilities to its members. The arts of politics, diplomacy, and compromise had become necessary. "But we can make it up to ourselves with humor," Freud wrote, "when we talk about these 'farts' together one day." Other great movements in history faced difficult times. "There are never more than one or two individuals who find the straight road and don't trip over their own legs."

Jung was far from finding the straight road, at least the road on which Freud wanted him to travel. He was about to choose a detour, led by his passion for mythology and archeology. That distraction prevented him from learning to cope with organizational problems. Jung was trying to find his own way, to propose his own faith, and that left him little time to defend Freud's.

Throughout 1910 Jung described his work in mythology with a growing excitement that should have made Freud wary. Jung's letters show that he was gripped by something beyond his control, a force sweeping him toward a destination he could not foresee. He derived what he called an almost autoerotic pleasure from pursuing these dreams. "I often feel I am wandering alone through a strange country, seeing wonderful things that no one has seen before and no one needs to see. I must just let myself be carried along, trusting to God that in the end I shall make a landfall somewhere."

Jung's ventures into the uncharted area of symbolism carried an air of mystery and furtiveness. He dropped only meager clues about his discoveries to his friends and for a long time did not divulge even that much to Freud. "Too much shouldn't be revealed yet. But be prepared for some strange things the like of which you have never yet heard from me."

Jung believed that Freud would never accept these new ideas, and that once they were fully developed, he would no longer be able to accept Freud's teachings. Although this was obvious to Jung, it was also threatening, and he had difficulty coming to terms with it. Yet he relished the secrecy, keeping his discoveries and thoughts to himself, just as he had done as a child.

In another parallel with his childhood, Jung became preoccupied with dreams and fantasies, dating from his dream about the house with different levels, the dream Freud interpreted in terms of a death wish. It was clear to Jung, however, that the various levels of the house symbolized different levels of the mind, what Jung preferred to call the *psyche*. The upstairs, the salon, represented the plane of conscious awareness. Despite its dated furnishings, it had a lived-in look. It was a room in daily use.

The floors below signified different layers of the unconscious mind. The ground floor stood for what Jung called the *personal unconscious,* essentially a storehouse or reservoir of memories and thoughts no longer in the conscious mind but that could easily be recalled. Personal experiences filed in this level of the unconscious could be extracted, examined, and restored or forgotten until the next time they rose into consciousness.

The most important level of the house was the cave containing remnants of cultures long dead. Jung interpreted this as the residue of primitive peoples and their animal ancestors, an accumulation of experiences of all our forebears that lies within the darkest region of the unconscious mind of every individual.

This *collective unconscious* was a deeper level of the psyche than any explored by Freud. In Freud's view, the contents of the unconscious mind were personal—the thoughts, memories, experiences, wishes, and fears that derived from one's past and were repressed into unconsciousness. These unconscious forces constituted the driving power for our behavior, and it was Freud's genius that first made scientists aware of this potent portion of the mind.

Jung's collective unconscious contained more than personal

experiences. It housed all the memories of our evolution as a species, repeated in the mind of each person in every generation. To Jung this primitive past was the foundation of personality, directing our behavior and thought.

Jung's interpretation suggested to him that dreams and other manifestations of the unconscious could not be analyzed solely in personal terms, as Freud believed. Rather, explanation must proceed at the more profound and less personal level of the universal images, symbols, and fantasies contained in the collective unconscious. In his continuing search to understand these universal experiences, then, Jung dug deeper into archeology and mythology.

It took considerable study for all this to come clear to Jung. It did not reveal itself in a blinding flash of insight but unfolded slowly, almost tortuously, after voracious reading and self-study. Layer by layer, like an archeologist tenderly scraping centuries of soil from ancient ruins, Jung proceeded to lay bare the various levels of the unconscious.

He was helped in his excavations by the unusual daydreams of an American woman with the masculine name of Frank Miller, who had been a patient of the Swiss psychiatrist Theodore Flournoy. Her fantasies had been published by Flournoy in 1906,* and Jung happened upon them in the course of analyzing his dream of the house. He was struck by the strong mythological nature of the woman's fantasies. "They operated like a catalyst upon the stored-up and still disorderly ideas within me. Gradually, there formed out of them, and out of the knowledge of myths I had acquired, my book *Wandlungen und Symbole der Libido* [*Metamorphoses and Symbols of the Libido*, later published in English as *The Psychology of the Unconscious* (1912)]."

This book, like the delineation of Jung's ideas, took a long time to become reality, and it disturbed him to know that Freud would never accept its premises. As the hypotheses took shape,

---

*"Quelques Faits d'imagination créatrice subconsciente," *Archives de psychologie* (Geneva) 5 (1906); *Journal of the American Society for Psychical Research* (New York) 1 (June 1907): 6.

Jung became more and more depressed. He proposed to trans-
form Freud's concept of libido from a psychic energy almost
entirely sexual in nature to a more generalized energy in which
sex played a minimal role. Jung's kind of libido expressed itself
in universal symbols that could be understood only through the
study of mythology, a conception that was a blatant refutation of
all Freud stood for.

Jung proceeded carefully and quietly with his work. He gave
tentative expression to his ideas in lectures to audiences in
Zurich, which made it unlikely that Freud would learn the details. To Freud himself Jung described the work in vague terms.

In January 1910 Jung spoke to some student scientific societies. He wrote to Freud that the topic was symbolism and said
that he tried to link individual fantasies and conflicts to their
basis in mythology. He said that he would like to discuss the
subject with Freud and ask his advice. Freud replied that Jung
had given him only a hint of his thinking, but he agreed with
Jung's suggestion about writing a paper on the topic for the
Yearbook. In May, Jung wrote to Freud about another talk, this
one to a group of Swiss psychiatrists. Again the topic was symbolism, "mythological stuff that aroused great applause." He sent
Freud a copy of the lecture.

Freud wrote that he read the paper with pleasure but offered
a number of specific objections. The work lacked "clarity,"
Freud said. Jung responded: "I am presenting myself in my shirt-
sleeves. The piece is only a very rough sketch." But even as he
made that disclaimer Jung's rough sketch was taking on finished
form. And the more complete it became, the more certain Jung
was that the split with Freud would come soon.

Often in Jung's life, his dreams foretold his future. The most
significant and obvious set of dreams at this time had as its
backdrop the mountains on the border between Switzerland and
Austria, separating Jung's homeland from Freud's. In one dream
Jung saw an elderly man dressed in the uniform of an Austrian

customs official. The man walked by, ignoring him, as though Jung were invisible. The man looked peeved, melancholy, and vexed. Other people appeared in the dream, one of whom told Jung that the old man wasn't really alive. He was the ghost of a customs agent long dead. "He is one of those who still couldn't die properly."

As soon as Jung awoke he set about uncovering the dream's meaning, focusing on such key words as *customs* and *border*. What could they signify in his unconscious? He associated *customs* with censorship. *Border* made him think of the boundary between the conscious and the unconscious, as well as the line between Freud's view of the mind and his own. What, he then asked, do customs agents do at borders? They open suitcases and examine the contents for contraband. This signified to Jung the technique of psychoanalysis. In the course of therapy the analyst uncovers and examines the unconscious assumptions or contraband—the forbidden contents—of the psyche.

And what of the customs agent himself, the man who could not die properly? To Jung he had a sour view of life because his work brought little pleasure and satisfaction. Yet he persisted, in ghostly form, in preventing people from crossing the border. Obviously he represented Sigmund Freud.

Freud had already lost much of his authority and stature for Jung, but Jung was far from free of his influence. Freud "meant to me a superior personality," Jung wrote, "upon whom I projected the father, and at the time of this dream this projection was still far from eliminated."

Jung knew that whenever such a projection exists, the person under its power cannot be objective toward the target of the projection. Jung, therefore, could not be fair at that moment in his evaluation of Freud. "On the one hand we are dependent," he wrote, "and on the other we have resistances. When the dream took place I still thought highly of Freud, but at the same time I was critical of him. This divided attitude is a sign that I was still unconscious of the situation and had not come to any resolution of it."

Inspired by the customs-agent dream, Jung felt impelled to

clarify his standing with Freud, not in person—for that he was not yet prepared—but in his own mind. The longer he thought about it, the more he came to realize that he had been censoring his own opinions, judgments, and criticisms because of the weight of Freud's personality. He had been telling himself that Freud was wiser and more experienced, and this had prevented him from developing and propounding his own ideas.

But now Jung could contemplate Freud as the melancholy ghost of the customs agent. Perhaps this was evidence that he had a death wish toward Freud. If so, then Freud's interpretation of Jung's dream of the multilevel house was valid. Jung considered the problem and concluded that he could find no reason—conscious or unconscious—why he would desire Freud's death. Freud's friendship was still important to him. After considerable reflection Jung decided that the symbolism of the customs-agent dream meant that he should be more critical in his attitude toward Freud. He professed shock at that realization.

There was more to come in the shadowy world of Jung's dreams, more signposts to guide him on his detour from psychoanalysis. The image of the customs official was followed by a continuation of the dream in which Jung found himself downtown at noon. A fierce sun was blazing, and the streets reminded him of Basel, yet it also appeared to be an Italian city. The shops were closing, and people were streaming toward him, on their way home for the midday meal. In their midst walked a knight in full armor, clad in medieval chain mail, a helmet, and a white tunic adorned with a huge red cross. "One can easily imagine how I felt: suddenly to see in a modern city, during the noonday rush hour, a crusader coming toward me." No one else took any notice of the cavalier. He might have been invisible. Only Jung had the power to see this extraordinary figure.

A voice spoke to Jung in his dream, saying, "Yes, this is a regular apparition. The knight always passes by here between twelve and one o'clock, and has been doing so for a very long time, and everyone knew about it."

In analyzing the dream Jung was struck by the contrast between the two figures: the customs agent, ghostly and unable to die properly; and the knight, real and full of vitality. Jung associated the knight with the twelfth century, the period of the search for the Holy Grail, stories of which had fascinated him since adolescence. Thanks to his dream, he had an inkling of some supreme secret buried in those myths, an indication that his search for truth had nothing to do with Freud's. Like the multi-level house, this was Jung's alone, not to be built on Freud's work or shared with him in any way. "My whole being was seeking for something still unknown which might confer meaning upon the banality of life." Jung knew he had to seek his own grail and go his own way.

But he was not even close to finding it. That was made clear in another dream toward the end of 1910, while he was taking a bicycle trip with a friend through northern Italy. They spent a night at Arona on the southern end of Lake Maggiore. Jung dreamed he was among a group of spirits of distinguished people who lived centuries ago. They were speaking Latin. A man wearing a curly wig asked Jung a difficult question. He understood the question but in the dream did not know enough Latin to answer it. He was overcome with humiliation and woke up.

The first thought that entered his mind was about the book he was writing on his concept of libido. The dream appeared to have relevance for that work. He said he developed such "intense inferiority feelings about the unanswered question that I immediately took the train home in order to get back to work. It would have been impossible for me to continue the bicycle trip and lose another three days. I had to work, to find the answer."

Jung's obsession with seeking the answer haunted him, and when he finally found it, it left him confused and miserable. Freud was sure to find it unacceptable.

Jung faced other unresolved problems and worries, mostly dealing with his father complexes toward Freud and Bleuler and his relationship with his new surrogate son, Johann Honegger.

Bleuler remained a thorny issue, although Jung had left the Burghölzli and was no longer in daily contact with him. Under persistent pressure from Freud, Jung attempted to force Bleuler into membership in the Zurich society. Bleuler—sometimes friendly and affable and other times sulking and irritable—refused. He was unyielding and threatened to disassociate himself publicly from the group. Such a spectacle on the part of one of Europe's most prominent psychiatrists would have had fateful consequences for the movement.

Jung eventually took the rejection personally and came to believe that Bleuler's refusal to ally himself formally with the Zurich branch of the International Psychoanalytic Association resulted not from Bleuler's attitude toward psychoanalysis but from his attitude toward Jung. He wrote to Freud that Bleuler's opposition was a matter of revenge because, after the trip to America, Jung had resigned from the anti-drinking societies Bleuler supported. This placed Jung in an awkward situation. He admitted to Freud that leaving the Burghölzli and breaking with Bleuler had had a severe impact on him. "Once again I underestimated my father complex."

As if his own complexes, the Zurich society, and his libido book were not enough, letters from Freud arrived so frequently that Jung could not keep up with them. There were often long delays between replies. Jung admitted encountering resistances when he had to write to Freud. His conscious reason was that he could respond only during an uninterrupted period of time adequate for reflection. Such a time, he confessed, never seemed to arise, and he had great difficulty in arranging it for himself. But the more profound reason for the delays was once again Jung's father complex, his "inability to come up to expectation."

Freud responded to this confession four days later, thus maintaining the pressure for Jung to correspond. After assuring Jung that the bond between them was built on shared feelings and mutual efforts on behalf of their cause, he added that occasionally he was irritated because Jung remained under the influence of his father complex.

Then, in an effort to boost Jung's spirits, Freud reminded him of the legacy that would one day be his. Alluding to Jung as Alexander the Great, Freud wrote, "Just rest easy, dear son Alexander. I will leave you more to conquer than I myself have managed, all psychiatry and the approval of the civilized world, which regards me as a savage. That ought to lighten your heart."

Jung's relationship with Johann Honegger, the young Zurich psychiatrist he desired to mold into his disciple, was rocky. Honegger has been described as a "radiant young man, keen and subtle minded, a witty debater with an easy charm and a cheerful intensity that greatly appealed to Jung." There was, however, a dark side to Honegger's radiance. On one occasion he lost all sense of reality, a state that lasted several days. Jung diagnosed the condition as neurotic and proposed a program of analysis that he would supervise.

Honegger's problems were more severe, however. He was a borderline psychotic, which Jung failed to recognize in a manner reminiscent of his misdiagnosis of Otto Gross. In a near replay of the Gross case, Jung's analysis of Honegger became a mutual therapeutic enterprise. Honegger helped Jung interpret some of his more disturbing and elusive dreams to the extent that Jung told Freud that Honegger had done him a lot of good.

Jung wanted Honegger to assist him with his patients so that he could spend more time on the libido book, but he never got around to formally offering Honegger the position. Needing employment and losing patience with Jung, Honegger accepted a staff job at a sanatorium outside of Montreux. Jung was hurt and vowed to do everything in his power to win Honegger back.

He asked Honegger to return to Zurich but made that return conditional on Honegger's completing his medical dissertation. Only then, Jung said, could he allow Honegger to become his assistant. Jung also expressed dissatisfaction with Honegger's personal discipline and work habits, telling Freud that the young man depended too much on inspiration and did not read enough. Jung opposed what he considered Honegger's self-indulgent and shiftless behavior.

Jung also told Freud that he might be judging Honegger too harshly. Would Freud offer some grandfatherly advice? Freud extolled Honegger's positive qualities and agreed that Jung was being unreasonable in expecting Honegger's work habits to parallel his own; Jung should not want Honegger to be a duplicate of himself.

Honegger returned to Zurich in the fall of 1910, but Jung was not the most considerate of bosses. His treatment of Honegger was peremptory and dictatorial. He made certain that Honegger understood that his role was a subordinate one. He criticized Honegger's work habits and a lifestyle Jung claimed was dedicated to the pursuit of pleasure. Jung expected Honegger to carry a fair share of the burden of his patients so that he would not feel so overworked.

Jung was especially critical of Honegger's fiancée, Helene Widmer, who had once been Jung's secretary. Jung thought she had done excellent work, but his favorable opinion of her did not carry over to her role as Honegger's intended wife. Jung told Honegger that they were unsuited for each other, and he did everything he could to break the engagement.

Jung's campaign against Helene Widmer was successful, and he gleefully told Freud that the breaking of the engagement would probably save Honegger's career. Jung was wrong. Honegger left him and joined the staff of an asylum nearby. Four months later he committed suicide by injecting himself with a concentrated dose of morphine. At first, Jung claimed to be unaffected, reporting the death to Freud in a brief note. He said that Honegger's motive was a desire to avoid becoming a psychotic because he was unable to give up his pursuit of pleasure. Jung gave no indication of any sense of personal loss or even involvement in Honegger's situation.

Freud was more upset. He expressed sorrow at the tragedy and praised Honegger as an intelligent and gifted person. He said he was certain that Jung must be more deeply affected than he admitted, and, in truth, it took several weeks before Jung could accept the loss. When he did, he felt overwhelmed with guilt. Surely, he wrote to Freud, it was his fault that Honegger had committed suicide. After all, Jung had been his analyst. He had made a mistake. He should have followed the orthodox Freudian approach rather than pursuing an unproven technique stemming from his own work on the libido. Jung was convinced that his failure led directly to Honegger's death.

To deal with the blow, Jung prescribed a course of therapy for himself: to work even more energetically on his new theories and to try to understand the universal, historical bases of unconscious fantasies, those signs and symbols found in the collective unconscious, the deepest region of the psyche. It was a realm only he could enter. Freud could not explore it with him. The dreams of the multilevel house and the knight told Jung that this work was his alone.

Freud's problems during the summer and fall of 1910 centered on the Viennese dissenters led by Adler and Stekel, on Bleuler, and on his loyal friend Ferenczi. To make matters worse, his summer vacation was not as restorative as usual. He had planned to go to the spa at Karlsbad, expecting the sulfur springs to alleviate his stomach trouble, which he persisted in attributing to American cooking. From there he would take the family to the mountains in Switzerland, then north to Zurich, ending the holidays with a long visit with the Jungs.

But those plans had to be abandoned when Freud's mother-in-law became ill, so the family spent their vacation near her home in Hamburg. Freud decided to tour Holland, which was not far away, and to cancel the visit to Zurich, saying that he was just too tired. If Freud visited Jung, he knew he would get no rest. He and Jung would exhaust themselves in conversation. Freud told Jung that he could not assimilate any more that summer, adding, in English, that he was "full to the brim."

Jung also planned a restful summer and made up his mind not to journey to Holland to meet Freud. Instead, he had his boat shipped to Lake Constance and went sailing for two weeks. Freud stayed in Holland six weeks, first at Scheveningen—a seaside resort at The Hague—and then up the coast at Noordwijk.

Two of Freud's sons traveled with him for the first two weeks; then the rest of the family joined them. Ernest Jones visited for a few days, and the two men took long walks on the beach. Freud "would stride along swiftly," Jones said, "and I noticed that he had to poke every bit of seaweed with his stick, his quick eyes darting here and there all the time. I asked him what he expected to find, but got the noncommittal answer 'Something interesting. You never know.' "

Freud seemed to enjoy himself at the seaside but admitted to missing his beloved mountains. He wrote to Jung that it was difficult to know what to do with himself on a beach. He held a brief but interesting therapeutic session in August with the composer Gustav Mahler. He met Mahler in the old university town of Leyden, and they walked the streets for four hours. During this peripatetic psychoanalytic session Freud reportedly cured Mahler of impotence.

Ferenczi arrived to accompany Freud on a three-week trip to Florence, Rome, and Naples. Freud always enjoyed Italy, but this time Ferenczi made undue demands on his emotional energy, depriving Freud of the opportunity to devote himself to sightseeing and his own mental relaxation.

Freud complained to Jung about Ferenczi's infantile attitude. "He never stops admiring me, which I don't like, and is probably sharply critical of me in his unconscious when I am taking it easy. He has been too passive and receptive, letting everything be done for him like a woman, and I really haven't got enough homosexuality in me to accept him as one. These trips arouse a great longing for a real woman."

Ferenczi sulked and could not be depended on to manage the day-to-day travel arrangements. Jones analyzed Ferenczi's problems and declared that they stemmed from an insatiable need for his father's love, which he transferred to Freud. This explained why Ferenczi demanded so much emotional sustenance from Freud during the trip. Unable to express his needs openly, he could only wait for Freud to reveal his innermost self through discussions of his dreams.

Freud, however, wanted nothing to do with Ferenczi's neuroses, transference, conflicts, or anything else connected with psychoanalysis. He was on vacation and wanted to tour the sights with a person of compatible interests. After the trip he wrote to Ferenczi, "I was probably most of the time a quite ordinary elderly gentleman, and you in astonishment kept measuring the distance between me and your fantasy ideal. On the other hand I often wished that you would pull yourself out of the infantile role and place yourself beside me as a companion on an equal footing, something you were unable to do."

Jung agreed with Freud's assessment of Ferenczi. That sort of behavior irritated him, he told Freud, and he still had an aftertaste of it from their trip with Ferenczi to America. How Jung wished he could have gone with Freud to Italy, he said, although he had never suggested to Freud that he might join him.

When Freud returned to Vienna he was forced to confront the dissension within the ranks of his Viennese followers. He had appointed Adler and Stekel editors of the new *Central Journal* to give them a feeling of independence from Jung. He had resigned as president of the Vienna society of the International Psychoanalytic Association so that Adler could take his place. He had hoped these moves would make them more tractable, but they seemed to have had the opposite effect.

Adler distrusted Jung and thought that Freud favored the Swiss at the expense of himself and the other loyal Viennese. He was also developing his own ideas, which focused on conscious rather than unconscious aspects of the psyche. Adler refused to accord sex a primary place in human motivation, speculating instead about something he called the "will to power." A highly ambitious man, Adler chafed in the modest role he was assigned to play in the psychoanalytic movement. "Do you think it gives me such great pleasure to stand in your shadow my whole life long?" he asked Freud.

Freud's relations with Adler and Stekel deteriorated on both professional and personal levels. In November Freud complained to Ferenczi that "the tactlessness and unpleasant behavior of Adler and Stekel make it very difficult to get along together." Two weeks later he wrote to Ferenczi: "I am having an atrocious time with Adler and Stekel. I have been hoping that it would come to a clear separation, but it drags on and despite my opinion that nothing is to be done with them I have to toil on. It was often much pleasanter when I was alone."

Two days later Freud complained to Jung. All the irritation caused by Adler and Stekel had dampened his spirits. Stekel, who was undergoing a manic episode, was driving him to despair. Adler was decent and intelligent but also paranoid, and his theories were unintelligible. Their publication in the new journal would only confuse readers.

In addition, Freud wrote, Adler was "always claiming priority, putting new names on everything, complaining that he is disappearing under my shadow, and forcing me into the unwelcome role of the aging despot who prevents young men from getting ahead." Adler and Stekel were also rude. He would like to get rid of both. The problem was that they did not want to leave the movement. Instead, they expected to change it. Freud could not allow that to happen.

He was also annoyed by what he called the absurd pride of the Viennese dissenters and their jealousy of Jung and the Zurich analysts. One would think that their personal experience with psychoanalysis would help them, Freud said, but they had no understanding of their true motives. The rest of the Vienna disciples did not offer much more solace; they were not a brilliant lot.

Freud continued to grumble about the Adler situation. The most alarming aspect, he wrote to Jung, was the way Adler minimized the role of sex. Our opponents, Freud said, "will soon be able to speak of an experienced psychoanalyst whose conclusions are radically different from our own." The prospect was intolerable. If Adler did not mend his ways, he would have to leave the psychoanalytic family.

As the year drew to a close, Freud also had to contend with

Bleuler and his contentious relationship with Jung. It had become obvious that friction between them was the cause of Bleuler's failure to affiliate himself with the Swiss psychoanalytic society.

Freud found Bleuler's moodiness distressing. The man was sometimes supportive and sometimes critical. Occasionally Freud could not discern what position Bleuler was taking. His arguments, Freud wrote to Binswanger in Zurich, are "so cloudy, imponderable, and ungraspable that I find it difficult to make him out." But Freud still desired the prestige of Bleuler's name and continued to court him in an exhausting correspondence.

"I have taken great trouble over Bleuler," Freud wrote to Oskar Pfister, a Protestant pastor and Freudian loyalist in Zurich. "I cannot say that I want to hold him to us *at any cost*, since after all Jung is rather close to me, but I will willingly sacrifice for Bleuler anything provided it will not harm our cause."

Making no headway with Bleuler through letters, Freud decided on a personal confrontation. He told Jung he was willing to travel to Zurich over the Christmas holidays. Jung recommended instead that Freud meet Bleuler on neutral ground, perhaps in Munich. If Freud visited Bleuler at home in Zurich, Jung wrote, "you would have to grit your teeth and lodge with him. You can't possibly spend a whole day alone with him; he is thoroughly exhausting because he is quite inhuman." Jung suggested a meeting of four or five hours, beginning at six o'clock in the evening and ending when the night train departed Munich to take Bleuler back to Zurich.

As an inducement for Freud to agree to his plan, Jung proposed to arrive in Munich the same evening so that he and Freud could spend the next day together. They agreed that it would be best if Bleuler did not know of their arrangement. Freud accepted Jung's advice. "I am happy as a lark about the little intrigue," he wrote.

Freud wrote to Bleuler to request a meeting in Munich. A flurry of letters and telegrams followed between Freud and Bleuler and Freud and Jung, full of precise travel schedules and a warning for Jung to keep out of Bleuler's sight. The date was set for December 26.

The talk between Freud and Bleuler was productive, and relations between them improved. Bleuler promised to join the International Psychoanalytic Association. "I came to a complete understanding with him," Freud wrote to Ferenczi, "and had achieved a good personal relationship. After all he is only a poor devil like ourselves and in need of a little love which perhaps has been neglected in certain quarters that matter to him," no doubt a reference to Bleuler's disappointment with Jung. Freud was convinced that the breach between Bleuler and Jung could be healed after Bleuler joined the organization.

Bleuler did apply for membership two weeks after his meeting with Freud, but the cordiality established in Munich did not last. Three months later Freud referred to Bleuler as a "nuisance" whose behavior had to be tolerated for the good of the movement. Jung reported that his relations with Bleuler were still tense.

Freud wrote that dealing with Bleuler was like "embracing a piece of linoleum. But we must bear it." But in less than a year Freud's patience snapped. Bleuler resigned from the Zurich society, and Freud acknowledged, finally, that the psychoanalytic movement could manage without him.

The day Freud and Jung spent in Munich following the Bleuler meeting was a happy one. "Jung was magnificent," Freud wrote to Ferenczi, "and did me a power of good." Freud talked to Jung about the problems with Adler and also expressed concern about Jung's excursions into mythology. He hoped that before long Jung would return to their fundamental work on neuroses. "There is the motherland where we have first to fortify our dominion against everything and everybody."

At the time, Freud considered the trip to Munich an unqualified success. He had apparently won Bleuler over and had achieved harmony and understanding with Jung. To Ferenczi, Freud exclaimed, "I am more than ever convinced that [Jung] is the man of the future."

---··◦∞◦··---

CHAPTER NINE

You Are a Dangerous Rival: 1911–1912

The debate was a thinly disguised trial; the charge was heresy. The verdict—guilty—was quickly pronounced. The punishment was excommunication, banishment. Sigmund Freud was the judge and jury, Alfred Adler the defendant.

As the year 1911 began, the situation with Adler worsened. He deviated so openly from the official line that he became a menace to the faith. Every utterance, every paper, every meeting of the Vienna society showed his divergence from Freud's teachings. Freud had to confront him, air their differences in public—and then get rid of him. The palace revolution, as Freud called it, would be stamped out.

Adler's dissension had gone beyond redemption. He was suggesting that the conscious mind, not the unconscious, was the center of the psyche, that personality was shaped by the social environment and not by the continuing effort to satisfy biological needs. That people were motivated by aggression, by a will to power, not by sex. And even that the sex act was motivated by aggressiveness and not by desire. These ideas had no place in psychoanalysis, and neither did the man who was proposing them.

Freud arranged for the "trial" as the first order of business for the new year. He scheduled a formal debate over four meetings of the Vienna branch of the International Psychoanalytic Association. Adler was to present his case on January 4 and February 1; Freud had February 8 and 22 for a rebuttal. Freud tore apart each of Adler's arguments in detail. What Adler touted as new ideas were trivial, and the rest of his work stemmed directly from psychoanalysis without due acknowledgment or credit to their source.

Wilhelm Stekel, attempting to act as peacemaker, argued that there really were no major differences between the positions of Adler and Freud, but Freud countered by saying that both he and Adler disagreed with Stekel's contention. "I feel the Adlerian teachings are incorrect," Freud said, "and therefore dangerous for the future development of psychoanalysis."

A few days later Adler and Stekel resigned as president and vice-president, respectively, of the Vienna society. Freud was asked by the membership to assume the presidency. He told Jung that he was taking the reins into his own hands and would keep a tighter hold on them this time.

The members of the Vienna society, in an independent gesture, voted unanimously for a resolution thanking Adler and Stekel for their efforts on behalf of the group and expressing the wish that they would remain affiliated with the society. This did not reflect Freud's views, however. He had won the first round by getting the dissenters out of office, and the next step was to force them out of the organization. "Naturally I am only waiting for an occasion to throw them both out," he wrote to Jung. In his heart, he added, he was finished with them. He was exasperated with all the members of the Vienna society—none of them would ever amount to much—but his hatred was reserved for Adler and Stekel, who, together, "might add up to one human being."

Over the next few months Freud appeared to reconsider his judgment of Stekel, who showed signs of toeing the official psychoanalytic line. Freud told Jung that Stekel was a "good-natured fellow" who perhaps was still devoted to the cause. Freud said he felt an obligation to Stekel, the kind one would feel toward a faithful family servant.

Freud's attitude toward Adler did not soften. By June he was able to report that he had succeeded in ousting him. Adler resigned as coeditor of the *Central Journal* and left the Vienna society, taking three members with him. He established a group he called the Society for Free Psychoanalysis. Freud was offended by the obvious implication that *his* psychoanalysis was not free.

Some of Freud's disciples asked if they could also attend Adler's meetings. Freud strongly opposed this practice. His members would have to make a clear choice between his group and Adler's. The matter was put to a vote and Freud won, but six more members resigned. In all, the break with Adler cost Freud about one-third of his Viennese supporters. Not all of those who left did so out of open support of Adler. Some chose to resign because they believed Freud was violating their scientific freedom of choice by restricting the ideas to which they could be exposed.

On the same evening that Freud lost the six members, three newcomers joined, including Sabina Spielrein from Zurich. She told Freud that he did not seem as malicious as she expected.

As Freud described the deepening confrontation with Adler and Stekel in his letters, Jung became alarmed. He knew that in their own way, the ideas he was developing contradicted Freud's teachings as much as Adler's did. Jung had to assume that a similar trial would one day befall him.

Jung was still unprepared for the break with his surrogate father. Something in him craved Freud's approval. In the summer of 1911 he reacted to a bit of praise from Freud by gushing about how overjoyed it made him feel. He told Freud that he was "very receptive to any recognition the father sees fit to bestow." His situation pained him greatly. On the one hand, Jung was increasingly driven by the challenge of elaborating his own views on libido deriving from his work in mythology, and he expected to publish them soon. On the other, he remained reluctant to take a public stance out of fear of Freud's reaction.

Freud certainly did not want to break with Jung. Adler was

expendable, but Jung was the son and heir. In March 1911 Freud wrote to Ludwig Binswanger: "When the empire I founded is orphaned, no one but Jung must inherit the whole thing." Freud recognized that Jung was exploring different paths and that the work in mythology was diverting him from the study of neuroses, sex-based libido, and the rest of orthodox psychoanalysis. Freud did not care for Jung's paper on the symbols of the libido or his questioning of Freud's definition. But Freud understood that these were temporary diversions, the young scholar flexing his muscles to see what he could achieve on his own. Such testing was common in every family, but loyal sons always returned to the fold. Freud was content to wait.

Yet Freud must have harbored doubts about Jung. However reluctant he may have been to admit it, he surely noticed the warning signs. Even before their first meeting five years earlier, Jung had told Freud that he was unable to accept fully the pivotal role of sex. The years had not diminished Jung's objections. And Jung's dreams of skulls, skeletons, and death, of Freud as an old man—their meaning was transparent to Freud. The incident in Bremen involving the peat-bog corpses? A mistake on Jung's part so obvious and ominous that Freud had fainted. Perhaps Freud had not wanted to see the signals—perhaps he had repressed some and misrepresented others—but certainly he knew a feeling of disquiet, of vague discomfort if not outright distrust.

There was Jung's irritating behavior with regard to Adler. Just when Freud was celebrating his victory over the heretic, Jung nearly ruined it all and placed Freud in an embarrassing position. A month after Freud reported to Jung his joy at forcing Adler out of the Vienna psychoanalysts' group, Jung received a letter from Adler charging that Jung was responsible for Adler's dismissal. Jung denied it. Indeed, Jung said he found Adler's loss to the psychoanalytic movement regrettable.

Jung wrote to Freud to tell him of the exchange of letters with Adler, and he asked Freud who could have started the rumor that he had demanded Adler's removal.

Freud was furious and dashed off a letter to Jung. Freud

knew precisely who had started the rumor—Adler himself! "I also know why," Freud wrote to Jung. "In writing you things which he knew you could easily refute, he was counting on the automatism of good manners. He knew you would say, 'No, on the contrary, sorry to hear about it.' And you let yourself be taken in."

Freud then pointed out that Adler had in his hands a letter from Jung, the president of the International Psychoanalytic Association, expressing regret at Adler's resignation, telling Adler what a loss it was. Think of the use to which Adler could put that, Freud said. The traitor had an official statement expressing, in effect, disapproval of Freud's actions, suggesting to Adler and the rest of the world that Freud and Jung disagreed over this matter. It was too late for Jung to undo the harm, Freud added, and he implored Jung to handle Adler in the future "with psychiatric caution."

Jung did not respond to this verbal flogging for four days, and his reply offered no apology for putting Freud in an awkward position. Jung did not blame Adler for precipitating the misunderstanding. He simply expressed annoyance at having been deceived but defended his expression of regret over Adler's resignation.

Jung told Freud that he had treated Adler with proper "psychiatric caution." He had reacted in accordance with accepted psychiatric belief: it was best not to argue with a paranoiac but to offer calm denials of any and all accusations. In time, Jung said, Adler would learn that Jung's position was far from his own. (That statement could just as easily have been intended for Freud.) Nothing more was said about the Adler affair, but Freud, who detected hidden meanings in most human acts, must have wondered what Jung's behavior signified.

Then there were the letters Emma Jung wrote to Freud during the fall of 1911, in which she seemed to be warning him about something. Freud had visited with the Jungs for four days in mid-September and had discussed his own marital situation with

Emma. He told her that there was nothing left of his marriage and that he was, therefore, resigned to his own death. His children were such a worry to him and subject to so many illnesses and mishaps that he wondered if the causes were not psychological. Emma suggested that he psychoanalyze the children, but Freud said he did not have time. He had to write and lecture and treat patients to earn an income so that the children would have a leisurely life.

Perhaps it was because Freud had been so personally revealing that Emma summoned up the courage to write to him about her own concerns. She confided to Freud that since his visit to Zurich she had been tormented by the conviction that things were not right between Freud and Jung. She was writing in the hope of improving their relations. She reminded Freud that he had said nothing about Jung's new work on the metamorphoses and symbols of the libido. Was he displeased with it? Was the problem something else altogether? "If so, please tell me what, dear Herr Professor; for I cannot bear to see you so resigned and I even believe that your resignation relates not only to your real children (it made a quite special impression on me when you spoke of it) but also to your spiritual sons; otherwise you would have so little need to be resigned."

Emma wrote to Freud again two weeks later. She told him that she believed that his talk about his children was intended just for her and referred, symbolically, to Jung. She also mentioned again Freud's failure to comment on Jung's libido book.

She told Freud how eagerly Jung awaited Freud's opinion and how often he had mentioned his worry that Freud would not like it. She recognized that Jung's trepidation was related to his father complex, which she felt was being resolved by his work on the book. She suggested that Freud had been right not to mention the book because that would have reinforced the father-son relationship.

Emma wrote of Freud's feeling of resignation about his own work. Evidently he had expressed the belief that, like his marriage, his work was at an end. She told Freud that he was ceding too much of the development and promotion of psychoanalysis to Jung. Why, she asked, should Freud give up at the very time he should be enjoying his success? He was not so old and still had many worthwhile ideas to pursue. He had struggled too hard not to savor the victory within his grasp.

Emma seemed to be cautioning Freud against his assumption that Jung would take over the movement, as a son might rightly be expected to run a family business. The son might have his own plans and goals. "Do not think of Carl with a father's feeling," she added, "but rather as one human being thinks of another, who like you has his own law to fulfill."

Freud wrote to Sandor Ferenczi that he replied to Emma Jung with affection but that he had no idea what she was trying to tell him. A Freud biographer speculated that Emma was "more perceptive and more prescient than the protagonists. Something was wrong." Unfortunately, Freud's letters to Emma have not survived.

Emma was correct about her husband's anxiety over Freud's reaction to the libido book. "I knew in advance," Jung wrote, "that its publication would cost me my friendship with Freud." He talked at length to Emma about his misgivings. She tried to reassure him that Freud would not object to Jung's revisionist views, but Jung was not convinced. He became so distraught in anticipation of Freud's opinion that he was unable to write for two months. He told Sabina Spielrein that Freud would never understand his work and would banish him as soon as the book was published.

Emma was also perceptive about Freud's continued dependence on Jung to play the role of the son. She pleaded with Freud to consider that Jung had his own identity, his own destiny to fulfill. They needed to redefine their relationship as colleagues instead of parent and child if they were to promote psychoanalysis together. Jung echoed these thoughts in a letter to Sabina. "[Freud] wants to give me love, while I want understanding. I want to be a friend on an equal footing, while he wants to have me as a son."

Jung revealed apprehension about his work in a letter to Freud early in 1911. The libido book was fascinating, and he felt confidence in its worth, but he acknowledged that it was a "risky business for an egg to try to be cleverer than the hen. Still, what is in the egg must eventually summon the courage to creep out. So you see what fantasies I must resort to in order to protect myself against your criticism."

Freud wrote that he could not understand why Jung should be afraid of his criticism. He was looking forward to reading more about Jung's extension of the concept of libido into the area of mythology.

Four months later Jung announced that he was incorporating ideas from astrology and the occult in his research. He described the new development in almost lyrical terms. "There are strange and wondrous things in these lands of darkness," Jung wrote, but Freud should not worry about "my wanderings in these infinitudes. I shall return laden with rich booty for our knowledge of the human psyche. For a while longer, I must intoxicate myself on magic perfumes in order to fathom the secrets that lie hidden in the abysses of the unconscious."

Freud confided his qualms about Jung's wanderings to Ferenczi, who shared Jung's interest in the occult. It was obvious, Freud wrote, that there was no restraining the two of them from such excursions. He hoped that Ferenczi would make the journey into those uncharted areas with Jung. As for himself, it was too dangerous. They would have to go without him.

Freud told Jung that although he should always follow his impulses, he would be criticized for it. He could be accused of mysticism, Freud said, which had no place in science. Jung's reputation, based on solid scientific work on dementia praecox, would protect him for a time. "Just don't stay in the tropical colonies too long," Freud warned. "You must reign at home"—that is, in Freud's realm, psychoanalysis, and not in any other.

A month later Jung told Freud that he was devoting most of his evenings to astrology and was even using horoscopes to treat his patients. He was uncovering the most remarkable things, which Freud would think so extraordinary that he probably would have a hard time believing them. For one patient Jung calculated the positions of the stars at the instant of her birth and reported that the result was a phenomenally accurate description of the character of her mother. That was significant, Jung said, because he had diagnosed the woman as suffering from a mother complex. Jung's enthusiasm for astrology was boundless. "I dare say that we shall one day discover in astrology a good deal of knowledge that has been intuitively projected into the heavens."

Whatever Jung was doing, it was certainly not science. Using signs of the zodiac to foretell personality? This was not a proper method for probing the unconscious mind. Freud did not scold Jung for his excesses, however, nor did he try to reason with him. He simply said that he would "promise to believe anything that can be made to look reasonable," although he would not do so with any pleasure.

Three months after that, Jung was the one to be surprised by a new dimension to Freud's research. At first Freud was mysterious and would say only that Jung would be amazed by his unusual, even uncanny, discoveries. Surely, Freud challenged, Jung was shrewd enough to guess what he was up to. But Jung could not guess. "Your letter has got me on tenterhooks because for all my 'shrewdness,' I can't quite make out what is going on so enigmatically behind the scenes." He implored Freud to reveal the secret.

Freud could not long contain his excitement. He was delving into the source of religion, a topic developed in his book *Totem and Taboo*. He had concluded that the origin of religion was related to the Oedipus complex, a point he claimed Jung had suggested in a paper on libido. But Jung had made no such point, and the reasons behind Freud's statement remain unclear.

Jung was distressed to hear about Freud's interest in the psychology of religion. It was too close to his own area. Jung was staking his claim to his own territory, fulfilling his own law independent of Freud's, only to find Freud shoving him aside. Was the father again to overshadow the son?

Freud finally commented on Jung's libido research two months after his visit to Zurich. He was glad to see that there were issues on which Jung agreed with Freud's public positions and also that there were points with which Freud could agree. But, referring to his own work on religion, Freud added, "it is a torment to me to think, when I conceive of an idea now and then, that I may be taking something away from you or appropriating something that might just have well been acquired by you. When this happens, I feel at a loss. Why in God's name did I allow myself to follow you into this field?"

Jung's concern that Freud's studies on religion would overlap his own work on mythology and symbolism was not eased by this letter. "You are a dangerous rival," Jung wrote, bringing out in the open the formerly unspoken competition between them. Not friends, not colleagues, but *rivals.* That single word then defined their relationship.

But that was the natural order of things, Jung assured Freud. That was progress; it could not be stopped. They were different people, and the differences between them would naturally be reflected in their work. But as Freud's junior, Jung believed he was destined to appear second best in their newly acknowledged rivalry, and this was difficult for him to accept.

Jung offered Freud a preview of the latest part of his book on mythology and libido in a letter that provided a hint, a clue— perhaps even another warning. Freud's definition of libido, restricting it to sexual energy, was too narrow for Jung to embrace. It had to be broadened to become a generalized psychic energy so that it could be applied to dementia praecox.

Freud demanded to know more precisely why Jung felt the need to extend the libido concept. That sort of disagreement had arisen before, Freud reminded him, when Jung claimed that Freud believed libido applied to *any* kind of desire. Not so; only the sexual drive could be called libido. That was a fundamental tenet of psychoanalysis, and to Freud there was no confusion about the meaning. Although Freud referred to a "misunderstanding" in his letter, he knew that what Jung was suggesting was not a revision or a modification but a basic departure. It was nothing short of heresy.

"It has not been a brilliant year for our cause," Freud wrote to Jung at the end of 1911. The final weeks of the year had brought more vexations, not the least of which was Jung's research. Freud noted only two bright spots in recent months—his visit to Jung in mid-September and the Third Psychoanalytic Congress, which convened in Weimar, Germany, just after that. The congress, with fifty-five members in attendance, was a great success, with none of the overt acrimony between the Viennese and the Swiss that had marred the previous meeting. Jung was elected by acclamation to another term as president of the International Psychoanalytic Association (his previous term would expire six months after the Weimar meeting). He announced that the organization boasted 106 members, evidence that psychoanalysis was gaining adherents throughout the world.

The papers presented at the conference were of a uniformly high quality and included several that have since become classics. Newspaper reporters attended several of the sessions. Otto Rank delivered a lecture entitled "The Motif of Nudity in Poetry and Legends," and the next day's newspaper noted that "interesting papers were read on nudity and other current topics." Reporters were discouraged from covering future congresses.

Freud's paper dealt with the importance of myths in human history, the first time he had talked publicly about the field in which Jung was laboring. In statements that foreshadowed Jung's notion of the collective unconscious, Freud told his audience that the unconscious mind contains not only material from the individual's past but also memories and vestiges from previous generations. He gave due credit to Jung and extolled his work on mythology. "Jung had excellent grounds for his assertion that the mythopoeic forces of mankind are not extinct, but that to this very day they give rise in the neuroses to the same psychical products as in the remotest past age." Jung's paper dealt with the symbols found in mythology and in the psychoses.

Freud and Jung appeared to be in harmony at Weimar. Any underlying tensions were not evident to the others. Ernest Jones said that one participant complained about the coarseness of Jung's jokes. "It's a healthy coarseness," Freud responded, defending his son and heir.

Emma Jung attended the meetings and can be seen in a group photograph sitting up straight in the front row, an enigmatic smile on her face. Jung stands behind her and slightly to her right. On her left, beyond a woman from Berlin wearing a large hat, is Toni Wolff, who looks tense, almost angry. Sabina Spielrein planned to come but declined because of an illness, which Jung said was psychosomatic in origin.

In the center of the second row in the photograph, clearly at the group's heart, stands Freud, looking every inch the patriarch. On his right is the loyal Ferenczi and on his left is Jung, but there is something odd about this trio. Freud dwarfs Ferenczi and appears almost a head taller than Jung! Freud posed for the picture while standing on a box, whereas Jung, still the dutiful son (who was some seven inches taller than Freud), stooped over.

By all accounts the conference was fruitful, but it was the last at which Freud and Jung would meet as friends. A month later Freud reminisced in a letter to Jung about the splendid days he had spent in Zurich and Weimar. "The exchange of ideas, the hopes and satisfactions that were the substance of those days stand out in all their purity." Jung, in his next letters to Freud, made no mention of their time together that September.

At the beginning of 1912 Freud wrote to Karl Abraham in Berlin: "We have a gloomy time in front of us." Disturbing news had come from Zurich. Freud and psychoanalysis were coming under attack in the city's newspapers. A series of inflammatory and misleading articles excoriated the "radical" notions from Vienna that allegedly had been foisted upon the Swiss by the local contingent of analysts. Jung was so stung by these revilements that he consulted an attorney to find out if he could sue for libel. The lawyer advised against it.

The attacks coincided with public revelations about Oskar Pfister, the Freudian loyalist and Protestant preacher in Zurich. His parishioners were indignant because he left his wife and embarked on an affair with a girl Jung described as "much too young and infantile." This was what happened when a man of the cloth became infected with Freudian teachings about sex—so declared the good burghers of the city. If a clergyman was not safe from this nefarious influence, who was?

The journalistic offensive continued throughout January and well into February, with no relief in savagery or intensity. "Zurich is seething," Jung wrote to Freud. Psychoanalysis was "the talk of the town." The attacks coalesced on Pfister. Critics of psychoanalysis had found a vulnerable spot, a chink in the armor, and were defaming both the pastor and the movement by spreading increasingly vicious rumors about his behavior.

Jung fought back by writing his own newspaper articles in defense of psychoanalysis. At first he signed them "Dr. J" but soon used his full name and title as president of the International Psychoanalytic Association. He lambasted his critics for having the poor taste to discuss such matters in print before a lay audience. Without proper training in psychoanalysis, even the most highly educated readers could not be expected to understand them. They were proper subjects for medical and psychoanalytic circles only. Further, Jung charged, much of what was being published in the newspapers about psychoanalysis was simply wrong. These people did not know what they were talking about.

Jung justified the concept of sexuality in neurosis by arguing that it had a "much wider meaning than the vulgar one," as anyone could verify from the books and articles he and Freud had written. He tried to shift the blame for the emphasis on sexuality to its source. "The sexual indelicacies which unfortunately occupy a necessarily large place in many psychoanalytic writings are not to be blamed on psychoanalysis itself. Our very exacting and responsible work merely brings these unlovely fantasies to light, but the blame for the existence of these sometimes repulsive and evil things must surely lie with the mendaciousness of our sexual morality."

The newspaper stories gradually subsided, but the damage to the reputation of psychoanalysis lingered long after the last word was printed. The effects were financially devastating for the Swiss analysts; many of their patients stopped coming. Even Jung's practice shrank. The secretary of the International Psychoanalytic Association, Franz Riklin, begged Freud to send some patients to Zurich. The campaign so undermined the movement that within two years, virtually all the Swiss analysts renounced their sinful past and abandoned the sexual foundation of psychoanalysis. Jung would be the first to recant.

Preparing articles to counter the newspaper scandal consumed much of Jung's time at the beginning of 1912. In addition, he was absorbed in his work on mythology and the libido, hurrying to complete his book. He took a brief trip to St. Moritz and spent a few days touring art galleries in Germany. Then, to make matters worse, he was bitten by a dog.

All this explains why he began the year as a "niggardly correspondent," keeping Freud waiting days, even weeks, for letters. "I have been racking my brains for a fortnight, wondering why I had received no answer from you," Freud wrote. Meanwhile, he received a note from Pfister reporting the dog bite. Pfister assumed that Freud knew of the incident, that Jung had told him. But Freud had not known, and he reproached Jung for his silence. Freud said that he understood Jung's reluctance to talk about it but would have preferred to learn of it from Jung and not from someone else. The question of why Jung had not told him nagged at Freud, and he suspected some unconscious motivation behind the omission.

Jung let three weeks pass between letters and then sent a brief note to let Freud know, as he put it, that he was still alive. Freud was miffed by the delay and the curtness of Jung's long-awaited communication. "I was very glad to receive a letter from you," Freud replied. "I am not fond of breaking habits and find no triumph in it."*

Jung commented on Freud's resentment of his habits as a correspondent. He confessed to being irresponsible but laid the blame on work, saying it captured all his libido. He was focusing on the problem of a son's incestuous feelings toward his mother. He asked Freud to be tolerant and promised to deliver wonderful findings from his descent into the unconscious realm of mothers, all for the greater glory of psychoanalysis.

But Freud was in no mood to be tolerant. He challenged Jung's assertion that he resented Jung's neglect of their correspondence. That assertion, Freud wrote, demanded a complete psychoanalytic explanation to determine Jung's unconscious feelings.

Freud admitted to being a demanding correspondent. He welcomed hearing from Jung and always replied immediately, but that would stop. "I disregarded your earlier signs of reluctance. This time it struck me as more serious; my suspicion was aroused by your refusal to inform me of the state of your health after the dog bite. I took myself in hand and quickly turned off my excess libido. I was sorry to do so, yet glad to see how quickly I managed it. Since then I have become undemanding and not to be feared." The message was clear: Freud would not bother Jung with further demands for letters.

But Freud was not finished. He complained that Jung had diverted too much energy from the International Psychoanalytic Association, investing it instead in mythology. The organization

---

*It has been suggested that Freud made an error, writing *Ihnen*, meaning "you," instead of *ihnen*, meaning "them" (which translates into English as "it"). Freud's unconscious mind was saying that he could find no triumph in *you*—in Jung. If Jung noticed the mistake, he made nothing of it.

was not functioning smoothly; Jung was inattentive to his duties. The various national societies were not kept informed of one another's activities because Jung failed to publish the *Bulletin* on schedule. Freud reminded Jung of all the sacrifices they had made to establish the association, the people they had alienated to do so. And it was not operating as Freud had hoped. He still had to spend too much time on details. That was Jung's job, and he was not doing it.

And there was the matter of the next congress, for which Jung had not made preparations. It would suit Freud if there was no meeting that year. It would leave him free to travel and relax during the month of September.

Although Freud believed that the formal structure of the psychoanalytic movement was weakening, he was even more concerned about the future. He had to ensure that psychoanalysis would be in good hands "when the time comes."

"Your letter has made me very pensive," Jung responded, before launching a litany of refutation. The failure to publish the *Bulletin* regularly was the fault of Riklin, the association's secretary, who had neglected to carry out Jung's instructions. Jung promised to fire Riklin if such omissions continued.

As for the congress, that was not Jung's fault either. He was required to do annual military service with the Swiss army and had not been told when he would have to report. Until he knew those dates, he could not schedule the conference, for no one would want to hold it without the president in attendance.

With regard to the remainder of Freud's quarrels—notably devoting insufficient time to the association—Jung offered two excuses. First, his responsibilities in editing the *Yearbook* were substantial, and second, his work in mythology was so exhausting that it allowed no further fragmentation of his energy. That work had priority and would, in the long run, be more important for psychoanalysis than anything else he might do. Freud would surely understand once the book was published.

And the dog bite? Well, the matter was too inconsequential. Had it been a serious illness, something that might have jeopardized the progress of their work, of course Jung would have mentioned it. He was not deliberately neglecting Freud but was simply too busy. Did Freud mistrust him? If so, there was no basis for it. True, his opinions about some aspects of psycho-analysis diverged from Freud's, but that was attributable to the difficulty of discussing such complicated issues through the mail. Surely Freud would not take offense over a difference of opinion.

Jung wrote that he was always ready to modify his opinions in line with the judgments of those who were wiser and more experienced, but heresy ran in his blood. If it hadn't, he would never have allied himself with Freud in the first place. Surely Freud did not want only passive followers. "One repays a teacher badly," Jung quoted from Nietzsche, "if one remains only a pupil."

Freud replied the day he received Jung's letter. "Why so 'pensive' when the situation is so simple?" Jung had satisfac-torily answered Freud's complaints about the management of the association. With regard to his lapses in correspondence, that, too, had been resolved. "You make it clear to me," Freud wrote, "that you don't wish to write to me at present, and I reply that I am trying to make the privation easy for myself. Isn't that my right? Isn't it a necessary act of self-defense?"

Otherwise, Freud said, they were in agreement about every-thing. Their personal relationship was based on the "indestruc-tible foundation" of their shared work in psychoanalysis. Freud had hoped to build an intimate friendship on that foundation. Wasn't that something they should continue to try to develop?

Freud also expressed accord with Jung's need to be intellec-tually independent and with the quotation from Nietzsche. Freud did not think he had ever attempted to squelch Jung's indepen-dence. He reminded Jung that Adler had made the same com-plaint, and they both knew that had been Adler's neurosis speaking. "Still," Freud wrote, "if you think you want greater freedom from me, what can I do but give up my feeling of urgency about our relationship, occupy my unemployed libido elsewhere and bide my time until you discover that you can tolerate greater intimacy?"

But Freud continued to worry the point. He asked again why Jung was so troubled by these matters. Did he think Freud was looking for another son and heir? Did he expect Freud to have found a replacement so quickly? If not, then all was well between them. Freud assured Jung of his continuing affection. Jung should think of him as a friend, even if Jung did not write very often.

CHAPTER TEN

The Rest Is Silence:
1912–1913

The second installment of Jung's work on the libido was scheduled for publication in the *Yearbook*. This was the part that would propose new definitions of *libido* and *incest*. Few letters had passed between Freud and Jung in the previous month. Freud wrote to say he was eager to read Jung's paper, and he reminded Jung of the Nietzsche quotation, calling it, in English, Jung's "declaration of independence." Freud added that Jung should not be concerned about Freud's reaction to the paper. He was capable of considering Jung's ideas impartially, and if he could not accept them initially, he would wait until they became clear.

Jung had described the conclusions of his research in three letters to Freud prior to the paper's publication. His deviation from orthodox psychoanalysis was striking. Jung proposed that the Oedipal drama not be taken as literally as Freud believed. Children did not lust after parents of the opposite sex; girls did not want to sleep with their fathers and boys did not want to sleep with their mothers. These alleged incestuous wishes were symbols and fantasies. Jung admitted that boys developed an intense attachment to their mothers, but that was not because of sexual needs. Jung explained it in terms of a generalized dependence children feel toward their mothers.

Mothers are protective and nurturing figures. The Oedipal symbolism, Jung thought, served as a warning to prevent "psychological incest" between parent and child. It was vital that "children and parents should respect scrupulously their differences of personality and need, be free from spiritual bondage, and live their own lives." The purpose of the incest myth was for sons to free themselves psychologically from their mothers, and daughters from their fathers, so that the children could assume their individual roles in life.

Thus Jung explained his position to Freud, the results of his long and concentrated period of work. For eight days he heard nothing. Finally he sent Freud a note. "I hope nothing untoward has happened that would account for your delay in answering my last letter. If I have the assurance that there are no weightier reasons behind the delay, I shall naturally go on waiting and not make any exorbitant demands on your time and nervous energy."

Jung's note and Freud's response to Jung's work must have crossed in the mail. It is likely that Jung received Freud's reaction later on the same day he wrote the note.

Freud was puzzled. He could not understand why Jung had forsaken his views. As for Jung's new ideas, Freud considered them repugnant, regressive, and disastrously similar to the heretic Adler's.

Nearly three weeks passed before Jung wrote to profess grief at witnessing the powerful emotional forces Freud was bringing to bear against Jung's innovations. Jung had no choice but to defend his ideas because they were supported by reason. The comparison with Adler was a "bitter pill; I swallow it without a murmur. Evidently this is my fate." Jung reminded Freud that he had undertaken this work with nothing more in mind than supporting Freud's view—which he now called the old view—but was forced by the evidence he had uncovered in mythology to come to a different interpretation. He hoped they might be able to reach an understanding about any such differences in the future, but in the meantime, Jung would have to go his own way. "You know how obstinate we Swiss are."

❖

A more prosaic misunderstanding arose between Freud and Jung at about the same time. Freud mentioned that he would be paying a visit to Ludwig Binswanger at the end of May. Binswanger had left the Burghölzli Hospital and was director at Bellevue, a private clinic at Kreuzlingen, near the town of Konstanz, less than 40 miles from Jung's home. Freud wrote that the trip would be only for the weekend, but the implication was clear that he hoped Jung would offer to come to see him at Kreuzlingen.

The reason for Freud's visit was a long-delayed promise he had made to see Binswanger. The matter had assumed some urgency; Binswanger had just undergone surgery for a malignant tumor and was not expected to survive. (As it turned out, he lived another fifty years.) After Freud returned to Vienna he wrote to Jung that the visit to Binswanger had been pleasant, but he was disappointed that he had not heard from Jung while he was so close by.

Jung wrote two weeks later. "The fact that you felt no need to see me during your visit to Kreuzlingen must, I suppose, be attributed to your displeasure at my development of the libido theory." Jung was wrong, Freud said. The reason he had not journeyed on from Kreuzlingen to Zurich had nothing to do with their current professional disputes. Freud outlined in considerable detail why he had no time to ago to Zurich, but, he added, Jung should have come to him.

Freud had not specifically asked Jung to come—he considered that an imposition—but he felt Jung should have thought of it on his own. It pained Freud that Jung was misinterpreting his motives. A few months ago, Freud suggested, Jung would not have drawn such a hasty and unfortunate conclusion.

Neither man wrote for six weeks, the longest period they had been out of contact. Then Jung sent a cryptic note to say that he understood Freud's "Kreuzlingen gesture" and that only the ultimate success or failure of Jung's ideas would show if Freud's policy was correct.

Freud sent Jung's puzzling letter to Ferenczi, citing it as an example of how active Jung's neurosis had become. Freud told Ferenczi that the effort to integrate Jews and non-Jews in the promotion of psychoanalysis had collapsed. "They separate themselves like oil and water."

Freud wrote to Karl Abraham in Berlin, reminding Abraham of his warning to Freud that he should not trust Jung. The "old prophecy of yours, which I had wanted to ignore, is being confirmed."

To Ernest Jones Freud wrote that Jung's letter was a disavowal of their friendly relations. Freud admitted to being disappointed, but he "resolved to let things go and not try to influence him more."

And to Binswanger Freud said, "I am completely indifferent. Warned by earlier experiences, and proud of my elasticity, I withdrew my libido from him months ago, at the first signs, and I miss nothing now." Later he said he would be interested in working toward a public reconciliation with Jung, but that "inwardly nothing will change anymore."

The relationship was over, and both Freud and Jung knew it. If anyone harbored doubts, those doubts were dispelled by what Jung did next. He went to America and made his heresy public.

Jung had been invited to deliver a series of lectures at Fordham University in New York City. He accepted the invitation even though it meant being away in September, the month when the psychoanalytic congresses were usually held. He believed he should go, he told Freud, to win converts for the cause, and suggested rescheduling the congress for mid-August in Munich.

Freud congratulated Jung on the invitation but .disagreed about the psychoanalytic conference. An August date would interfere with his traditional holiday, and the heat in Munich then would be unbearable. So little had happened since the previous congress that there really was no need for another one. Jung's invitation provided ample justification for skipping a year, Freud added, and his lectures in the United States would serve the broader interests of the movement. That was one of the worst predictions Freud ever made.

By the time Jung informed Freud, in August, that his American lectures were prepared, both the so-called Kreuzlingen gesture and Jung's incest paper had come between them. Freud no longer expected any benefits for psychoanalysis from Jung's talks in New York. Jung said that he expected to advance "tentative suggestions for modifying certain theoretical formulations." Freud knew what that meant. Jung planned to give the American audience *his* version of psychoanalysis, not Freud's. The son was taking over, openly challenging the dangerous rival.

Before departing for New York, Jung relinquished his responsibility for editing the current issue of the *Yearbook*, turning it over to Bleuler. He also raised the question of continuing as president of the International Psychoanalytic Association. Could he remain the head of an organization whose teachings he could not support? He told Freud he would leave the matter for the next congress. Finally, in what could be seen as a direct threat, Jung said that he would "let the association decide whether deviations are to be tolerated or not."

Jung delivered nine lectures on what he called "the theory of psychoanalysis." He was a great success, and his hearty, open, boisterous manner was appreciated by the New Yorkers. He also spoke to groups at the New York Psychiatric Institute and the New York Academy of Medicine and gave a daily two-hour seminar at Bellevue Hospital for two weeks. Reporters for *The New York Times* interviewed Jung and published a three-quarter-page photograph and a long article. He toured the country for eight weeks, visiting Chicago, Baltimore, and Washington, making a highly favorable impression wherever he went.

It was not only Jung's personal appeal that was responsible for his triumph in America. It was the message he preached in his lectures. He stated that psychoanalysis had changed since Freud first proposed it and that there was now considerably less emphasis on sex. This declaration was received with much relief.

Jung did not say, however, that it was he and not Freud who was responsible for the change.

Jung explained to his audiences—composed mostly of psychiatrists and neurologists—that the libido was no longer equated solely with the sex drive. It was, instead, a generalized psychic energy. He talked about his innovations in incest theory and contradicted Freudian ideas on the origin of neuroses.

Neuroses, Jung said, did not have their roots in childhood traumas and conflicts but rather rose out of current situations and events. Thus it was not necessary to delve into the past to treat a patient's neurotic disorder. Furthermore, Jung said, all of these changes in psychoanalytic theory and practice had resulted from the efforts of what he called the "Zurich school."

Jung gave credit to Freud for his early work and his courage to be dogmatic and immoderate—faint praise, indeed. He insisted that he was not really deviating from orthodox psychoanalysis but was defending Freud. In introductory remarks Jung wrote for the published version of his American lectures, he said that the talks were an "attempt to outline my attitude to the guiding principles which my honored teacher Sigmund Freud has evolved. It has been wrongly suggested that my attitude signifies a 'split' in the psychoanalytic movement. I am far indeed from regarding a modest and temporary criticism as a 'falling away' or a schism; on the contrary, I hope thereby to promote the continued flowering and fructification of the psychoanalytic movement."

On the day Jung began his lectures in New York, Emma Jung sent Freud an advance copy of the long-awaited second part of Jung's work on the symbols of the libido, scheduled for publication in the next issue of the *Yearbook*. Freud started to read it but could not finish. He wrote to Ernest Jones that when he reached the exact page on which he knew Jung had gone wrong, he had no interest in reading further.

Jung wrote to Freud in mid-November of 1912, after his return from the United States. His letter was boastful and daring, beginning with the casual remark that he probably should have written from New York but had been too busy. And once he had returned home, he had neither the time nor the inclination to write to Freud about the trip.

Jung praised the vitality of the psychoanalytic movement in the United States. It was full of intelligent people, and Jung was able to do much to advance the cause. His lectures had been quite well received. Naturally, he reported to Freud, he included some of his own views, and his version of psychoanalysis gained many converts among those made uneasy by Freud's emphasis on sexuality. He promised to send Freud a copy of his lectures and expressed the hope that Freud would accept his innovations.

Then, abruptly, Jung's tone changed. "I feel no need to let you down provided you can take an objective view of our common endeavors." He regretted Freud's supposition that Jung's modifications of psychoanalysis had been initiated by a personal resistance to Freud. "Your Kreuzlingen gesture has dealt me a lasting wound. I prefer a direct confrontation. With me it is not a question of caprice but of fighting for what I hold to be true. In this matter no personal regard for you can restrain me."

Nevertheless, Jung wrote that he had no desire to end their personal relationship. He had always tried to be fair to Freud and would continue to do so regardless of the outcome. He preferred that their relations remain friendly because he owed Freud much, but he would insist on being judged objectively, unhampered by personal feelings. After all, Jung had accomplished more for the movement than all of Freud's other followers combined. "I can only assure you that there is no resistance on my part," Jung wrote, "unless it be my refusal to be treated like a fool riddled with complexes."

"Dear Dr. Jung," Freud wrote three days later, abandoning the salutation "Dear Friend." "I greet you on your return from America, no longer as affectionately as on the last occasion in Nuremberg—you have successfully broken me of that habit." Freud had read of Jung's success in America with interest and satisfaction. But regarding Jung's modified version of psychoanalysis being more palatable to the Americans, that was nothing to boast about. Obviously, the more Jung omitted of orthodox psychoanalysis, the more it would appeal to some, but the future of the movement did not lie in America. Jung's so-called victory there was of minor importance to the cause.

As for Freud being able to judge Jung and his work objectively, certainly Jung could count on that. Consequently, Jung could depend on the continuance of their personal relationship. Freud assured Jung that there was nothing wrong with deviations and that he, too, felt the need to maintain their collaboration. However, Freud added, he was annoyed about Jung's repeated references to the Kreuzlingen incident. He did not understand it and found it "incomprehensible and insulting."

Freud said that he looked forward to receiving a copy of Jung's American lectures. Perhaps that would help to clarify the nature of Jung's innovations, which, Freud maintained, the lengthy paper for the *Yearbook* had not. Freud also mentioned a disturbing letter that was circulating among the Vienna society, in which Adler described his impressions of the Zurich group, charging that the Swiss were fleeing in panic from the idea of sexuality. Adler said that he was unable to keep the Swiss from appropriating his ideas, an allegation that confirmed Freud's growing distrust of Jung.

The remainder of Freud's letter to Jung was devoted to association business, specifically Stekel's duties as editor of the *Central Journal*. Although his editorial policies were increasingly at odds with Freud's views, he refused to give up his position. Freud decided to let Stekel have the journal and to start a replacement as the official organ for the psychoanalytic movement. Freud noted that he should have left the matter to Jung as president of the association, but Jung had gone to America without leaving anyone in charge. As a result, Freud had been forced to deal with Stekel himself. The new periodical would be edited by Ferenczi and Otto Rank, but before Freud could add Jung's name to the masthead he would need an official statement formally endorsing the new journal and renouncing the old one.

Uncharacteristically, Jung responded to Freud's long letter on the same day he received it. He would continue to pursue his own ideas, he said. He would sever relations with Stekel's journal but did not want to be associated formally with the new one. "Since you have disavowed me so thoroughly, my collaboration can hardly be acceptable."

Jung said that he would prefer to work with Freud on more neutral ground, such as the *Yearbook*, of which Jung agreed to remain editor unless Freud became too restrictive. Jung would let tolerance rule in the pages of the *Yearbook*, so that analysts could develop their ideas in their own way. It is only when people are free, Jung lectured, that they are able to perform at their highest level.

Jung concluded on an angry and defensive note: "Adler's letter is stupid chatter and can safely be ignored. We aren't children here. If Adler ever says anything sensible or worth listening to I shall take note of it, even though I don't think much of him as a person. As in my work heretofore, so now and in the future, I shall keep away from petty complexes and do unflinchingly what I hold to be true and right."

In his capacity as president of the International Psychoanalytic Association, Jung requested an emergency meeting of the heads of the various branch societies to discuss Freud's proposal to abandon the *Central Journal* to Stekel and replace it with the *International Journal*. The meeting was scheduled for November 24 at the Park Hotel in Munich. Present were Freud and Jung, Ernest Jones, Karl Abraham, Franz Riklin, Leonhard Seif from Munich, and J. H. W. van Ophuijsen of Holland.

In dispatching the invitations, Jung committed a psychopathological slip. Jones was in Florence, Italy, and had supplied Jung with his address, but Jung sent the invitation to Jones's family home in Wales. Jung also gave the wrong date for the meeting—one day later than it was to be held. Jones learned about the meeting from other sources and arrived on time. He reported that Jung seemed surprised to see him. "The look of astonishment on Jung's face told me the mistake belonged to the class called 'parapraxes' [Freud's term for chance acts, mistakes, and slips of the tongue], but when I told Freud of Jung's unconscious slip he replied: 'A gentleman should not do such things even unconsciously.' "

The group met at nine o'clock in the morning. Jung proposed that they accept Freud's idea for the new journal without further discussion. Freud, however, insisted on recounting his problems with Stekel and explaining at length why he felt the change was necessary. No one dissented, and the issue was resolved in a couple of hours.

Freud and Jung went for a long walk together. Freud asked Jung to explain his continual references to the "Kreuzlingen gesture," as Jung called it. Jung said that he had been unable to dismiss his resentment of the fact that Freud had not informed him of the trip to Kreuzlingen in time for Jung to arrange to meet him there. Jung had not received Freud's letter until Monday, the day Freud left Kreuzlingen to return to Vienna.

Freud agreed that his behavior appeared, on the surface, to be suspicious. If Freud wanted Jung to come to Kreuzlingen, then he should have notified him by the previous Friday or Saturday. But Freud was certain he had done just that. Something was amiss. Suddenly Jung remembered that he had been away over the weekend. That explained why he had not seen Freud's letter until Monday!

Freud continued to question Jung about his motives. Why had he not examined the postmark or asked Emma when the letter arrived rather than making irresponsible charges against Freud? Did Jung's resentment derive from something else, something he could not admit to himself but was displacing onto the Kreuzlingen trip?

Jung apologized. He confessed that there were nasty and difficult aspects to his personality. Freud was not about to let the matter rest there. As Ernest Jones recalled, Freud also had "steam to let off and did not spare [Jung] a good fatherly lecture. Jung accepted all the criticisms and promised to reform."

Freud felt that the Munich meeting had been satisfying. The journal problem was solved, and there was reason to believe that Jung would be easier to deal with. Freud knew that they could not recapture their former closeness, but he hoped they would maintain a cordial professional relationship. As a result of these events, Freud was content and jovial at lunch with the group.

During the meal, conversation turned to a paper published by Abraham about the Egyptian pharaoh Amenhotep. Abraham explained Amenhotep's revolutionary accomplishments as an outgrowth of his hostility toward his father. That was why, Abraham contended, Amenhotep had scratched out his father's name wherever it was inscribed and put his own in its place. Abraham interpreted all the pharaoh's achievements—in art, religion, and poetry—in terms of his death wish toward his father.

Jung protested vigorously against this interpretation. Other pharaohs had erased their fathers' names, too, believing that they had the right to do so because they were incarnations of the same god. Yet although they had replaced their fathers' names, they had not created anything, as Amenhotep had done. Jung said that Abraham's arguments denigrated Amenhotep's accomplishments, which had nothing to do with a death wish.

Freud changed the subject, or so it seemed at first. He mentioned that Jung had erased his surrogate father's name. Freud said that Jung and other Swiss analysts published articles on psychoanalysis in Swiss journals and failed to credit Freud properly. Not only were they dismantling his work through Jung's innovations, but they were also deleting his name from the movement.

Jung remarked that he thought it no longer necessary to mention Freud's name in print; everyone knew that Freud was the founder of psychoanalysis. But Freud was not satisfied. "He persisted," Ernest Jones wrote, "and I remember thinking he was taking the matter rather personally." Then Freud fell over in a dead faint.

"I picked him up," Jung recalled, "and carried him into the next room, and laid him on a sofa. As I was carrying him, he half came to, and I shall never forget the look he cast at me. In his weakness he looked at me as if I were his father."

When Freud revived, he said, "How sweet it must be to die." Freud recovered and spent the rest of the afternoon with

Jung. Although neither man wrote about their discussion, they presumably made some attempt at a reconciliation. Before Freud boarded his train at five o'clock, Jung assured him, "You will find me fully on the side of the cause."

A few days later Freud wrote to the American psychiatrist James Jackson Putnam about the Munich meeting. "Everybody was charming to me, including Jung. A talk between us swept away a number of unnecessary personal irritations. I hope for further successful cooperation. Theoretical differences need not interfere. However, I shall hardly be able to accept his modifications of the libido theory since all my experience contradicts his position."

Lou Andreas-Salomé, a new member of the Vienna society and later a close friend of Freud's, confided to her daily journal that "Freud has returned almost too refreshed and content from the trip to Munich. Is the understanding with Jung really such a certainty?"

No psychoanalyst, least of all Freud, could ignore the symbolism in his second fainting spell in Jung's presence, and the episode became the topic of much speculation. On both occasions, the loss of consciousness had been preceded by a spirited discussion of the death wish. In Munich, as in the previous occasion in Bremen, Jung had criticized Freud for placing too much emphasis on that notion. As Jung recalled, "the fantasy of father murder was common to both cases."

There was another interesting twist. Freud had on two occasions experienced heart palpitations while dining in the same Munich hotel in the company of Wilhelm Fliess, with whom he had had a deep friendship before meeting Jung. Writing about these nervous symptoms to Ernest Jones, Freud speculated that there was "some piece of unruly homosexual feeling at the root of the matter."

Like heart palpitations, fainting was an indication of anxiety, and this realization prompted Freud to subject himself to considerable self-analysis. He suggested several possible explanations in a letter to Binswanger:

My attack in Munich was surely provoked by psychogenic elements, which received strong somatic reinforcements (a week of troubles, a sleepless night, the equivalent of a migraine, the day's tasks). I had had several such attacks; in each case there were similar contributory causes, often a bit of alcohol for which I have no tolerance. Among the psychic elements there is the fact that I had had a quite similar seizure in the same place in Munich, on two previous occasions, four and six years ago. In the light of a most careful diagnosis, it seems scarcely possible to attribute my attacks to a more serious cause, for instance a weak heart. Repressed feelings, this time directed against Jung, as previously against a predecessor of his [Fliess], naturally play a main part.

Freud's fainting spells may have also revealed an inability to tolerate the intense hostility he felt toward Jung. On both occasions he believed that he hated Jung because of what he perceived as Jung's death wish toward him. Freud was convinced that fainting symbolized death. By losing consciousness in Jung's presence, Freud may have been symbolically making reparations or atoning for his hatred.

Also, the act of fainting could be taken as Freud's attempt to remove himself from an unpleasant or threatening situation. By fainting, Freud abandoned his position in the discussion in a dramatic way, telling Jung that their disagreement was of great importance.

Jung viewed the incidents less charitably, interpreting the fainting spells simply as Freud's desire to surrender, to give up their personal confrontation. In Jung's opinion, Freud could avoid the unpleasantness by fainting. Freud "could not stand a critical word," Jung wrote. "Just like a woman. Confront her with a disagreeable truth: she faints."

Two days after the Munich meeting Jung wrote a contrite letter to Freud, saying that he had only just come to understand Freud and to realize how different they were. That recognition would radically alter his attitude in the future. Jung assured Freud that he would not abandon their friendship, and he asked Freud to forgive him for his mistakes. If only Jung had understood their true natures earlier, he could have prevented Freud's many disappointments in his behavior.

Jung expressed concern about Freud's return trip to Vienna. Had the night train ride been difficult? Would he please let Jung know how he was feeling? Jung was feeling so abject that he even expressed his willingness to contribute to the new journal. He mentioned several organizational matters to which he was diligently attending and closed the letter with the hope that all was well with Freud and his family.

Freud's reply, although friendly, was not effusive. He did not indicate that all was forgiven or that their relationship might regain its former level of intimacy. He thanked Jung for his "friendly letter" and said that it was clear that Jung had rid himself of certain beliefs and misconceptions about Freud. That action, Freud said, encouraged him to hope for the best in their future collaboration.

But Freud recognized that the path would not be smooth. He wrote:

> Believe me, it was not easy for me to moderate my demands on you; but once I had succeeded in doing so, the swing in the other direction was not too severe, and for me our relationship will always retain an echo of our past intimacy. I believe we shall have to lay by a fresh store of benevolence toward one another, for it is easy to see that there will be controversies between us and one always finds it rather irritating when the other party insists on having an opinion of his own.

The fainting attack had not been serious, Freud added, no more so than the one in Bremen. He diagnosed it as the result of a migraine headache, although he accepted the idea of a psychological component, which he did not have time to investigate. He told Jung of the anxiety attacks he had suffered while with Fliess at the same hotel and called them "a bit of neuroses that I ought really to look into."

Five days later, on December 3, 1912, Jung lashed out at Freud with a savagery never before displayed. It was a brutal assault with no prefatory pleasantries. A line boldly scrawled across the top of the page warned: "This letter is a brazen attempt to accustom you to my style. So look out!" Jung noted Freud's reference to his "bit of neuroses" with regard to the fainting episodes. Freud should take his neurosis seriously, Jung said, because it had led to the "semblance of voluntary death." Jung felt that he had suffered because of Freud's neurosis throughout their relationship, although Freud had been unaware of it.

If Freud would look at the situation clearly, without the blinders of his neurosis, he would see Jung's work differently. As it was, he misjudged Jung's ideas and was unlikely to comprehend them. Jung demanded again that he and his work be evaluated in objective and intellectual terms rather than emotional ones.

Jung reminded Freud of two other incidents involving Freud's neurosis. One was in Freud's own book *The Interpretation of Dreams*, where he confessed to the neurosis and the need for treatment. The other incident had occurred on the voyage to America when Jung analyzed Freud's dreams. Freud had refused to supply some clarifying information for fear of losing his authority. "These words are engraved in my memory," Jung wrote, "as a symbol of everything to come."

Jung insisted that from now on he would address Freud in the same direct manner he would use with any friend, and he hoped that Freud would not be offended by his "Helvetic bluntness." He begged Freud to accept his comments as an effort to be honest. Freud should not "apply the depreciatory Viennese criterion of egoistic striving for power or heaven knows what other insinuations from the world of the father complex." That, Jung said, was all he had been hearing as the explanation for his innovations. He had come to the conclusion that most psychoanalysts use psychoanalysis as a tool for devaluing the work of others, and such thinking caused him much apprehension about the future of the movement.

Freud answered this remarkable letter at once but devoted most of his reply to association business. He did say that he had no objection to Jung's announced new style; frankness was permissible between analysts. Freud, too, was disturbed by controversies and arguments over novel ideas but was not sure how to prevent them unless each analyst focused more on his or her own neuroses rather than on those of colleagues. The only point in Jung's letter that Freud specifically denied was the accusation that Jung had been harmed by Freud's neurosis. Not so, claimed Freud.

Over the next nine days, from December 7 to 16, several innocuous letters passed between them that dealt with organizational affairs. But on December 16 Freud caught Jung in a revealing slip of the pen. Jung had written, "Even Adler's cronies do not regard me as one of yours." He had meant to say "as one of *theirs*." Freud asked Jung if he were objective enough to analyze this mistake without becoming angry.

Jung exploded with rage. "May I say a few words to you in earnest?" Jung wrote, plunging on to express his "honest and absolutely straightforward view of the situation." Freud erred, Jung said, in treating followers as though they were patients. "In that way you produce either slavish sons or impudent puppies." Not so with Jung. *He* was too objective about the situation to be deceived by Freud's trick of uncovering symptoms in the simplest acts, of reducing his followers to the level of children who were expected to blush and confess their imperfections and transgressions, while Freud remained in the domineering and commanding position as father to the brood.

> You see, my dear Professor, so long as you hand out this stuff I don't give a damn for my symptomatic actions; they shrink to nothing in comparison with the formidable beam in my brother Freud's eye. I am not in the least neurotic—touch wood! If ever you should rid yourself entirely of your complexes and

stop playing the father to your sons and instead of aiming continually at their weak spots took a good look at your own for a change, then I will mend my ways and at one stroke uproot the vice of being in two minds about you. Do you *love neurotics* enough to always be at one with yourself? I shall continue to stand by you publicly while maintaining my own views, but privately shall start telling you in my letters what I really think of you. I consider this procedure only decent. No doubt you will be outraged by this peculiar token of friendship, but it may do you good all the same.

Freud's immediate reaction, as he told Ernest Jones, was a feeling of humiliation. Four days later, however, he wrote a mild reply to Jung that gave no indication of his pain. But Freud did not mail the letter. On reflection, he decided that something stronger was needed, and two weeks later, on January 3, 1913, he sent his final reply to Jung:

Your letter cannot be answered. It creates a situation that would be difficult to deal with in a personal talk and totally impossible in correspondence. It is a convention among us analysts that none of us need feel ashamed of his own bit of neurosis. But one who while behaving abnormally keeps shouting that he is normal gives ground for the suspicion that he lacks insight into his illness. Accordingly, I propose that we abandon our personal relations entirely. I shall lose nothing by it for my only emotional tie with you has long been a thin thread—the lingering effect of past disappointments.

Jung replied three days later: "I accede to your wish that we abandon our personal relations, for I never thrust my friendship on anyone. You yourself are the best judge of what this moment means to you. 'The rest is silence.' "*

*A quotation from *Hamlet*.

CHAPTER ELEVEN

We Are at Last Rid of Them: The Final Years

*F*reud and Jung met for the last time in September 1913, nine months after their personal correspondence ceased. The occasion was the Fourth Psychoanalytic Congress, which was held in Munich.

The circumstances were awkward. Despite the harsh words that had passed between them, they were forced to work together. Jung retained his position as president of the International Psychoanalytic Association and editor of the *Yearbook*. His reference to "silence" at the conclusion of his last letter applied only to the personal side of the relationship with Freud. They continued to exchange notes—formal, precise, and stiff—on association and editorial matters.

As the date of the congress approached, concern was growing among the Viennese analysts about how best to deal with Jung. The situation was potentially explosive. If Jung and the rest of the Swiss group withdrew from the association, a rift would likely open among the remaining members. That had occurred after Adler and his followers departed. Also, the divisiveness would provide additional evidence for all the world to see of the splits in the movement. And what if Jung was able to win acceptance of his innovations? That would mean the dissolution of psychoanalysis as Freud had created it.

Throughout the summer months Freud spent many hours discussing the problem with Ferenczi and Jones. They agreed that a working relationship with Jung should be upheld and that efforts should be made to prevent an open quarrel at the congress. The Viennese contingent was advised to secure reservations at the same hotel where the Swiss were staying to avoid the outward appearance of discord between the two groups.

Freud's daughter Anna recalled this period as the only time she saw her father depressed. His animosity toward Jung made the thought of a meeting with him hard to bear. Freud poured out his feelings in letters to colleagues and friends. When Jung announced a five-week lecture tour to the United States in March, Freud wrote to Abraham, "Jung is in America. He is doing more for himself than for psychoanalysis. I have greatly retreated from him, and have no more friendly thoughts for him. His bad theories do not compensate me for his disagreeable character. He is following in Adler's wake, without being as consistent as that pernicious creature."

Three months later Freud wrote to Abraham, "Jung is crazy, but I have no desire for a separation and should like to let him wreck himself first." To Putnam in Boston, Freud mentioned the affection he had once felt for Jung and how much he had overestimated him. He told G. Stanley Hall at Clark University that Jung was no longer his friend and that their collaboration would probably not last much longer. That was regrettable, Freud added, but unavoidable.

Freud's most caustic comments about Jung were reserved for Sabina Spielrein, Jung's former mistress, who had since become a Freudian analyst. In May 1913, Freud told her that he was

> sorry to hear that you are consumed with longing for [Jung], and this at a time when I am on such bad terms with him, having almost reached the conclusion that he is unworthy of all the interested concern I have bestowed on him. I feel he is about to destroy the work that we have built up so laboriously, and achieve nothing better himself. Quite apart from our scientific differences, his personal behavior merits severe criticism.

Freud suggested to Sabina that she must still be in love with Jung because she had not yet "brought to light the hatred he merits." On August 28, fewer than two weeks before the congress, Freud told her that he would not present her compliments to Jung when they met, as she had asked him to do. He went on to comment on her pregnancy. Freud said he was "cured of the last shred of my predilection for the Aryan cause, and would like to take it that if [your] child turns out to be a boy he will develop into a stalwart Zionist. We are and remain Jews. The others will only exploit us and will never understand or appreciate us."

Freud had overcome his desire to have a non-Jew lead the psychoanalytic movement. If Jung could not be trusted, then none of them could. A month later he urged Sabina to "think again about the blond Siegfried and perhaps smash that idol before his time comes."

With Jung a liability and a threat, Freud looked to his loyal followers, especially Ferenczi and Jones, for comfort, and soon he had transferred much of his dependency needs to them. Writing about the future of his symbolic child, psychoanalysis, Freud told Ferenczi, "That assurance that the children will be provided for, which for a Jewish father is a matter of life and death, I expected to get from Jung; I am glad now that you and our friends will give me this."

Freud blamed himself for the crisis facing the movement. After all, he was the one who had designated Jung as his successor, who had forced the Viennese to accept Jung as president of the association, and who had so severely misjudged Jung's personality. Freud had been warned, but he had not listened.

He told Ferenczi and Jones that if his judgment was so poor, he had better leave the presidential choice up to the members. But the fact remained that Jung was still president, and they would all have to try to get along with him as long as he remained in that position.

"I consider there is no hope of rectifying the errors of the Zurich people," Freud wrote to Ferenczi, "and believe that in two or three years we shall be moving in two entirely different directions with no mutual understanding. The best way to guard against any bitterness is an attitude of expecting nothing at all, in other words, the worst."

In another letter to Ferenczi before the meeting Freud expressed the possibility that "this time we shall be really buried, after a burial hymn has so often been sung over us in vain." Ferenczi, Jones, and the other disciples would have the task of defending true psychoanalysis at the congress, Freud said, because he was loath to take part in the dispute. "My habit is to repudiate in silence and go my own way."

Lou Andreas-Salomé described the tension at the 1913 meeting in Munich:

> At the congress the Zurich members sat at their own table opposite Freud's. Their behavior toward Freud can be characterized in a word: it is not so much that Jung diverges from Freud, as that he does it in such a way as if he had taken it on himself to rescue Freud and his cause *by* these divergences. One glance at the two of them tells which is the more dogmatic, the more in love with power. Two years ago Jung's booming laughter gave voice to a kind of robust gaiety and exuberant vitality, but now his earnestness is composed of pure aggression, ambition, and intellectual brutality. I have never felt so close to Freud as here; not only on account of this break with his "son" Jung, whom he had loved and for whom he had practically transferred his cause to Zurich, but on account of the manner of the break—as though Freud had caused it by his narrow-minded obstinacy. Freud was the same as ever, but it was only with difficulty that he restrained his deep emotion.

The roster for the conference included eighty-seven members and guests, but Jones recalled the papers as a mediocre lot. He wrote that one of the Swiss contributions was so tedious that Freud remarked, "All sorts of criticisms have been brought against psychoanalysis, but this is the first time anyone could have called it boring."

Jung presided over the sessions in what Freud described as a "disagreeable and incorrect manner." Officious and overbearing, Jung restricted the time available to each speaker. The tone of his paper made it obvious that he was no longer a disciple of Freud.

"I found it necessary to clear up this confusion," Freud wrote, "and I did so by declaring that I did not recognize the innovations of the Swiss as legitimate continuations and further developments of the psychoanalysis that originated with me." Freud wanted to tell the psychiatric world that psychoanalysis was not changing; only Jung's version of it was. Ferenczi made the point with a pithy observation: "The *Jung* [the young] no longer believe in Freud."

Because of the offensive manner in which Jung conducted the meetings, many of the participants, particularly the Viennese, decided to indicate their dissatisfaction through some type of protest. Abraham suggested that those who disapproved of Jung's actions abstain from voting when Jung's name was introduced for election to another term as president.

While the ballots were being counted, the tension in the room was great. There were no other candidates. Out of the fifty-two members present who were eligible to vote, twenty-two submitted blank cards. Jung's election would not be unanimous.

Jung was furious, and he lashed out first at Jones. "I thought you had ethical principles," he said. Jung had counted on Jones's support because he was one of the few non-Jews in attendance. Some Freudian analysts interpreted Jung's comment to mean "I thought you were a Christian," and, indeed, that is the way Jones recorded it in his biography of Freud. In his autobiography, however, it is written as "ethical principles." Nevertheless, Freudian loyalists believed that Jung was appealing to racial differences and giving voice to his latent anti-Semitism.

After the congress Jung chastised Ferenczi for not supporting his reelection to the presidency. Ferenczi responded,

> It is altogether untrue when you ascribe our attitude to Freud's reaction to your "own scientific views." So little is that the case that in spite of our deep differences we had decided, in

accord with Freud's own suggestion, to vote again in favor of your being president. It was only the absolutely improper way in which you as chairman of the congress dealt with the suggestions we put forward, the quite one-sided partial comments you made on all the papers read, and also the personal behavior on the part of your group, that caused us to protest by voting with blank cards.

Jung accepted the presidency for another term despite the lack of support, and the Fourth Psychoanalytic Congress was adjourned. "We dispersed without any desire to meet again," Freud said.

Freud left Munich for Italy. Minna Bernays joined him on the train at Bologna, and they went to Rome for "seventeen delicious days."

It was obvious to all concerned, on both sides of the controversy, that Jung and his Swiss contingent were no longer members of the psychoanalytic family, despite Jung's title as president and his duties as editor of the leading journal. Freud was particularly upset about Jung's control over the *Yearbook*, fearing that Jung might usurp it to promote his own views and restrict the contributions from Freud and his followers.

Several weeks after the Munich congress Freud's worries about the *Yearbook* were relieved. On October 27 Jung resigned as editor because, he explained, he had received information from Alphonse Maeder, a Swiss psychotherapist, about allegations Freud had made against him. The substance of these charges—and whether they were real or products of Maeder's imagination—are unknown, but evidently Jung took them seriously.

"It has come to my ears through Dr. Maeder that you doubt my [good faith]," Jung wrote to Freud. "I would have expected you to communicate with me directly on so weighty a matter.

Since this is the gravest reproach that can be leveled at anybody, you have made further collaboration impossible. I therefore lay down the editorship of the *Yearbook* with which you entrusted me."

Jung wrote to Maeder that it was impossible to continue an association with Freud, and he suggested the establishment of a journal strictly for the Zurich school of psychoanalysis. He told Maeder that he hoped to have news from a publisher soon—and from Freud, "if the latter does not deem it beneath his papal dignity to answer me." Freud did not reply.

There remained only the matter of the presidency of the International Psychoanalytic Association. Jung lingered in that capacity for five more months before unexpectedly announcing his resignation on April 20, 1914. Jones suggested that Jung's decision was precipitated by a barrage of criticism published in the *International Journal*, the Vienna periodical started by Freud to replace the dissident Stekel's journal.

In his letter of resignation Jung referred simply to the "latest developments" that had persuaded him that his ideas were in "such sharp contrast to the views of the majority of the members of the association that I can no longer consider myself a suitable personality to be president. I therefore tender my resignation with many thanks for the confidence I have enjoyed hitherto."

Jung had removed himself from both positions of influence within the International Psychoanalytic Association, but even his continued membership annoyed Freud. Heretics could not be allowed to retain any affiliation; no one would be tolerated who suggested that conflicting varieties of psychoanalysis could co-exist. Further, outsiders could not be permitted to believe that Jung's views enjoyed the approval of the official organization.

There was only one psychoanalysis, and the international community had to be made aware that the works of Jung, Adler, and other dissenters had no place in it. Freud devoted the months of January and February of 1914 to writing *On the History of the Psychoanalytic Movement*. This classic essay was published in the *Yearbook* in July and later in book form. Freud referred to it affectionately as the "bomb" he threw at Jung and Adler.

Freud stated his position forcefully in the opening paragraph: "Psychoanalysis is my creation; for ten years I was the only person who concerned himself with it. Even today no one knows better than I do what psychoanalysis is, how it differs from other ways of investigating the life of the mind, and precisely what should be called psychoanalysis and what would better be described by some other name."

He noted that the views of Jung and Adler would best be described by some other name. They had abandoned psychoanalysis; their ideas in no way resembled his.

Freud's work had the desired effect. Shortly after the essay was published, Jung and most of the other Swiss analysts resigned from the International Psychoanalytic Association.

The banishment was complete. Freud wrote to Abraham on July 26, 1914: "So we are at last rid of them, the brutal, sanctimonious Jung and his disciples. All my life I have been looking for friends who would not exploit and then betray me."

The break with Freud was devastating for Jung's emotional health, plunging him into a psychic abyss where he remained for three agonizing years. "After the parting of the ways with Freud," he wrote, "a period of inner uncertainty began for me. It would be no exaggeration to call it a state of disorientation. I felt totally suspended in midair." He thought he was going insane and believed he was exhibiting psychotic symptoms. He felt a constant state of inner pressure and loneliness, burdened by torments he dared not mention for fear of being misunderstood.

In October 1913, when Jung resigned as editor of the *Yearbook*, he reported that he was

> seized by an overpowering vision. I saw a monstrous flood covering all the northern and low-lying lands between the North Sea and the Alps. When it came to Switzerland I saw

that the mountains grew higher and higher to protect our country. I realized that a frightful catastrophe was in progress. I saw the mighty yellow waves, the floating rubble of civilization, and the drowned bodies of uncounted thousands. Then the whole sea turned to blood. The vision lasted about an hour. I was perplexed and nauseated, and ashamed of my weakness.

Two weeks later the vision recurred, stronger and more vivid. A voice told Jung not to doubt the reality of what he had seen.

Another dream of catastrophe visited Jung in the spring, first in April, the month he resigned as president of the association, and again in May and June, just before he relinquished membership in the organization. In all three dreams it was midsummer, yet a brutal cold wave had descended over Europe, turning everything to ice. The third such dream, however, had a different ending. One tree remained green amid the desolation and death. Jung perceived it as his "tree of life." The frost had transformed the leaves of this tree into grapes that were full of juices that had healing powers. In the dream Jung saw himself plucking the grapes from the branches and distributing them to a waiting crowd.

Forewarned by these terrifying visions, Jung waited for a calamity to strike Europe. He devoutly believed he had seen symbolic glimpses of the future. And on August 1, the Great War erupted, leaving him the daunting task of trying to understand how his own mental torments had anticipated reality.

Jung determined that he had to withdraw as much as possible from the external world to explore the depths of his unconscious, to discern the meaning of his dreams and visions. He needed to give free rein to his long-dormant Number Two personality. His conscious ego, the Number One personality, had been dominant since adolescence. Now he needed to reverse that situation and suppress the conscious aspects of the psyche to permit greater expression of the unconscious. To accomplish this, he had to free himself from everyday concerns.

Accordingly, he abandoned the final formal links with Freud and the psychoanalytic establishment—the editorship of the *Yearbook* and the presidency and membership in the association. He gave up his teaching position on the medical faculty of the University of Zurich and stopped reading professional books and writing scientific papers. He also retreated from his wife and children and his few friends.

There was a danger in this attempt to isolate himself in the world of his unconscious. He could not do so totally without risking the kind of loss of contact with reality that was the primary symptom of psychosis. Jung knew that it was necessary to maintain some minimal contact with the environment to avoid the psychotic state. He needed to keep reminding himself that he had a wife and family to care for and patients to treat. These, he wrote, "were actualities that made demands upon me and proved to me again and again that I really existed, that I was not a blank page whirling about in the winds of the spirit."

Jung's personal course of therapy began with an examination of his childhood in the hope of uncovering some traumatic incident that might be at the root of his present disturbance. In doing this he was subscribing to Freud's hypothesis that neurosis has its origin in childhood experiences, rather than to his own belief that such problems arise from current circumstances. He reviewed his memories of his childhood systematically and found nothing unusual, despite what biographers have judged a singularly disturbed childhood.

In desperation, Jung abandoned his effort to understand his problems in a rational and intellectual fashion and decided to do whatever occurred to him, no matter how nonsensical or irrational it seemed. "I consciously submitted myself to the impulses of the unconscious," he wrote.

The first thing his unconscious led him to do was build a miniature village out of small stones. That, he instantly recognized, was a re-creation of his life at age ten or eleven when he played avidly with building blocks. "There is still life in these things," he said to himself, searching the lakeshore for rocks.

"The small boy is still around, and possesses a creative life which I lack." He became obsessed with this activity, rushing outdoors after each patient left. His first efforts were hesitant; he was embarrassed by the feeling that he could do nothing but play childish games. Later he said it became the turning point of his life.

The construction of the toy village out of stones was only the beginning of what Jung termed his "confrontation" with his unconscious. He pursued the fantasies, dreams, and visions released by his games actively and eagerly, carefully heeding what they told him. Initially he held back, out of fear of losing control, but after a while he decided that he had no choice. "I knew that I had to let myself plummet down into them." That was the only way to grasp their meaning and master them. On the afternoon of December 12, 1913, Jung remembered, he resolved to commit himself to that most dangerous of enterprises, to submerge himself in his fantasy life.

"I was sitting at my desk once more, thinking over my fears. Then I let myself drop. Suddenly it was as though the ground literally gave way beneath my feet, and I plunged down into dark depths." He experienced an instant of panic, which quickly turned to relief as he landed on his feet in some soft, sticky substance.

He found himself outside the entrance to a cave. He squeezed past a leather-skinned dwarf and waded through ice-cold water into the cave, where he saw a glowing red crystal. A body floated past, a young man with blond hair and a head injury of some kind. This was followed by a giant black Egyptian scarab or beetle. A red sun rose out of the water, and a thick stream of blood spurted high in the air for a long time.

After the vision ended, Jung reflected on its meaning and thought he recognized some of the symbolism. The scarab, for example, was held by ancient Egyptians to indicate resurrection and immortality. The essence seemed to him to be death and rebirth, the very process he was undertaking by confronting his unconscious.

Other visions followed. He dreamed he was in the mountains accompanied by a dark-skinned savage. They were armed with rifles and were lying in wait for Siegfried, the hero of the Nibelung legend. When Siegfried appeared, riding in a chariot made of bones, they fired at him and he fell dead. Jung was horrified and ran away, but a heavy rain erased all traces of the murder. His fear of being discovered eased, but he was assailed by a terrible guilt.

When he awoke and tried to analyze the dream, he found that he could not. He tried to fall asleep again but a voice told him that it was imperative that he understand the dream at once. If not, the inner voice said, he would have to shoot himself. Jung habitually kept a loaded pistol at his bedside, and he suddenly became fearful that the voice would command him to use it.

The meaning of the dream became apparent a moment later. Siegfried symbolized Germany's increasing military power and its attempt to impose its will on others—to have its own way, just as Jung wanted to do. The dream signified that the attitude of the hero, Siegfried, with whom Jung long identified, was no longer appropriate. That was why Siegfried had been put to death in the dream. This interpretation reinforced Jung's belief that he had to abandon his conscious attitudes and sacrifice the will of his ego for higher goals. The dark-skinned savage indicated the dark, primitive side of Jung's unconscious, revealing that it was being brought into balance with his conscious ego. In time, the unconscious would become an equal partner within the psyche, rather than being subordinate, as it had been since Jung's adolescence.

Other fantasies involved an old man and a blind girl who called themselves Elijah and Salome. Elijah, a prophet, symbolized knowledge and understanding. Salome represented the erotic element of life. Although she was unable to see into life's meaning, she was a necessary companion for the wise old man. Jung discerned many examples in mythology to parallel the story of Elijah and Salome, a wise old man traveling with a sensuous young girl. He decided that no one should undertake a journey such as his without companionship. Toni Wolff served as his Salome.

The vision of Elijah gradually metamorphosed into another old man, Philemon, who had the horns of a bull and the wings of a kingfisher (a long-billed, brightly colored bird). Philemon became Jung's inner teacher, the guide for his spiritual enlightenment. He was a person of superior insight, not unlike an Indian guru, and Jung received instruction from him in his imagination. A biographer noted that Jung spent many hours in his garden talking to Philemon, who "represented what Jung had looked for, apparently found, and then tragically lost in Freud: paternal wisdom and guidance, readiness to minister to his spiritual needs." In Philemon, Jung had a new surrogate father, one who would never desert or disappoint him.

Jung's bizarre journey eventually proved fruitful. Out of his three-year exploration of the depths of his psyche he fashioned a new meaning and center for his own life and a new way of describing the human personality. There is no doubt of the importance of those introspective years to Jung's growth, following his break with Freud. His unfolding unconscious, Jung wrote, was like a "stream of lava, and the heat of its fires reshaped my life. The years when I was pursuing my inner images were the most important in my life—in them everything essential was decided."

Not surprisingly, Jung came to look upon the middle years, around age forty, as the most crucial in the formation of the personality. Freud, in contrast, saw the time of early childhood, his own most traumatic years, as decisive. Thus each man reflected in his theory the reality of his own life's experiences.

Jung's confrontation with his unconscious had begun when he was thirty-eight years old. Freud experienced a similar crisis that started when he was forty-one. Freud resolved his neurotic episode by exploring his unconscious through an analysis of his dreams. Like Jung, Freud concluded his period of self-examination by achieving enhanced understanding and a fresh way of describing the human personality. Both men accomplished their most creative work during and after their emotional crises at midlife.

In another parallel, neither man was able to embark on that search for self-knowledge until after the death of his father. Freud was forty when his father died. Freud said that the death revolutionized his soul and made him feel sufficiently free to write the autobiographical *The Interpretation of Dreams*, which resulted from his confrontation with his unconscious.

Jung, thirty-eight when his spiritual and symbolic father died—when Freud ceased to have an impact on his life—had hesitated to formulate his own approach to the mind, making little progress for fear of offending Freud. Jung was tormented by the conflict between the need to assert his independence and the need for a father figure. Only after the split with Freud was he able to develop his own ideas fully, to go his own way. Thus he, too, was liberated by the loss of the father.

A final similarity between Freud and Jung in the resolution of their midlife crises was that each was sustained by a supportive relationship with a woman, who helped him through the difficult period. Jung had Toni Wolff, who became his lover. Freud had Minna Bernays, his sister-in-law, to whom he transferred many of his emotional needs.

While Jung was being plagued by dreams and fantasies during the spring and summer of 1914 following his break with Freud, Freud was having bowel troubles. Whether they were real or symbolic, he was disturbed because he feared they indicated some form of cancer. This proved not to be the case, however, "so this time I am let off," he commented. Nine years later, however, cancer of the jaw and mouth was diagnosed. Over the next sixteen years he endured thirty-three operations as a result of the disease.

Freud did not experience the emotional upheaval that overwhelmed Jung after their separation. In the language of psycho-analysis, Freud had already withdrawn his libido from Jung by that time. His emotional ties to Jung had been weakened, then severed, beforehand.

Freud did notice a kind of liberation. According to one biographer, it was only after Jung was banished from the movement that Freud "felt certain of his identity" and "confident enough to take full responsibility for his ideas." Previously he had chosen to share much of the credit for psychoanalysis with his early mentor, Josef Breuer.

At that point, Freud could boldly state that "psychoanalysis is my creation," as he did on the first page of his essay *On the History of the Psychoanalytic Movement*. In it, Freud was more critical of Jung than of Adler. "Of the two movements under discussion," Freud wrote, "Adler's is indubitably the more important; while radically false, it is marked by consistency and coherence." Jung's work, on the other hand, was "so obscure, unintelligible, and confused as to make it difficult to take up any position upon it."

Freud may have been unable or unwilling to take a position on Jung's work, but he had no difficulty in doing so with respect to Jung himself. Even Freud's most loyal disciples agreed that he could hold a grudge for a lifetime. Freud never forgave Jung, Adler, and their followers for their treason, for defecting from his cause. One of Adler's disciples recalled that Freud would not even look at him (the disciple) if he passed by on the street.

When Adler died in 1937 in Aberdeen, Scotland, twenty-six years after he and Freud had parted, Freud wrote to a friend, "I don't understand your sympathy for Adler. For a Jew boy out of a Viennese suburb, a death in Aberdeen is an unheard-of career in itself and a proof of how far he had got on. The world really rewarded him richly for his service in having contradicted psychoanalysis."

Adler equaled Freud in his bitterness and anger, referring to Freud's work as "filth" and to Freud himself as a swindler and a schemer.

Freud and his adherents continued to refer to Jung and Adler as heretics. Binswanger once asked Freud why the two disciples who were perhaps the most talented had broken with him. "Precisely because they too wanted to be popes," Freud answered, a statement that clearly reveals as much about Freud as about the dissenters.

In 1915 Freud wrote to Putnam to complain of Jung's "lies, brutality, and anti-Semitic condescension toward me." In 1924, in a letter to Ferenczi, he called Jung an "evil fellow." As late as the 1930s, when Wilhelm Fliess's son asked about Jung, Freud "grimaced in disgust and muttered, 'Bad character.'"

In 1938, shortly after the Nazi occupation of Austria, Jung and Franz Riklin sent the latter's son to Vienna with $10,000 for Freud to use to get himself and his family out of the country. When the younger Riklin asked to see Freud, Anna Freud said that her father would not receive him. Freud himself appeared in the doorway and said, "I refuse to be beholden to my enemies."

Freud was not alone in his resentment. For years Jung claimed that Freud's followers had ruined his private practice. He also spread stories about Freud's neurosis. In 1941, writing to an American admirer, Jung noted that "Freud himself was neurotic his life long. I myself analyzed him for a certain very disagreeable symptom which in consequence of the treatment was cured."

Jung complained to a Swedish psychotherapist of the "papal policies of the Viennese." He condemned Freud and all the Viennese analysts:

Vienna is working against me with methods which are so unfair that I cannot defend myself. Personal insinuations are being bandied about. In a breach of medical discretion, Freud has even made hostile use of a patient's letter—a letter which the person concerned, whom I know very well, wrote in a moment of resistance against me. Supposing I were to publish what people have already told me about Freud! These practices are characteristic of Viennese policies. Such an enemy is not worth the name.

As recently as 1960 Jung discussed Freud's neurosis and his analysis of Freud during the 1909 trip to America. "He was unquestioningly a neurotic," Jung said. And Jung denied ever being a disciple or pupil of Freud's. "I am a pupil of Bleuler's," he insisted, yet in his memoirs Jung mentioned Bleuler only in passing. To Freud he devoted twenty-three pages.

Jung talked about Freud's sourness and anger. In a seminar in 1925 he said that every word Freud uttered was loaded with bitterness and that "his attitude was the bitterness of the person who is entirely misunderstood, and his manners always seemed to say: 'If they do not understand, they must be stamped into hell.'"

A biographer noted that Jung "never quite completely made his peace with the pain inflicted on him both by the association and the parting with Freud." Although this pain lingered, Jung was able, toward the end of his life, to be charitable toward Freud. In written answers to questions from *The New York Times*, Jung described Freud as a man "to whom I owe so much." And to a German psychiatrist nearly twenty years after Freud's death he wrote, "I had the privilege of knowing Freud personally. Despite the blatant misjudgment I have suffered at Freud's hands, I cannot fail to recognize, even in the teeth of my resentment, his significance as a cultural critic and psychological pioneer." He added that without Freud's psychoanalysis, he would not have had a clue about how to proceed with his own investigation of the human mind.

Jung was even more complimentary in his autobiography, *Memories, Dreams, Reflections*, published in English in 1961. There he paid tribute to Freud's achievements, courage, understanding, and freedom from bias. "Like an Old Testament prophet, he undertook to overthrow false gods, to rip the veils away from a mass of dishonesties and hypocrisies, mercilessly exposing the rottenness of the contemporary psyche. He did not falter in the face of the unpopularity such an enterprise entailed."

Perhaps the son, at last, was coming to terms with the father. Or perhaps he was remembering a letter he received from a Freudian analyst in 1918. "You should have the courage to recognize Freud in all his grandeur, even if you do not agree with him on every point, even if in the process you might have to credit Freud with many of your own accomplishments. Only then will you be completely free." That writer had come to understand Freud and Jung better than they understood each other. Her name was Sabina Spielrein.

In 1936 Jung received one of the highest honors of his career. He was invited to Harvard University to be given an honorary degree as part of the celebrations attending the three-hundredth anniversary of the school's founding. He had achieved international recognition. His books were widely read, his ideas discussed and accepted in many quarters. Visitors came to Zurich from all over the world to meet him, to learn from him, and, in many cases, to undergo analysis by him. He had a large and loyal coterie of followers—Jungians—just as there were Freudians in the psychiatric world.

Jung had successfully overcome the influence of his surrogate father. In his own mind he had vanquished Freud and no longer felt that he was living and working under Freud's influence. The accolade Harvard chose to bestow on him was proof of his stature, visible and coveted recognition of how far he had come by following his own path.

But there was something Jung did not know about the invitation. He was Harvard's second choice. Initially they had wanted to honor Sigmund Freud. University officials had been informed that Freud was too old and ill to make the trip and, consequently, would decline the invitation. The psychologists on the planning committee did not want the award to go to someone from another field, so they agreed to invite Jung.

Introducing Jung at the ceremonies in Cambridge, Massachusetts, was Stanley Cobb, an American neurologist who counted Freudian analysts among his friends. He suffered from a speech defect that caused him to stammer, forcing the distinguished audience to pay close attention to his words. He described Jung's accomplishments lavishly—and introduced him as "Doctor Freud."

Notes

INTRODUCTION: *An Uneasy Alliance*

xiv. "breezy personality": Gay, *Freud,* 198.   **xiv.** "from the depths": Ibid., 156.

CHAPTER ONE: *The Medallion: 1906*

1. "Who divined": Quotation from Sophocles cited in Jones, *Life and Work* 2: 13.   **2.** "odd states of mind": S. Freud, *Origins of Psychoanalysis*, 210. **3.** "No notice": S. Freud, *Autobiographical Study,* 48.   **3.** "I now feel quite uprooted": Schur, *Freud,* 109.   **4.** Reviews of *The Interpretation of Dreams:* Ellenberger, *Discovery of the Unconscious,* 783–784.   **6.** Freud's daily routine: Jones, *Life and Work* 2: 382–385.   **7.** "making a funny sound": Young-Bruehl, *Anna Freud,* 43.   **9.** "I could not contemplate": Jones, *Life and Work* 2: 396; Engelmann, *Berggasse 19,* 45.   **9.** Freud's indigestion: Roazen, *Freud and His Followers,* 46.   **10.** "paradise": Jones, *Life and Work* 1: 336. **10.** "I was one of those": S. Freud, *On the History,* 21, quoting the German dramatist Friedrich Hebbel.   **13.** "where you worked": Ellenberger, *Discovery of the Unconscious,* 667.   **14.** "all intention": Jung, *Memories, Dreams, Reflections,* 112.   **15.** "within monastic walls": Ibid.   **15.** "understood nothing": Hannah, *Jung,* 78.   **15.** "Frosty old bachelor": Stern, *C. G. Jung,* 55.   **16.** "a mere intellect": Ibid., 69.   **19.** "the hard work": S. Freud, *Freud/Jung Letters,* 6.   **20.** "I would so much": S. Freud, *Complete Letters to Wilhelm Fliess,* 198.   **20.** "unavoidable necessity": S. Freud, *Freud/Jung Letters,* 12.   **21.** "You cannot be": Ibid., 13.

CHAPTER TWO: *The Dream of the Three Fates: Freud's Early Years*

23. Freud's dream of his mother's death: S. Freud, *Interpretation of Dreams,* 622–623.   **24.** *"mein goldener Sigi"*: Jones, *Life and Work* 1: 3.   **24.** "You are a lucky mother": Bernays, "My Brother Sigmund Freud," 335.   **24.** "A man who has been": Jones, *Life and Work* 1: 5.   **24.** "the mother": Roazen, *Freud and His Followers*, 46.   **25–26.** Freud's dream of the three fates: S. Freud, *Interpretation of Dreams*, 237–238.   **26.** Freud's dreams and fears: Fromm, *Sigmund Freud's Mission*, 11, 16–18.   **26.** "I came to know the helplessness of poverty": Schur, *Freud*, 63; S. Freud, *Complete Letters to Wilhelm Fliess*, 374.   **27.** "You see, I have come to something": Roazen, *Freud and His Followers*, 37; S. Freud, *Interpretation of Dreams*, 216.   **27.** "Don't worry, Papa": Fromm, *Sigmund Freud's Mission*, 55.   **27.** Freud's father as a "weakling": Krüll, *Freud and His Father*, 154.   **28.** Jakob Freud and his cap: Fromm, *Sigmund Freud's Mission*, 55, 60.   **28.** Freud's nanny: Schur, *Freud*, 120.   **29.** Three generations of the Freud family: Jones, *Life and Work* 1: 10.   **29.** "All my friends": Roazen, *Freud and His Followers*, 31; S. Freud, *Interpretation of Dreams*, 472, 483, 486.   **29.** "Freud's sexual constitution": Jones, *Life and Work* 1: 11.   **30.** The cupboard and Freud's mother's "inside": Schur, *Freud*, 121–123; S. Freud, *Complete Letters to Wilhelm Fliess*, 270–272; S. Freud, *Psychopathology of Everyday Life*, 51.   **31.** "I have often felt": Roazen, *Freud and His Followers*, 22.   **32.** "This was a time": Gay, *Freud*, 21.   **32.** Anti-Semitism in Vienna: Ellenberger, *Discovery of the Unconscious*, 422.   **32.** "charged the hostile crowd": M. Freud, *Sigmund Freud*, 71.   **32.** "the strength to defy public opinion": Robert, *From Oedipus to Moses*, 13.   **32.** "suppressed anti-Semitism": Roazen, *Freud and His Followers*, 24; S. Freud, *Psychoanalytic Dialogue*, 46.   **32–33.** "completely estranged" and "Not very much": Ellenberger, *Discovery of the Unconscious*, 463; S. Freud, *Totem and Taboo*, 15.   **34.** "They were hard times": Jones, *Life and Work* 1: 15.   **34.** Jakob Freud's income: Ellenberger, *Discovery of the Unconscious*, 425.   **35.** "pained expression": Jones, *Life and Work* 1: 18.   **36.** Study mates, not playmates: Bernays, "My Brother Sigmund Freud," 336.   **36.** Gisela Fluss: Jones, *Life and Work* 1: 25.   **37.** Freud's father's objections to medical school: Bernays, "My Brother Sigmund Freud," 340.   **37.** "lost opportunity": Jones, *Life and Work* 1: 25–26.   **37.** "I lack that passion": Ibid., 28.   **38.** Brücke: Ellenberger, *Discovery of the Unconscious*, 433; Jones, *Life and Work* 1: 39, 60.   **39.** "happiest years": Jones, *Life and Work* 1: 43.   **40.** "No doubt [Freud] found": Robert, *From Oedipus to Moses*, 44.   **40.** Meynert: Jones, *Life and Work* 1: 65.   **41.** Cocaine: Ellenberger, *Discovery of the Unconscious*, 434–435; Roazen, *Freud and His Followers*, 67–68; Jones, *Life and Work* 1: 62, 81.   **42.** "It was the fault": S. Freud, *Autobiographical Study*, 14–15.

CHAPTER THREE: *He Died in Time for You: Jung's Early Years*

43. "There was a rattling": Jung, *Memories, Dreams, Reflections*, 96. **43.** "How quickly": Ibid.   **43.** "He died in time": Ibid.   **44.** "to be free": Hannah, *Jung*, 63.   **44.** "He looked drained": Stern, *C. G. Jung*, 23. **45.** "The gay spirit": Jung, *Memories, Dreams, Reflections*, 95. **45.** "To this day": Ibid., 8.   **46.** "stale and hollow": Ibid., 43.   **46.** "You always want": Ibid.   **46.** Jung's father as a failure: van der Post, *Story of Our*

Time, 79. **46.** "I must take": Jung, *Memories, Dreams, Reflections*, 47. **46.** "You can ride": Ibid., 77. **47.** "what she said": Ibid., 49. **47.** "One night I saw": Ibid., 18. **47.** "shook like an aspen leaf": Stern, *C. G. Jung*, 26. **48.** Associated women with unreliability: Jung, *Memories, Dreams, Reflections*, 8. **48.** "It took him completely": Stern, *C. G. Jung*, 29. **48.** "This story": Jung, *Memories, Dreams, Reflections*, 25. **49.** "From then on": Ibid., 52. **49.** "Her chatter": Ibid., 48. **49.** Jung's parents' marriage: Ibid., 25. **50.** "for it clearly": Ellenberger, *Discovery of the Unconscious*, 662. **50.** Influence of religion: Storr, *C. G. Jung*, 3. **51.** "I began to distrust": Jung, *Memories, Dreams, Reflections*, 10. **51.** "a harmless": Ibid., 11. **51.** "skin and naked flesh": Ibid., 12. **52.** Jung kept the matter to himself: Stern, *C. G. Jung*, 28. **52.** "So that is the": Jung, *Memories, Dreams, Reflections*, 17. **52.** "The world is beautiful": Ibid., 36. **53.** "Don't go on thinking": Ibid. **53.** "I saw before me": Ibid., 39. **53.** "and make all comprehensible": Ibid., 40. **54.** "The pattern of my relationship": Ibid., 41–42. **54.** Jung's communion: Ibid., 55. **55.** "I found this extraordinarily interesting": Ibid., 8. **56.** "asocial monster": Wehr, *Jung*, 29. **56.** "I knew not a soul": Jung, *Memories, Dreams, Reflections*, 21. **56–57.** Jung stresses inner growth; Freud stresses outer growth: Storr, *C. G. Jung*, 4–5. **57.** "a whiplash": Hannah, *Jung*, 29. **57.** "For the first time": Jung, *Memories, Dreams, Reflections*, 24. **57.** "I didn't even know": Ibid., 27. **58.** "It would be dreadful": Ibid., 31. **58.** "I had seen how poor": Brome, *Jung*, 49. **58.** "The whole bag of tricks": Jung, *Memories, Dreams, Reflections*, 32. **59.** Plagiarism incident: Ibid., 64–65. **59.** Jung's carriage dream: Ibid., 34. **60.** "It occurred to me": Ibid., 33–34. **60–61.** Jung's career dreams: Ibid., 75, 85. **61.** "Opportunism": Hannah, *Jung*, 57. **62.** Jung's uncles: Ibid., 64. **62.** Jung at University of Basel: van der Post, *Story of Our Time*, 92; Wehr, *Jung*, 58; Ellenberger, *Discovery of the Unconscious*, 665. **63.** Jung and Krafft-Ebing: Jung, *Memories, Dreams, Reflections*, 108–109.

CHAPTER FOUR: *The Future Belongs to Us: 1907*

64. Jung's letter of January 8: S. Freud, *Freud/Jung Letters*, 20. **65.** "I much regret": Ibid., 24. **65.** "I am sorry": Billinsky, "Jung and Freud," 42. **65.** "the debate": M. Freud, *Sigmund Freud*, 109. **65.** "I found [Freud] extremely intelligent": Jung, *Memories, Dreams, Reflections*, 149. **66.** "My first impressions": Ibid. **66.** "There was one characteristic": Ibid., 152. **67.** "It was a shocking discovery": Billinsky, "Jung and Freud," 42. **68.** "You will doubtless": S. Freud, *Freud/Jung Letters*, 25. **68.** "The last shreds": Ibid., 26. **68.** "You have gone into it": Ibid., 27. **69.** Freud on Jung's dementia praecox book: Ibid., 17. **69.** "I rejoice every day": Ibid., 56. **69.** "long-cherished": Ibid., 86. **69.** "Heartiest thanks": Ibid., 91. **70.** "Something of the character": Ibid., 95. **70.** "Consequently, I skirt": Ibid. **70.** "The dream sets my mind": Ibid., 96. **70.** "chalked on the inside of doors": Ibid., 19. **71.** "The 'leading lights'": Ibid., 18. **72.** "but

I am still young": Ibid., 20. **72.** Jung on the sexual theory: Ibid., 25. **72.** "sweeten the sour apple": Ibid., 28. **72.** "I detest gladiatorial fights": Ibid., 33. **73.** "Since I am not so deeply committed": Ibid., 36. **73.** "It's a hard nut!": Ibid., 76. **73.** "Your lecture in Amsterdam": Ibid., 77. **73.** "As usual": Ibid., 78. **74.** "I know you are now in Amsterdam": Ibid., 82. **75.** Aschaffenburg's verbal slips: Ibid., 85; Jones, *Life and Work* 2: 112. **75.** Jones and Jung: Jones, *Life and Work* 2: 112. **75.** Jung on Jones as an asset to the movement: S. Freud, *Freud/Jung Letters*, 86. **75.** "impatient and already prejudiced": Jones, *Life and Work* 2: 113. **75.** "What a gang": S. Freud, *Freud/Jung Letters*, 83, 84. **76.** "manner in which Freud's disciples": Ellenberger, *Discovery of the Unconscious*, 798. **76.** "don't want to be enlightened": S. Freud, *Freud/Jung Letters*, 87. **76–77.** Freud on professional opposition: Ibid., 54. **77.** "As we know": Ibid., 54–55. **77–78.** Freud and Jung on professional publications in psychoanalysis: Ibid., 59, 88, 104. **79.** "He will be a staunch supporter": Ibid., 101. **79.** "I suppose I should be": Ibid., 102. **79.** "You deceive yourself": Ibid. **79.** "What magnificent plans!": Ibid., 104.

CHAPTER FIVE: *My Own Fatherhood Will Not Be a Burden: 1908*

80–81. Participants at the Congress of Freudian Psychology: Jones, *Life and Work* 2: 40–41. **82.** "We begged him": Jones, *Free Associations*, 166. **82.** "hailed him as a destroyer": Stekel, *Autobiography*, 122. **82.** "The congress is a great success": S. Freud, *Letters of Sigmund Freud*, 273. **82.** On the loyal Viennese: Jones, *Life and Work*, 2: 44; Stern, *C. G. Jung*, 89. **83.** Freud and Emanuel: S. Freud, *Letters of Sigmund Freud*, 273. **84.** "impudent invitations": S. Freud, *Freud/Jung Letters*, 110–111. **84.** Freud on Bleuler: Ibid., 112, 121–122. **84.** "above all that": Ibid., 123–124. **84.** "They are not all fit": Ibid., 116, 119–120. **85.** Jung on Freud's topic: Ibid., 134–135. **85.** "under the reverberating impact": Ibid., 144. **85–86.** "Every suspicion": Ibid., 144–145. **86.** "I have done bad work": Ibid., 138–139. **87.** "spirit of my spirit": Ibid., 114–115. **87.** "I thank you": Ibid., 119, 122, 125. **87.** "I need you": Ibid., 165, 168, 172. **87.** "I have had your photograph": Ibid., 115. **87–88.** Jung and Abraham: Ibid., 145–146, 149; Jones, *Life and Work* 2: 46–51. **90–92.** Otto Gross: S. Freud, *Freud/Jung Letters*, 147, 153, 159–162, 414–416; Stern, *C. G. Jung*, 80–90; Jones, *Life and Work* 2: 33. **92–93.** On the *Yearbook*: S. Freud, *Freud/Jung Letters*, 185–188, 207; S. Freud, *Letters of Sigmund Freud*, 277; Ellenberger, *Discovery of the Unconscious*, 694–695. **94.** "delightful man": Brome, *Jung*, 107. **94.** Freud/Jung visit in Zurich: S. Freud, *Freud/Jung Letters*, 167, 171–173; Jones, *Life and Work*, 2: 50–53. **94.** Jung and Freud on Bleuler: S. Freud, *Freud/Jung Letters*, 171, 185–189; Jones, *Life and Work* 2: 50. **95.** "ideal hero-father": S. Freud, *Freud/Jung Letters*, 184, 186. **95.** Invitation to America: Ibid., 192–193; Jones, *Life and Work* 2: 54.

CHAPTER SIX: *The Peat-Bog Corpses: 1909*

97. Fainting episode in Bremen: Jung, *Memories, Dreams, Reflections*, 156; Jones, *Life and Work* 2: 146. **97.** "Why should I want him to die?": Brome, *Jung*, 115. **98.** "I think this side": S. Freud, *Freud/Jung Letters*, 193–194. **98.** Freud on psychoanalysis in America: Ibid., 196. **99.** "I am to go to America": Jones, *Life and Work* 2: 54; S. Freud, *Freud/Jung Letters*, 210. **99.** "a good deal": Ernest Jones quoted in Roazen, *Freud and His Followers*, 357. **99.** "The thought of America": Jones, *Life and Work* 2: 54. **99.** Freud and Jung on their American lecture topics: S. Freud, *Freud/Jung Letters*, 228–229, 233, 234. **99–100.** The voyage to America: Jones, *Life and Work* 2: 55; Roazen, *Freud and His Followers*, 245–246; Jung, *Memories, Dreams, Reflections*, 158; van der Post, *Story of Our Time*, 145; Billinsky, "Jung and Freud," 42. **101–102.** Jung's dream of the multistory house: Jung, *Memories, Dreams, Reflections*, 158–160. **102–103.** The death-wish interpretation: Ibid.; Hannah, *Jung*, 87. **103.** "Won't they get a surprise": Roazen, *Freud and His Followers*, 229–230. **104.** "They escort you": Jones, *Life and Work* 2: 55–56, 60. **104.** "plump, jolly": Jung, *Memories, Dreams, Reflections*, 365, 366. **104.** "Jung used to say": Hannah, *Jung*, 92. **105.** "Kill his father": Jones, *Life and Work* 2: 58. **105.** "I'm a married man": Puner, *Freud*, 134. **105.** Freud's talk at Clark University: Jones, *Life and Work* 2: 56–57. **106.** "received great applause": Jung, *Memories, Dreams, Reflections*, 367. **106–107.** Clark University festivities: Ellenberger, *Discovery of the Unconscious*, 460, 557, 801–802. **107.** "There was a tremendous amount": Jung, *Memories, Dreams, Reflections*, 367–368. **107.** "In Europe": S. Freud, *Autobiographical Study*, 52. **108.** Putnam camp: Jung, *Memories, Dreams, Reflections*, 369; Jones, *Life and Work* 2: 58–59. **109.** America's mother complex: Jung, *Memories, Dreams, Reflections*, 368; Stern, *C. G. Jung*, 97; S. Freud, *Freud/Jung Letters*, 258. **109.** "a mistake": Jones, *Life and Work* 2: 59–60. **110.** Correspondence after the American trip: S. Freud, *Freud/Jung Letters*, 196–197, 207–209, 222, 248, 250, 259. **111.** "Why, after all, should there not be ghosts?": Jung, *Memories, Dreams, Reflections*, 98–100. **112.** Helene Preiswerk: Carotenuto, *Secret Symmetry*, 105, 178; Jung, *Memories, Dreams, Reflections*, 104–107. **112.** "Pale as a ghost," Stern, *C. G. Jung*, 41–45. **112.** "deep bond," Hillman, "Some Early Background," 123–136. **113.** Jung on spiritualism: Stern, *C. G. Jung*, 45; Ellenberger, *Discovery of the Unconscious*, 687. **113.** Freud on supernatural phenomena: Jung, *Memories, Dreams, Reflections*, 155; Roazen, *Freud and His Followers*, 235; Jones, *Life and Work* 3: 392; Schur, *Freud*, 251–252. **115–116.** Bookcase incident: Jung, *Memories, Dreams, Reflections*, 155–156. **116.** Letters on Freud's paternal authority: S. Freud, *Freud/Jung Letters*, 215–222. **117.** "Beware of this brilliant": Schur, *Freud*, 254. **117–118.** Sexual theory as dogma: Jung, *Memories, Dreams, Reflections*, 150–151; Ellenberger, *Discovery of the Unconscious*, 682; S. Freud, *Freud/Jung Letters*, 216. **119.** Jung's house: Jung, *Memories, Dreams, Reflections*, 7; Ellenberger, *Discovery of the Unconscious*, 682; Hannah, *Jung*, 93–94. **119–120.** Jung's interest in mythology: Jung, *Memories, Dreams, Reflections*, 162; Stern, *C. G. Jung*, 101–102; S. Freud, *Freud/Jung*

Letters, 251–252, 255, 260, 263, 265, 269, 279.   **121–122.** Letters on libido: S. Freud, *Freud/Jung Letters*, 270, 277, 280.

CHAPTER SEVEN: *A Brutal Reality: Wives and Other Women*

123. "Four and a half": Carotenuto, *Secret Symmetry*, 93, 137–139. **124.** Jung's letter to Freud about Sabina: S. Freud, *Freud/Jung Letters*, 7. **124.** "I was still a baby": Carotenuto, *Secret Symmetry*, 6–12, 30, 33, 101, 167–169.   **124–126.** Freud and Jung on Sabina: S. Freud, *Freud/Jung Letters*, 207–212, 226–232; Carotenuto, *Secret Symmetry*, 91–104.   **127–128.** Jung's new version of the relationship: S. Freud, *Freud/Jung Letters*, 235; Carotenuto, *Secret Symmetry*, 103–105.   **128–131.** Freud's reaction: S. Freud, *Freud/Jung Letters*, 236–238.   **133.** Outcome of Jung's relationship with Sabina: Ibid., 469; Carotenuto, *Secret Symmetry*, 181–182, 191, 207.   **134–136.** Toni Wolff: Hannah, *Jung*, 103–104, 119–120, 138–142; Stern, *C. G. Jung*, 137; S. Freud, *Freud/Jung Letters*, 440; van der Post, *Story of Our Time*, 173–174, 177. **136–137.** Jung and women: Stern, *C. G. Jung*, 18–19, 69, 70, 73; Hannah, *Jung*, 83–84; Carotenuto, *Secret Symmetry*, 95; Jung, *Memories, Dreams, Reflections*, 8–9.   **138.** "Honeymoons are tricky": Brome, *Jung*, 83.   **138.** Emma Jung: S. Freud, *Freud/Jung Letters*, 463, 467.   **138–140.** "Carl, oddly eloquent," Stern, *C. G. Jung*, 70–73, 78.   **140.** Martha Freud: S. Freud, *Freud/Jung Letters*, 456; Roazen, *Freud and His Followers*, 56–57, 556; Gay, *Freud*, 60; Sachs, *Freud*, 74; Puner, *Freud*, 149; Fromm, *Sigmund Freud's Mission*, 19, 22–24.   **141.** "if any acceptable": Young-Bruehl, *Anna Freud*, 27. **142.** "All is well": S. Freud, *Freud/Jung Letters*, 424–425.   **142.** Freud's views on sex: S. Freud, *Letters of Sigmund Freud*, 50–51; S. Freud, *Psychopathology of Everyday Life*, 3, 175, 237; S. Freud, *Origins of Psychoanalysis*, 227; Jones, *Life and Work* 2: 386; Fromm, *Sigmund Freud's Mission*, 29–30; Roazen, *Freud and His Followers*, 52, 53, 62, 83–84, 556; Puner, *Freud*, 27; Young-Bruehl, *Anna Freud*, 61, 68; S. Freud, *Freud/Jung Letters*, 292, 308, 419.   **145.** Minna Bernays: "Seemed a bit miffed," Roazen, *Freud and His Followers*, 59–62; Sachs, *Freud*, 74; Young-Bruehl, *Anna Freud*, 449; Jones, *Life and Work* 1: 164–165; Brome, *Jung*, 264; Gay, *Freud*, 76, 752–753; Gay, "Sigmund and Minna?" 1; Elms, "Freud and Minna," 42–43; Billinsky, "Jung and Freud," 42.

CHAPTER EIGHT: *The Swiss Will Save Us: 1910*

149–150. Adler and Stekel at Nuremberg: Jones, *Life and Work* 2: 68–69; Stekel, *Autobiography*, 128.   **151–152.** Freud's confrontation with Viennese loyalists: Jones, *Life and Work* 2: 69–70; Stekel, *Autobiography*, 128–129; S. Freud, *On the History*, 42–43; Wittels, *Sigmund Freud*, 140.   **152–153.** The new journals and Freud's opinion of the Viennese: S. Freud, *Freud/Jung Letters*, 304; S. Freud, *On the History*, 43–45; Jones, *Life and Work* 2: 70–71; Wittels, *Sigmund Freud*, 142, 177.   **153.** Preparations for Nuremberg and Jung's departure for America: S. Freud, *Freud/Jung Letters*, 282, 292, 301–304. **154.** Freud's reaction to Nuremberg congress: Jones, *Life and Work* 2: 70–71. **154–155.** Freud and Jung on meetings of Zurich society: S. Freud, *Freud/Jung Letters*, 329–331, 338. **156.** Jung as an administrator: Ibid., 343–346, 363–366, 370; Jones, *Life and Work* 2: 142. **158–160.** Jung's dreams and interests in archeology and mythology: S. Freud, *Freud/Jung Letters*, 285, 308, 378; Jung, *Memories, Dreams, Reflections*, 160–161. **160–161.** Jung's new work on libido: S. Freud, *Freud/Jung Letters*, 288–289, 318, 331–335; Jung, *Memories, Dreams, Reflections*, 162–163; Hannah, *Jung*, 98–99; Ellenberger, *Discovery of the Unconscious*, 695–697. **161–162.** Jung's dream of customs agent: Jung, *Memories, Dreams, Reflections*, 163–164. **163–164.** Jung's knight and Latin dreams: Ibid., 164–165, 306–307; S. Freud, *Freud/Jung Letters*, 359. **164–165.** Letters on Jung's father complex: S. Freud, *Freud/Jung Letters*, 297, 300, 312–313, 328. **166–167.** Johann Honegger: Ibid., 289, 304–305, 325–327, 330, 337–338, 412–416, 426; Stern, *C. G. Jung*, 101–104. **168–170.** Freud and Ferenczi: S. Freud, *Freud/Jung Letters*, 340–342, 353, 355; S. Freud, *Letters of Sigmund Freud*, 283; Jones, *Life and Work* 2: 78–84. **170–171.** Freud and Adler: S. Freud, *Freud/Jung Letters*, 373, 376; S. Freud, *On the History*, 51; Jones, *Life and Work* 2: 130. **171–173.** Eugen Bleuler: S. Freud, *Freud/Jung Letters*, 374–376, 381–384; Jones, *Life and Work* 2: 72–73, 140; Binswanger, *Sigmund Freud*, 26.

CHAPTER NINE: *You Are a Dangerous Rival: 1911–1912*

174–175. "Trial" of Adler and Stekel: S. Freud, *Freud/Jung Letters*, 400–404, 418, 428; Jones, *Life and Work* 2: 131–133; Roazen, *Freud and His Followers*, 184–186. **177.** Freud's doubts about Jung: S. Freud, *Freud/Jung Letters*, 433–435, 438, 447; Binswanger, *Sigmund Freud*, 31. **178–180.** Emma Jung: S. Freud, *Freud/Jung Letters*, 452–453, 456–457. **180.** "more perceptive and more prescient": Gay, *Freud*, 225. **180–181.** "[Freud] wants to give me love": Jung, *Memories, Dreams, Reflections*, 167; Carotenuto, *Secret Symmetry*, 184. **181–184.** Freud and Jung on libido and mythology: S. Freud, *Freud/Jung Letters*, 384–385, 388, 421–422, 427, 429, 438–439, 441, 459–461, 469. **184–185.** Zurich visit and Weimar Congress: Ibid., 443, 448, 475; Jones, *Life and Work* 2: 84–86; Carotenuto, *Secret Symmetry*, 182. **185–186.** Zurich scandal: S. Freud, *Freud/Jung Letters*, 482, 484, 487, 493; Ellenberger, *Discovery of the Unconscious*, 811–813; Jones, *Life and Work* 2: 91–92, 141; Brome, *Freud and His Inner Circle*, 119. **187–188.** Dog-bite incident: S. Freud, *Freud/Jung Letters*, 478–489. **190–191.** Quarrel over personal relationship: Ibid., 490–493.

CHAPTER TEN: *The Rest Is Silence: 1912–1913*

192–193. On Jung's libido work: S. Freud, *Freud/Jung Letters*, 500–509; Ellenberger, *Discovery of the Unconscious*, 698; Roazen, *Freud and His Followers*,

256; van der Post, *Story of Our Time*, 142. **194–195.** Kreuzlingen incident: S. Freud, *Freud/Jung Letters*, 508, 509, 514; Jones, *Life and Work* 2: 92, 142; Schur, *Freud*, 262; Binswanger, *Sigmund Freud*, 45, 46. **195–197.** Jung's trip to America: S. Freud, *Freud/Jung Letters*, 496–497, 512, 513; Jones, *Life and Work* 2: 143–144; Ellenberger, *Discovery of the Unconscious*, 697–698; Roazen, *Freud and His Followers*, 253–254; Jung, *Freud and Psychoanalysis*, 85–86. **198–200.** Professional matters and the end of the personal relationship: S. Freud, *Freud/Jung Letters*, 512–521; Jones, *Life and Work* 2: 144; S. Freud, *On the History*, 58. **200–202.** Munich meeting: Jones, *Life and Work* 1: 317; Ibid., 2: 145–147; Jung, *Memories, Dreams, Reflections*, 156–157; Jung, *C. G. Jung Letters* 2: 133. **202–204.** Freud's fainting episode: S. Freud, *Freud/Jung Letters*, 522; Schur, *Freud*, 266–268; Roazen, *Freud and His Followers*, 248–250; Jones, *Life and Work* 1: 317; Ibid., 2: 146; Jung, *Memories, Dreams, Reflections*, 157; Andreas-Salomé, *Freud Journal*, 58. **204–208.** Post-Munich letters and the loss of authority: S. Freud, *Freud/Jung Letters*, 522–535. **208.** "The rest is silence": Ibid., 537–540; Jones, *Life and Work* 2: 147.

CHAPTER ELEVEN: *We Are at Last Rid of Them: The Final Years*

209–212. Freud on Jung before the Munich Congress: S. Freud, *Letters of Sigmund Freud*, 299–305; Carotenuto, *Secret Symmetry*, 119–121; Jones, *Life and Work* 2: 99, 101, 148–149; S. Freud, *Psychoanalytic Dialogue*, 137, 141. **212–214.** Munich Congress: S. Freud, *On the History*, 45, 60; Roazen, *Freud and His Followers*, 262; Brome, *Freud and His Inner Circle*, 133; Jones, *Life and Work* 2: 102–103, 149; Andreas-Salomé, *Freud Journal*, 168–169. **214–215.** On Jung's resignation from the *Yearbook* and the association: S. Freud, *On the History*, 7; Roazen, *Freud and His Followers*, 264; S. Freud, *Psychoanalytic Dialogue*, 186; Jung, *C. G. Jung Letters* 1: 28; S. Freud, *Freud/Jung Letters*, 550–551; Jones, *Life and Work* 2: 150. **217–222.** Jung's confrontation with his unconscious: Jung, *Memories, Dreams, Reflections*, 170–183, 189, 199; Stern, *C. G. Jung*, 115–123. **222–224.** Freud's response to the break with Jung: Gay, *Freud*, 779; Hannah, *Jung*, 245; Jones, *Life and Work* 2: 105; Roazen, *Freud and His Followers*, 181, 207–210, 244, 280–288; S. Freud, *Freud/Jung Letters*, 55; S. Freud, *On the History*, 7, 60. **224–226.** Jung's response: Jung, *Freud and Psychoanalysis*, 438–440; Roazen, *Freud and His Followers*, 279, 296; van der Post, *Story of Our Time*, 137; Jung, *Memories, Dreams, Reflections*, 168–169; Ellenberger, *Discovery of the Unconscious*, 462; Carotenuto, *Secret Symmetry*, 189; Jung, *C. G. Jung Letters* 1: 122, 302; Ibid., 2: xxix–xxx, 347–350, 359.

Bibliography

Alexander, Franz, and Selesnick, Sheldon T. "Freud-Bleuler Correspondence." *Archives of General Psychiatry* 12 (1965):1–9.

Alexander, Irving E. "The Freud-Jung Relationship: The Other Side of Oedipus and Countertransference." *American Psychologist* 37 (1982):1009–1018.

Andreas-Salomé, Lou. *The Freud Journal of Lou Andreas-Salomé.* Edited by Stanley A. Leavy. New York: Basic Books, 1964.

Bernays, Anna Freud. "My Brother Sigmund Freud." *American Mercury* 51 (1940):335–342.

Billinsky, John M. "Jung and Freud: The End of a Romance." *Andover Newton Quarterly* 10 (1969):39–43.

Binswanger, Ludwig. *Sigmund Freud: Reminiscences of a Friendship.* New York: Grune and Stratton, 1957.

Brome, Vincent. *Freud and His Inner Circle.* New York: William Morrow, 1968.

———. *Jung: Man and Myth.* New York: Atheneum, 1978.

———. *Ernest Jones: Freud's Alter Ego.* New York: W. W. Norton, 1983.

Carotenuto, Aldo. *A Secret Symmetry: Sabina Spielrein between Jung and Freud.* New York: Pantheon, 1982.

Clark, Ronald W. *Freud, the Man and the Cause.* New York: Random House, 1980.

Drinka, George Frederick. *The Birth of Neurosis.* New York: Simon and Schuster, 1984.

Drucker, Peter. "What Freud Forgot." *Human Nature* 2 (1979):40–47.

Ellenberger, Henri F. *The Discovery of the Unconscious: The History and Evolution of Dynamic Psychiatry.* New York: Basic Books, 1970.

Elms, Alan C. "Freud and Minna." *Psychology Today* 16, no. 12 (1982):42.

Engelmann, Edmund. *Berggasse 19: Sigmund Freud's Home and Offices, Vienna, 1938.* New York: Basic Books, 1976.

Freeman, Lucy, and Strean, Herbert S. *Freud and Women.* New York: Continuum Books, 1987.

Freud, Martin. *Sigmund Freud: Man and Father.* New York: Vanguard, 1958.

Freud, Sigmund. *The Interpretation of Dreams.* In The Standard Edition of the *Complete Psychological Works of Sigmund Freud.* Edited and translated by James Strachey. Vols. 4–5. London: Hogarth Press, 1900.

———. *The Psychopathology of Everyday Life.* In the Standard Edition. Vol. 6. London: Hogarth Press, 1901.

———. *Three Essays on the Theory of Sexuality.* In the Standard Edition. Vol. 7. London: Hogarth Press, 1905.

———. *Jokes and Their Relation to the Unconscious.* In the Standard Edition. Vol. 8. London: Hogarth Press, 1905.

———. *Totem and Taboo.* In the Standard Edition. Vol. 13. London: Hogarth Press, 1913.

———. *On the History of the Psychoanalytic Movement.* In the Standard Edition. Vol. 14. London: Hogarth Press, 1914.

———. *An Autobiographical Study.* In the Standard Edition. Vol. 20. London: Hogarth Press, 1925–1926.

———. *The Origins of Psychoanalysis: Letters to Wilhelm Fliess, Drafts and Notes: 1887–1902.* Edited by Marie Bonaparte, Anna Freud, and Ernst Kris. New York: Basic Books, 1954.

———. *The Letters of Sigmund Freud.* Edited by Ernst L. Freud. New York: Basic Books, 1960.

———. *Psychoanalysis and Faith: The Letters of Sigmund Freud and Oskar Pfister, 1909–1939*. Edited by Ernst L. Freud and Heinrich Meng. New York: Basic Books, 1963.

————. *A Psychoanalytic Dialogue: The Letters of Sigmund Freud and Karl Abraham, 1907–1926*. Edited by Hilda C. Abraham and Ernst L. Freud. New York: Basic Books, 1965.

————. *The Freud/Jung Letters: The Correspondence between Sigmund Freud and C. G. Jung*. Edited by William McGuire. Princeton: Princeton University Press, 1974.

————. *Sigmund Freud: His Life in Pictures and Words*. Edited by Ernst Freud, Lucie Freud, and Ilse Brubrich-Simitis. New York: Harcourt Brace Jovanovich, 1978.

————. *The Complete Letters of Sigmund Freud to Wilhelm Fliess, 1887–1904*. Edited by Jeffrey M. Masson. Cambridge: Harvard University Press, 1985.

Fromm, Erich. *Sigmund Freud's Mission: An Analysis of His Personality and Influence*. New York: Harper & Row, 1959.

————. *Greatness and Limitations of Freud's Thought*. New York: Harper & Row, 1980.

Gay, Peter. *Education of the Senses*. New York: Oxford University Press, 1984.

————. *Freud: A Life for Our Time*. New York: W. W. Norton, 1988.

————. "Sigmund and Minna? The Biographer as Voyeur." *New York Times Book Review*, January 29, 1989.

Gifford, George E. "Freud and the Porcupine." *Harvard Medical Alumni Bulletin* 46 (1972):4.

Hale, Nathan G. *Freud and the Americans*. Vol. 1. *The Beginnings of Psychoanalysis in the United States, 1876–1917*. New York: Oxford University Press, 1971.

Hannah, Barbara. *Jung: His Life and Work*. New York: G. P. Putnam's Sons, 1976.

Hillman, James. "Some Early Background to Jung's Ideas: Notes on 'C. G. Jung's Medium' by Stefanie Zumstein-Preiswerk." *Spring* (1976):123–136.

Hogenson, George B. *Jung's Struggle with Freud*. Notre Dame, Indiana: University of Notre Dame Press, 1983.

Jaffé, Aniela. *The Myth of Meaning: Jung and the Expansion of Consciousness*. New York: G. P. Putnam's Sons, 1971.

Jahoda, Marie. *Freud and the Dilemmas of Psychology*. Lincoln: University of Nebraska Press, 1977.

Jones, Ernest. *The Life and Work of Sigmund Freud*. 3 vols. New York: Basic Books, 1953–1957.

————. *Free Associations: Memories of a Psychoanalyst*. London: Hogarth Press, 1959.

Jourard, Sidney M. *The Transparent Self.* Rev. ed. New York: Van Nostrand Reinhold, 1971.

Jung, C. G. *Memories, Dreams, Reflections*. New York: Pantheon, 1961.

————. *On the Psychology of the Unconscious*. In *The Collected Works of C. G. Jung.* Edited by Herbert Read, Michael Fordham, and Gerhard Adler. Vol. 7. Princeton: Princeton University Press, 1966.

————. *The Psychology of Dementia Praecox*. In *The Collected Works.* Vol. 3. Princeton: Princeton University Press, 1972.

————. *C. G. Jung Letters*. 2 vols. Edited by Gerhard Adler and Aniela Jaffé. Princeton: Princeton University Press, 1973.

————. *Freud and Psychoanalysis*. In *The Collected Works.* Vol. 18. Princeton: Princeton University Press, 1976.

————. *C. G. Jung Speaking: Interviews and Encounters*. Edited by William McGuire and R. F. C. Hull. Princeton: Princeton University Press, 1977.

Kaufmann, Walter. *Discovering the Mind*. Vol. 3. *Freud versus Adler and Jung*. New York: McGraw-Hill, 1980.

Krüll, Marianne. *Freud and His Father*. New York: W. W. Norton, 1986.

Lieberman, E. James. *Acts of Will: The Life and Work of Otto Rank*. New York: Free Press, 1985.

Loewald, H. "Review Essay on *The Freud/Jung Letters*." In *Papers on Psychoanalysis*. New Haven: Yale University Press, 1980.

Malcolm, Janet. *In the Freud Archives*. New York: Alfred A. Knopf, 1984.

Masson, Jeffrey M. *The Assault on Truth: Freud's Suppression of the Seduction Theory*. New York: Farrar, Straus, Giroux, 1984.

McGrath, William J. *Freud's Discovery of Psychoanalysis: The Politics of Hysteria*. Ithaca: Cornell University Press, 1986.

Puner, Helen Walker. *Freud: His Life and His Mind*. New York: Howell, Soskin, 1947.

Putnam, James Jackson. *James Jackson Putnam and Psychoanalysis: Letters between Putnam and Sigmund Freud, Ernest Jones, William James, Sandor Ferenczi and Morton Prince, 1877–1917*. Edited by Nathan G. Hale. Cambridge: Harvard University Press, 1971.

Roazen, Paul. *Freud and His Followers*. New York: Alfred A. Knopf, 1975.

Robert, Marthe. *From Oedipus to Moses*. Garden City, New York: Doubleday, 1976.

Rosenberg, S. *Why Freud Fainted*. Indianapolis: Bobbs-Merrill, 1978.

Sachs, Hans. *Freud: Master and Friend*. Cambridge: Harvard University Press, 1944.

Schur, Max. *Freud: Living and Dying*. New York: International Universities Press, 1972.

Shengold, Leonard. "The Freud/Jung Letters." In Vol. 1 of *Freud and His Self-analysis*, edited by Mark Kanzer and Jules Glenn. New York: Jason Aronson, 1979.

Silverstein, Barry. "'Now Comes a Sad Story': Freud's Lost Metapsychological Papers." In Vol. 1 of *Freud: Appraisals and Reappraisals*, edited by Paul E. Stepansky. New York: Analytic Press, 1986.

Singer, June. *Boundaries of the Soul: The Practice of Jung's Psychology*. Garden City, New York: Doubleday, 1972.

Staude, John-Raphael. *The Adult Development of C. G. Jung*. London: Routledge and Kegan Paul, 1981.

Steele, Robert S. *Freud and Jung: Conflicts of Interpretation*. London: Routledge and Kegan Paul, 1982.

Stekel, Wilhelm. *The Autobiography of Wilhelm Stekel: The Life*

Story of a Pioneer Psychoanalyst. New York: Liveright, 1950.

Stern, Paul J. *C. G. Jung: The Haunted Prophet*. New York: George Braziller, 1976.

Storr, Anthony. *C. G. Jung*. New York: Viking Press, 1973.

Sulloway, Frank J. *Freud: Biologist of the Mind: Beyond the Psychoanalytic Legend*. New York: Basic Books, 1979.

Swales, Peter J. "Freud, Minna Bernays, and the Conquest of Rome: New Light on the Origins of Psychoanalysis." *New American Review* 1 (1982):1–23.

van der Post, Laurens. *Jung and the Story of our Time*. New York: Pantheon, 1975.

von Franz, Marie-Louise. *C. G. Jung: His Myth in Our Time*. Boston: Little, Brown, 1975.

Walser, Hans. "An Early Psychoanalytical Tragedy: J. J. Honegger and the Beginnings of Training Analysis." *Spring* (1974):243–255.

Wehr, Gerhard. *Portrait of Jung*. New York: Herder and Herder, 1971.

———. *Jung: A Biography*. Boston: Shambhala, 1987.

Wittels, Fritz. *Sigmund Freud: His Personality, His Teachings, and His School*. Freeport, New York: Books for Libraries Press, 1971.

Young-Bruehl, Elisabeth. *Anna Freud: A Biography*. New York: Summit Books, 1988.

Index